*REWRITING
CHINESE HISTORY*

HÀ VĂN THÙY

REWRITING CHINESE HISTORY

TRANSLATOR: ĐẶNG THỊ HƯỜNG
EDITER: ALAN J. PATTERSON

NHÂN ẢNH
PUBLISHER
2021

REWRITING CHINESE HISTORY

Author: Hà Văn Thùy
Cover: Uyên Nguyên Trần Triết
Layout: Nguyễn Thành
Publisher: Nhân Ảnh 2021
ISBN: 9781989993682

INDEX

PREFACE

Dear friends,

You are reading the first few lines of the book that will shake faith and awaken your conscience.

So far, not only you but the whole world believe that Westerners bring civilization to China. Then, the Chinese brought civilization down to the Annamite people. Vietnamese language borrows 70% of Chinese. Vietnamese culture is the borrowing of Chinese culture imperfectively.

That is the great lie imposed becoming dogma throughout the last century!

From the knowledge of the new century, this book will tell you the opposite truth.

Thousands of years ago, when most of humanity was still alive in the ice, Vietnamese brought the stone ax - the superior tool of ancient time - to the China. Then also from Vietnam, the next migrants brought rice, millet, chicken breed, dog breed etc to build a brilliant agricultural civilization on the Mainland. Chinese language is born from Vietnamese. The iconography of the Chinese text was created by the Viet people. Y jing, Shi jing, Shu jing etc is also the creativity of the Viet people. If the history of a country is the history of the major population communities that make up that country, then Chinese history is the history of the Viet people who have been living in China.

You wonder, you doubt? No wonder many are as skeptical as you! What a moment to overturn the dogmahidden over two thousand years! Yes, two thousand years of pervert! The reason is that in the past, the Vietnamese lost land, lost the written words, it should lose its history. From the owner of the brilliant Oriental civilization, the Vietnamese were deprived of everything to become a bunch of ignorant people have to learn from others. Fortunately, into the new century, human science has illuminated the forgotten past, returning justice to history. The booklet in your hand will be the first lines, the first chapters of every Chinese history book in the future.

Finally, I would like to thank Dr. Nguyen Duc Hiep for writing precious introduction.

Thank my friend Do Ngoc Thanh by permission to use very valuable material for this book.

Lastly, thank the translator Đang Thi Huong and especially thank Mr Alan J. Patterson for his dedication to editing this book.

Sai Gon. The Winter 2020
Ha Van Thuy

FORWORD

Mr. Ha Van Thuy is a friend who I knew for over 10 years through his articles and my texts written on history and human origins in Southeast Asia and East Asia, based on discoveries of new genetics in the late 20th century and early 21st century. We have been in contact through e-mails and in exchange several times when I had occasions to go back Vietnam, through that I know him not only as a writer, journalist that previously he was a biologist, with biology bachelor's degree from the University (Hanoi University, 1963-1967) etc. This gave me an answer about a part of his passionate enthusiasm for the study of the origin of Vietnamese people and residents of Southeast Asia and East Asia through genetic evidence.

In Australia in the years 2003-2006, I, and Mr. Nguyen Văn Tuan, Mr. Cung Dinh Thanh collaborated together in writing articles on the subject published by Thought journal founded by Mr. Cung Dinh Thanh. We had the contacts, exchanges of information and sharing of ideas, research subjects with Mr. Thuy. Later when Mr. Thanh passed away, and I also by myself moving to other study fields, I did not contact much with Mr. Thuy.

Sending me an e-mail, Mr. Thuy said: "In the first step to look back ethnic origin, I was delighted to see the light from the group of Thought. I had to follow you with a lot of hope. But then Mr. Thanh passed away, you and Mr. Tuan are busy in your professional job, I become helpless."

Maybe being a little helpless but he did not give up. Being a Biologist and a Writer, he has a certain understanding of the process of national history, and he was lucky when was approaching Vietnamese Confucius ideology of Philosopher Kim Dinh (Viet Nho). And when he caught the findings of genetics, the seeds are sown from many sources, sparked flourishly.

Within five years from 2006 to 1011, he published three books: Finding again the origin of Viet culture (Literature Publishing House, 2006), Journey to find the origin (Literature, 2008) and Finding origin through genetics (Literature, 2011). Three books with the same theme, but each book is a revelation, the gradual maturation of knowledge and ideas.

In the preface to the third book, the author writes: "Because of the problems too new and too big that it can not be mentioned in two earlier books, the writer saw necessary to do another book, a collection of studies trusted and pioneer in the field." And he has done his work. The work laid the foundation for new scientific researches on the origin and migrations of human to Vietnam of J.Y.Chu, Stephen Oppenheimer, Wilhelm Solheim II etc previously which were only published in English, now they were translated into Vietnamese. Not just be satisfied with the translation, the author, in his ability, after each translation, he was willing to comment on the document separately on contributing guide the readers. Author said: "With such characteristics, the book could be the introductory document to help readers access to new scientific methods in the study of prehistoric Viet people.

After the third book, the author of the novel named Nguyen Thi Lo wanted to exit from prehistory to back the present with the novel is being written etc. But in time, he realized, all the findings about the origin and culture of Vietnamese had opened the secrets of Chinese world. So in the Spring of 2012 the book named Rewriting the Chinese history was drafted. The author said, when started writing, he thought that his documents were enough for a book. But when the chapters outlined, he found himself missing too much. So he stopped and thanked to the internet to decipher knowledge about China, from Zhoukoudian (周口店), Yangshao (仰韶), Lungsan (龍山) etc to the latest discoveries where The Fairy Cave on the bank of the Yangtze River early 2012, discovering a great storage of human intellect in the greatest civilization on the planet! And by special hustler mind, he connected and decoded, changed the known knowledge of each individual science, sublimated into new statements to surprise.

Mr. Thuy sent me a copy of the Rewriting Chinese history with the request me to write foreword. This is the honor and also the hard work, because with this book, we cannot write as an usual book review. In order to have an evaluable article, it should need much time and much dedication.

*
* *

If want to access this book, firstly we need to understand the history of the Vietnam's humanities. In a certain sense, the Vietnam's humanities appeared vague ideas from ancient primitive time, when human ancestors still even eat all aminal hairs and lived in caves with the story of the gourd fruit of the Dao ethnic: "The God born out a gourd. After the worldwide flood, the gourd was broken. Each seed was a peoples and they went to live on the ground." Then, from Chinese legends, old people told that Suiren (燧人) who found the fire, Mother Nuwa (女娲) who used the rocks to fix the sky, Mr. Phuc Hy (Fuxi- 伏羲) made Yi ching (易) and Mr. Than Nong (Shennong-神農) taught the ancients about planting cereals. Closer, Dragon Father Lac Long Quan and Fairy Mother Au Co born a bag with a hundred eggs etc. The Vietnamese ancient people said that: Vietnamese and Chinese are same race and same culture, so in the first line of Great Vietnamese Complete History wrote: "From the time Emperor built many nations ..."

However the human sciences of Vietnam really just born when France established French School of the Far East in Hanoi in 1898. At that time, knowledge of the French scholars about Far East was still poor, so the main characters in French School of the Far East were the Sinologists such as L. Aurousseau, H. Maspéro etc. Being Western scholars, they brought the European central notion - Europe was the center of human civilization. Intelligent weapons of the people who went to expand the civilization were two solid scientific postulates: human civilization from Mesopotamia passed through Greece and Rome to Europe and from there across Central Asia into China, eventually to Southeast Asia. And people, from the Tibetan plateau went to the Southeast, through China to Vietnam. As Confucian scholars, they naturally also had a conception that China was the center of Eastern civilization. In their eyes, Vietnam and Southeast Asia was just a pool of history! So in order to understand the savage Annam, French scholars started from ancient China.

In 1904, in the book Le Cambodge published in Paris, academician E. Aymonier proposed hypotheses: "Ancestors of the Mon-Khmer language's people originated from the Southern slopes of Tibet and then moved to the south in two directions – Southwest born Munda people in India, Southeast, born Mon-Khmer people in Indochina." From this theory, in the early 20th century, scholar L. Aurousseau exploited the Chinese bibliographies, said: "The Vietnamese lived in China before migrating across Northern Vietnam. Chu (楚) nation under the Bach Viet (Baiyue-百越) ethnics, the territory included the provinces of Hubei and Hunan today, appearing before the eleventh century BC. By the ninth century BC, a branch of Chu (楚) nation migrated to the South, along the Yangtze River, settled in Zhejiang, founding of Viet nation (Yue Wang Gou Jian - 越王勾踐) in the sixth century BC. In 333 BC, Chu (楚) nation defeated the Viet state, Viet people run to South in four groups: Dongou Group (東甌) or Viet Dong (越東) in Wenzhou (Zhejiang). Man Viet (Minyue 閩越) in Fujian. Nam Viet (Nanyue -南越) in Guangdong, Guangxi. Lac Viet (Luoyue 雒越) in South Guangxi and Northern Vietnam. These groups were being assimilated; only the Lac Viet (Luoyue 雒越) group existed. "Then we have enough evidence to say that the people of Annam today are direct descendants of Viet state perished in 333 BC, and ancient ancestor, in the sixth century Before Christ, were in Zhejiang province of China today, around the river basin with same name Zhejiang "(1)

Applying two theories on the field of linguistics, the leading linguist L. Maspéro of the French School of the Far East said: "Current Vietnamese language borrowed about 70% from Chinese language."

One famous scholar in that time, Coedes Georges, Director of the French School of the Far East from 1920 to 1950, through the Sanskrit inscription at the Cham temple towers in Vietnam, he said that Southeast Asia was only the reincarnation of two great civilizations of India and China.

Since the 1920s, French School of the Far East conducted many archaeological excavations, discovered Neolithic culture in Hoa Binh Vietnam. To 1930s found Dong Son bronze drum is cast exquisitely. Recognizing this, Austrian anthropologist Robert Heine-Geldern said Southeast Asia was the region has experienced many "cultural waves", and the continuous exodus brought to Southeast Asia the current technology. He believed that "The arch-shaped ax and the producer made them surely must come from Northern China. Dong Son bronze drum was the result of a wave of other cultures, came from Eastern Europe, who emigrated to the south at about 1000 BC and to Southeast Asia about 500 years later."

While leading scholar of French Orientalist prejudices so, the panorama of the world humanities science was more diverse

That time there were two theories about human origins. Out of Africa hypothesis stated that modern humans only emerged from Africa about 100,000 to 200,000 years ago. Contrary to it, the Multiregional hypothesis explained that modern humans evolved in many places in the world from Homo erectus about 1 to 2 million years ago.

Thought of the Multiregional hypothesis combined with ancient Chinese bibliographies have dominated French School of the Far East, making them have the preconceptions about the Far East.

In January 1932, the Conference of the International Archaeological History of the Far Eastern held in Hanoi confirmed: "Hoa Binh culture is the centre where invented first husbandry agricultural production in the world. Hoa Binh's agricultural center appeared earlier 3,000 years ago Mesopotamia." (Encyclopedia d'Archeologie). However, this finding was not supported by French School of the Far East.

Such conservatism is not just about archeology, but also in many other areas, especially linguistics. Until 1905, the French Colonel Frey, H, (1847-1932) worked in West Africa and Indochina had published three books related to Vietnam's language:

1. L'Annamite, mère des langues; communauté d'origine des races celtiques, semitiques, soudanaises et de l'Indo-Chine, Paris, 1892, 248p. (Vietnamese, the mother of the languages, the communities of the racial origins of Celtic, Jewish, Sudan and Indochina);

2. Annamites et extréme occidentaux, recherche sur l'origine des langues, Paris Hachette, 1894, 272 p. (An Nam and Far West, the study of the origin of language)

3. Les Egyptiens préhistoriques identifiés avec les Annamites, d'aprés les inscriptions hiéroglyphiques Paris, Hachette, 1905, 106 p. (The Egyptian prehistory contacted with Annam through hieroglyphic inscriptions. Several other authors also had a look closer to Frey's viewpoint: Vietnamese is the mother of the oriental languages.

However, the key scholars of French School of the Far East rejected this proposal. Specifically, from 1933 to 1937, have a debate among the Poland linguist Przilusky with Academician Maspero on the origins of Vietnamese language. While Przilusky agreed with Frey that Vietnamese born oriental languages, Maspéro was strongly opposed, keeping his views: Vietnamese borrowed 70% words from Chinese. Here, the winner was not scientific truth which is mogul of debate. Przilusky's view was rejected. The pioneering Vietnamese scholars from Tran Trong Kim, Nguyen Van To, Dao Duy Anh studied and then spread the mainstream knowledge in the Vietnamese community. While the academician of French School of the Far East followed their own preconception, in the scientific field appeared many contrary voices.

In 1952, as a continuation of the thinking of Conference of the International Archaeological History of the Far East held 20 years ago, an American scholar C. Sauer wrote in the book named "Agricultural origins and Dispersals": "It is true that agriculture has progressed through two stages where the first stage was the Hoa Binh culture. Paddy was planted simultaneously with taro". "I've proven that Southeast Asia was the cradle of the oldest agriculture. And I also proved that agricultural culture derived with fishing by net in this country. I also demonstrated that the most ancient animals originated from Southeast Asia, and this was an important center of the world of farming techniques and crops domesticated by plant reproduction".

In 1965, to rescue a relic where would be soon sunk in the hydropower reservoir, the research team of Professor Solheim

II was dispatched to Thailand. Through artifacts found in The Spirit Cave, Chester Gorman and his colleagues estimated that The Spirit cave has been used by humans about 10,000 years BCE. Here, he found an ax and knives dating back 7,000 years BC (this date was earlier than the ax found in China to 2,000 a year. Previously, it was thought that such tools were "exported" from Chinese to Southeast Asia around 3000 BC).

In 1972, Chester Gorman returned to Thailand. He found two other caves, and it can be concluded that there was a process of people residing here 10,000 years BC to 1000 years AD. He named this prosperous economy is the Hoa Binh economy (because these tools use the same forms with tools found at Hoa Binh, Viet Nam before). In 1966, Donn Bayard - a different disciple of Solheim II, excavated a prehistoric cemetery in Non Nok Tha (Thailand). Here, even digging down to 1.5 meters, he discovered 800 ceramic vases were buried along with their owners. Through analysis, Bayard estimated the ages of vestiges from 3,500 to 2,000 years BC (this time the city of Mesopotamia began to appear). Also, Bayard also explored some tools such as axes, bracelets made of copper and tin. The tools found here absolutely not have any sign of rude at all; on the contrary, they showed that their producers had smelted and casted the metals. The findings in The Spirit Cave and Non Nok Tha cemetery were a serious challenge to the hypothesis that had been circulated and accepted before. Since the above discovery, in 1967, Professor WG Solheim II wrote:

"I think that when we study a lot of evidence in the Southeast Asian mainland, we absolutely can discover that the first crops domesticated in the world was performed by residents in Hoa Binh (Vietnam) in about 10,000 years ago BC .... ". " Hoa Binh Culture was the local culture, not being influenced by outside, and it led to Bac Son culture." "That in the Northern and Central mainland of Southeast Asia, there were the progressive cultures in which there was the development of polished stone tools first in Asia, first times in the world ceramic was invented ... " "That there were not only the first domesticated plants like Mr. Sauer has suggested and proved, but also gone further, it has provided ideas of agriculture to Western region. And later some trees had been transmitted to India and Africa. And Southeast Asia continued to be an advanced area in the Far East until China replaced this momentum in the first half millennium 2nd BC, about 1500 years BC. "(2)

Same in this time, under the rain of bombs, archaeologists in northern Vietnam cheerfully discovered Dong Son culture with political goals, demonstrated to the age of Hung Kings in Vietnamese history.

Promoting the idea of Maspero in French School of the Far East, under the light of oil lamps in evacuation camps in Dai Tu Thai Nguyen, a leading professor of linguistics Vietnam, Nguyen Tai Can stared to elaborate the great linguistic works: Origins and the formation of Sino – Vietnamese pronounciation! Another scholar, Cao Xuan Hao, lonely rediscovered the essence of Vietnamese grammar which he has thought that it was being distorted by the Western scholars! In the anthropology department, Professor Nguyen Dinh Khoa daily measured again the index of more than 70 skulls in the ancient skull collection in Vietnam, and prepared the project "Anthropology in Southeast Asia".

In the 1980s, the works conceived in flames and smoke were born. Applying the concept of historical materialism of Marxism, historical science of Vietnamese Democratic Republic convicted that Trieu Da (Zhao Tuo) was a invader and expelled Zhao dynasty from the official history. Since the discovery of the Dong Son culture, Vietnam historians denied the legend of Xich Quy (赤鬼) nation in 2879 BC to affirm that, Vietnamese history began 2700 years ago only.

The book named Origins and the formation of Sino-

Vietnamese pronounciation way born. Professor Nguyen Tai Can discovered in Vietnamese language, there were layers of ancient Chinese words and layer Sino-Vietnamese words became to Viet. That implicitly acknowledged, Vietnamese language borrowed more than 70% from the Chinese! Being highly appreciated by domestic and international academic researchers, author received the Ho Chi Minh Prize. Meanwhile, in several studies, Cao Xuan Hao gradually rediscovered that the primitive grammar of Vietnamese has been modified according to the French grammar! And of course, he became an uncomfortable, unpopular person!

In the book of Southeast Asian Anthropology, Professor Nguyen Dinh Khoa gave the conclusions: "The Stone Age, on the territory of Vietnam two big races Mongoloid and Australoid appeared, they mixed blood together and their descendant cross each other continue born four races: Indonesian, Melanesian, Vedoid and Negritoid belonged the Australoid type. In which Indonesian and Melanesian were two main components. In the Copper and Iron ages, Southeast Asian resident has the strong transformation into Southern Mongoloid race. Australoid narrowed to the maximum in the area, don't knew due to immigration or assimilation."

From today look back, through the lens of genetics, we see that, it's extremely accurate detection, can say, it is the highest achievement that anthropology of "measured skulls" has reached. However, due to limitations of the science at the time, these discoveries as well as the questions posed by him still hanging there!

And until 2003, Professor Tran Quoc Vuong, one of "four pillars" of Vietnam historians, had claimed on BBC Vietnamese that: "Vietnam supports the Multiregional hypothesis of human ancestors."

We can say, until the end of the last century, the humanities in Vietnam, despite had discovery of many archaeological sites but ideological side was not beyond what was formed from the French School of the Far East, an unfortunate step back.

*
*   *

Signs of the crisis of science appeared when it could not answer the questions that life brought to. The crisis of the humanities in Vietnam is real but in fact, it is also located in the general crisis of world human science because there are no new breakthroughs, and unable to settle definitively the origin of the modern people and the formation of ethnic groups on earth.

And what should come it has come.

It was September 29, 1998, when a team led by Professor J.Y. Chu of Texas University published the studies on project "Genetic Relationship of the Chinese Population" with the following contents:

1. The Homo sapiens were born from East Africa about 160,000 to 200,000 years ago.

2. The prehistoric people of Africa went across the Red Sea, along the Indian Ocean coast to Vietnam 60,000 to 70,000 years ago.

3. In Vietnam, they was mixed blood then increased the number of people and 50,000 years ago, they went to the offshore islands of Southeast Asia, to India. 40,000 years ago the northern climate were improve, they went to China and about 30,000 years ago crossed the Bering Strait to conquer the America.

This information made the American scientists shocked because it means overthrowing the Multiregional hypothesis and opens enormous prospects for world humanities.

In Australia, we received this information as great pleasure and because of our expertise, we embarked on the study. Since 2001 we have had the first articles about this discovery and posted in the years 2003 to 2006 in the Ideology journal.

Mr. Ha Van Thuy approached the papers of group of J.Y. Chu in late 2004 and since then he had academic exchanges with us. Thuy's three books had mostly from the decision of this new discovery.

*
*   *

With more than 400 printed pages, "Rewriting the Chinese history" may hold the record for the few letters but contain a large amount of information:

1. So far, though boasted with 24 sets of national history (二十四史), the Chinese people have yet identified their ancestors. The leading scholars of China are scrambling to two perspectives: Classic group said that their ancestors were from Erectus Zhoukoudian. Modern group said that their ancestors were Arian people coming from the West. In Rewriting Chinese history, with solid evidence, the author asserted, Chinese people ancestor were Lac Viet people from Vietnam who went up, in the course of history had mixed blood with Mongoloid people of the North, also came from Vietnam.

2. A sensitive issue in China's history is the origin of Huaxia group. The author discovered that Huaxia people appeared after 2698 BC, from the invasion of the Northern Mongoloid people in areas of Lac Viet people in the Southern of Yellow River. Here, the crossbred generations of Mongolian-Lac Viet born. Thanks to the biracial and bicultural combination, the Huaxia people become the elite class, holding leadership of the crowded Viet population, creating brilliant period of China since Yao, Shun to Zhou. Thank to the glory of Huaxia tribe, after winning power, the Viet leaders as the Qin Shi Huang, Liu

Bang also self-recognized as Huaxia people.

3. Contrary to the firm belief among international linguists in theory of the Sweden linguist Bernhard Karlgren saying that Chinese language belonged to the Han Tibetan language group; Vietnamese language borrowed 60% from Chinese language etc. With many evidence difficult rejected, the author demonstrated that Chinese is the Lac Viet language were spoken by Mongol parlance and no so-called Proto Sino-Tibetan language.

4. So far, apart from the legendary of Emperor (皇帝) ordered Cangjie (倉頡) to create the letters, but Chinese still could not prove they created the figurative letters. In his work, with many hard evidences, the author showed that, the ancient Viet people invented the hieroglyphics, from the first signal in rock at Sapa to Jiahu, Gansang and highest in oracle bone script (甲骨文) at Anyang, Henan. When invading Henan, the En (殷代) dynasty learned from Lac Viet people and then grew up.

5. The author's fifth detection was to identify two cultures on Chinese land. In long time lived on the land of China, the Vietnamese people had built here a developed agricultural culture. With the invasion of Xuan Yuan and the appearance of Huaxia group, the cultures on Chinese land changed into a brilliant move on to the last Western Zhou. Then, due to the historical change, the nomadic tribe invaded, nomadic instincts in Huaxia grew and rised, pushed China into the terrible wartime. The Chinese empire appeared, expanded the nomadic instincts more, and created the face of modern Chinese culture.

6. In an article, the author requested "to return the justice to history." With his writings, the author not only returned the fairness for history, but also, found more valuable lessons from history.

We all know that, around 10,000 years ago when the last Ice Age ended, the Western people domesticated goat sheep, entered the nomadic way of life. But in 50-60000 years earlier, in the South-East Asia, the Lac Viet people had a social life and soon entered the agriculture.

Agriculture that created the brilliant culture of the East. 400 years ago, capitalism of nomadic civilization with their steel, bacteria and destroy weapons invaded the Eastern culture and up to now this has been threatening to destroy the humanity. Human mind is in crisis, have not found the exit. The leading minds of the West said that the problem of mankind today is that the feminism (women's rights) has been pinched. A fatal mistake! Not the women's rights but it is a bigger cosmic problem: the balance between Yin and Yang of the world was broken! Was the brainchild of nomadic civilization, capitalism has pushed world work with the Yang became too big, while the Yin became too small, leading to crashes. How could it save the mankind? Oriental wisdom points out that, to steer the world back of the harmonious relation of Viet ethnic agriculture culture, i.e., for the Father, the Yang three parts, it will take two parts for Yin, for Mother!

*

* *

Above, I spoke about the crisis of the Vietnamese humanities. Nothing is unusual because it is part of the general crisis of the world. Because wholehearted with same old methodologies, they are powerless to solve on origin and the formation of the peoples on the planet. All acts of history and culture are the activities of human society. Therefore, can only fully understand the cultural history when understood the owner of the culture and history

On the XXI century threshold, a new technology with a new methodology opens up great opportunities of humanities. Humans find the ancestral origins not through the artifacts or bones or fossils but knew exact from the line of his sacred blood.

It was lucky, but probably by karma, so while not spending

any pennies for genetics projects, the Vietnamese acquired a large volume of research findings of humanity. It is wonderful that all things discovered in early decades of the century illustrated that prehistoric humans from Africa went to Vietnam and then spreaded throughout the Asia; that Vietnam who have the highest genetic diversity in Asian ethnics ... Vietnam was the cradle of the people of Asia, implicitly also the cradle of Asian civilization!

In his works, researcher Ha Van Thuy, in fact, laid the foundation for modern Vietnamese human sciences and put Vietnamese humanities rank as the world's pioneer.

Realizing this is a valuable work, although there may be several explanations have not been agreed by many researchers today in Vietnam and abroad, I proudly present this carefully study of Mr. Ha Van Thuy to the readers.

Sydney, 15/06/2013
Ph.D. Nguyen Duc Hiep

Atmospheric Science Specialist. New South Wales, Australia - Department of Environment and Conservation, New South Wales, Australia

References:

1. L. Aurousseau. *Investigation of An Nam People Origin.* Translated by Hong Nhan Pham Quynh. Nam Phong magazine No. 84, May 6-1924, page. 480

2. W.G. Solheime II. *New light on Forgotten Past.* National Geographic, Vol. 139, No. 3, March 1971.)

3. J.Y. Chu et al. *Genetic Relationship of Population in China.* Proc. Natl. Acad. Sci.USA 1998 số 95 tr. 11763-11768)

CHAPTER I

THE FACTORS THAT FORMED THE CONCEPTION OF THE CHINESE ORIGIN

One man didn't know about his origin, he couldnot be mature. Likewise, a nation didnot understand its origin, it couldnot be mature. Therefore, each person, each nation has always wished to know its origin. As the nation has a long history and the largest population in the world, perhaps more than anyone else, Chinese people have desired to know about their origin.

However, with the too long prehistoric time, the exploration of a nation origin is extremely difficult, like looking for a needle in a haystack. So, like many other nations, first Chinese found their origin through the legends. The legends, like the vague memory of the community. It is not history but is the feedback of the most significant events occurred in the past. Because the time was floating too long, with extremely flexible means of language, so many events happened factly in the past, also greatly modified. Not believing the myth will miss the special information sources, almost only one from past resubmitted. But absolutely believing in the legend is the blind leading to delusions. Accurately decoding of past events sent in a legend is challenging but it is also the invaluable rewards for the study of history.

Therefore, here I would like to start with the most popular legend about the origins of the Chinese people.

I. The legend and history

1. Legend

Chinese legend says: "Yellow Emperor (Huangdi, 黃帝) was one of the leaders of the Yan Emperor (Yandi, 炎帝) tribe. When became strong, he defeated mighty Yandi in Banquan (阪泉) battle, and he became the new leader of the tribe. Then re-emerging conflicts occurred with the tribes of Chiyou (蚩尤) in the Southeast. At the Zhuolu (涿鹿) battle, Yellow Emperor defeated his rivals, established the hegemonic position. Then his descendants, Zhuanxu (顓頊), and Emperor Ku (帝嚳), held the positions of tribal leaders. Emperor Ku (Diku, 帝嚳) died, Emperor Yao (堯) was the next inherit. He was the sage king, founded the institutional system to throne to the sages, and he passed the throne to Emperor Shun (舜)

The legend also says, "The Yellow Emperor of Xuanyuan (軒轅) clan, had lived in the Ji land, so he had the Ji surname. Yan Emperor (炎帝) belonged to Shennong clan, living in their land so he had the Qiang (强) surname ." Zhoulu was located on the South bank of the Yellow River, today it is Zhoulu District, Hebei Province, North of Beijing. Zhoulu battle occurred in 2698 BC, led to the victory of Yellow Emperor, and played an important role in Chinese history.

However, Yellow Emperor was not the first emperor of China. Before that there were three legendary kings:

- Suiren (燧人), who made fire, appeared around 6000 BC;

- Fuxi (伏羲) who made Yì (易) with his wife Nuwa (女娲) (4480- 4369 BCE)

- Shennong (神農) who created the agriculture (3320-3080 BCE).

Anyway, legend is only the legend. More than 2,000 years, the legend had not helped much for finding the Chinese origin.

Statues of Yan Emperor, Yellow Emperor

On April 18, 2007, in the city of Zhengzhou, capital of Henan province, China inaugurated the Statue of Yellow Emperor and Yan Emperor with 106 meters high built on a mountain overlooking the Yellow River. Obviously, the statues were built according to the legend. The legend is vague memories of the community, both virtual and real, naturally exist in the mind, like fish swimming in water. Fish is taken out of the water, it will die. Legend when turned into naked truth with bronze statues and stone stele, then the translucent dreamy part was stripped away, leaving only the a block of lifeless stone thus statue became of a fake thing! Indeed, Yellow Emperor had the yellow skin of the North Mongoloid. Meanwhile, Yan Emperor was Lac Viet (Indonesian race), with the same dark skin as people living in West highland Vietnam today. Massive and solemn statue shows that the Chinese did not know who their ancestors were!

2. Historical documents.

Throughout the twentieth century, scholars and Chinese majority carry two firm beliefs:

a. Han population evolved from ancient people (Homo erectus), long lived on Chinese soil.

b. Central plains of Yellow River is also the fatherland of Han ethnic. From there, Chinese ancestors spread Southeast, carrying the Chinese culture to civilize the Southern barbarian.

Many Chinese history books expressed this view.

In the book Chinese Ethnography, Wangdong Ling wrote: "500,000 years ago, after four ice times, the survivors stayed in the Tianshan Mountains. Then they spread to West to become the white skin group. The group went to East and become the yellow skin people. This group was divided into two sides: A part followed the Tianshan North Road including Manchu, Mongolian, Hui. A part followed the Tianshan South Road include Miao, Chinese, Tibetan. In which Tibet, included Anhdone, Malaysia, Indonesia, Cambodia, Cham. Hua people is Han later. Miao is San Miao, Baiyue, including Ouyue (Cambodia, Thailand, Laos), Miaoyue (Meo, Man), Louyue (Viet, Muong). "[1].

In the book Chinese General History (中国通史), Zhougu Cheng wrote:

"Yanyue (炎越) entered into China first following the Yangtze River, then they went to seven provinces of North Changjiang then spread and occupied six provinces of Yellow River, as well as spread to five five provinces of south Yuejiang (越江) River, total up to 18 provinces. So when the Chinese entered, then Yanyue (炎越) ethnic lived scattered throughout China. Because Chinese ethnic also went following the Tianshan South Road but they lingered in the Xinjiang region of Qinghai at that time it was still a lucky place, then they followed to the Yellow River to occupy six provinces in the North and then gradually spread to the south, pushed the Yanyue (炎越) back. "[2]

Chinese cultural origin [3]:

"From ancient times, activities of Chinese people had widely dispersed, the Yuanmou man in about 1,7 million years ago were the earliest humans existed in ancient Chinese history. Later the Peking man were the delegate to the ancient Paleolithic Age. History of many clans and tribes could be called primitive peoples as Jiu li ethnics, ethnics of Yan Emperor and the Yellow Emperor, who resided in Central Highlands and the ethnics in the nearby area. Besides, there were also ethnics like Zushen, Sanrong, Xunhu, Shi, Kang, Ba, Yao Yi, Huai Yi." An important part created of above notions were result of anthropological discoveries on Chinese land.

II. Archaeological findings.

1. Peking man [4]

On October 22, 1926, Andersson a Swedish miner engineer announced the discovery of two teeth of ancient man from Zhoukoudian. This has brought sudden progress to the theory of the origin and evolution of man. The owner of two teeth was classified in new variety and new specie named Sinanthropus pekinensis of Hominidae. However, it is known under the name "Peking Man." Today known as Homo erectus pekinensis.

Before the excavation, the cave had been perfectly preserved with sediment over 50 meters deep. The entire sediment had been divided into 17 layers from top to bottom. Absolute age of the 13th layer is about 730,000 years. From the 14th layer to 17th had been formed before the middle Pleistocene. The 10th layer, the lowest layer, having the Peking man fossils, with about 500,000 years old; while the 3rd layer, the above layer having the man fossil, from 230,000 to 250,000 years ago. Thus, the Beijing man had lived in this cave 260,000 years.

The excavation had been conducted in 1973 at No. 4 Cave (New Cave). Here detecting one molar of the upper jaws on the left an early Homo sapiens, "an intermediate form between Homo erectus at position No.1 and late Homo sapiens" at the Upper Cave. Along with it, there were a few numbers of stone tools, ash, burnt stones, burned bones, seeds (Hackberry) and more than 40 fossil mammals. Their absolute ages were about 200,000 to 100,000 years ago, during the late Pleistocene geological age.

In the two years, 1933-1934, they excavated the Upper Cave, at No. 4. The bottom layer of the cave was adjacent to the top layer of sediment of the Peking man's cave. Three skulls (number 101, 102 and 103) are preserved and skull caps of the man in the Upper Cave were discovered from the lower chamber. Several pelvis and femur were found near the skull's place. All the bones represented approximately 10 individuals. The anthropologist said that people in Upper Cave belonging to the late Homo sapiens. Their absolute age was around 27 thousand years ago. There were 25 artifacts collected, a polished antler, a bone needle, 141 jewelries including 125 perforated animal teeth, three shell carvings, egg-shaped perforated stones, and seven hewn stones. In addition to the fossil fish and amphibians, 47 mammal fossils were found. Geological age was the final stage of Late Pleistocene period.

After many debates, old relics were extended from 10,175 ± 360 BP (ZK-136-0-4) for the upper part of the cave and 33,200 ± 2000 BP (OXA-190) for the bottom layer. When discussing on the race relations, the Skull 101 was considered to be of a primitive Mongoloid, the Skull 102 wass considered to be of a Melanesian and the Skull 103 was considered to be of an Eskimo.

Unfortunately, the original specimens, along with documentation of Homo erectus position 1, were lost in 1941, during World War II (Shapiro 1976) and now it can be only studied through the ingot casting.

The Zhoukoudian is the key finding with the universal humanity. It is the first and only one in the world there is a rich archaeological trace of human so in the long time. The appearance of Homo sapiens in early stage 100.000-200.000 years ago to Homo sapiens later period in the same place with the Homo erectus peikinensis 600,000 years old seems to say that, Zhoukoudian is the miniature of human race history. Detecting Zhoukoudian is strong evidence supporting the Multiregional hypothesis. And this leads to the concept that China is an oldest ethnic group in the world. Chinese people from ancient Beijing had evolved into. The detection of Yuanmou persons with 1.7 million years old, in rural Shangnuo, Yuanmou District Yunnan Province, in May 1965 reinforces the above notion.

2. The Yangshao (仰韶) man [5]

In 1916, a Sweden mining engineer, Andersson, while seeking copper ore, he accidentally discovered the stone artifacts. This changed his life, turned him to become a famous archaeologist, when in 1921 he discovered the Yangshao (仰韶) relics, Sanmenxia City, Henan Province. The Yangshao Culture was distributed on 3,000,000 m² area, throughout the provinces of Shaanxi, Shanxi, Gansu, Henan, Hebei, Inner Mongolia, Qinghai, Ningxia ... Exists from 5000 to 3000 BC, Yangshao Neolithic culture left following artifacts:

- A large number of pebble grinding tools including axes, hoes, spades, shovels, tools sowing.

- Many brown glaze red, black, finely crafted potteries.

- Many semi-submersible houses, with large number of jars containing millet shells in these houses.

- Many bones of pigs, chickens and dogs.

- In the cemeteries, they found remains of people which were close to the mordern Han people.

The Yangshao Culture place a great important role, because, with the emergence of indigenous cultures with new stone tools, pottery and cereal agriculture, it affirmed the role of the Eastern civilization, rejected the old idea that Western civilization spreaded to the East. With the Chinese, it was meaningful especially because the first time they found the remains "of Chinese ancestry," as the owner of a high-level culture. From here it appeared the concept "Chinese civilization was born in Yangshao then spreaded toward the Southeast."

3. The Lungshan man [6]

In Spring 1928, Wujin Ding (吾金鼎), an archaeologist in Lungshan Town of Jinan City, Shandong Province (now Zhangqiu city of Shandong province), discovered the Ziyai cheng famous relics of culture Lungshan, about 5000 – 3950 years ago. At the height of the earth station in west landslides, he found the stone tools, bone tools, thin pottery with shiny black. People here were mainly engaged in agriculture combined with hunting, fishing and animal husbandry. They had a tradition of divination bones and might have appeared the bronze items. Origins of the Xia, Shang and Zhou cultures, might be significantly associated with the Lungshan culture. The most important characteristics of the culture in this period were the discoveries of the relic city sites. Such as in Shandong province, besides the Lungshan Ziyai cheng, there were vestiges such as Yaowang cheng, Shouguang relics near the Shouguang City, Linzi dianzhuangtun relics etc ... Next, they discovered at Henan with the Pingliang Huaiyang relics, Luantai Luyi relics, Jiangcheng relics of Dengfeng Wangcheng, Yancheng Huojiatai relics, Huixian Mingzangtai relics etc.

In Shanxi Taosi cultre (4500 years ago), the ancient bone DNA studies can be sure that the residents of the Lungshan culture, the Y SNP chromosome is O3-M122 haplotypes, and only contains O3 and O3e subtype, no other kind. Lungshan man is fully consistent with all parts of modern Chinese people. In other words, "ancestor of the modern Han was completely from Zhongyuan man, ie. the ancient Lungshan man."

4 . The Hemudu (河姆渡) man [7]

It was first found in 1973 in Hemudu (河姆渡), Yuyao, Zhejiang Province. Hemudu culture of the Neolithic Period in the Yangtze River downstream, distributed mainly in the south bank of Hangzhou Bay, Ningbo, Shaoxing plain and Zhoushan Island, aged 5000-3300 years BC. According to matriarchy, the Hemudu people formed the villages with different sizes. In the village many houses built. But because the ground is the riparian wetland, so it formed the architecture and structure here differed significantly from the Central Highlands. The archaeological excavations at Hemudu failed to find the family cemetery, found only 27 tombs scattered with 13 complete skeletons. In 1978, after the end of second excavation, two anthropologists, Hanqiangxin and Fanqifeng arrived the excavation site, evaluated the ages, genders, fitness, races of the remains. Among them were 9 immature people, 4 adults, skull No. M23 and No. M17 were fully preserved.

(1). About the age – the M23 skull of the [3rd] cultural layer - a huge skull, wide forehead, cheekbones out wide in sudden, large jaw, obviously male. Pursuant to the skull bone, it resembled the modern humans and the wear of the teeth, for that he was around 30 years old. The M17 skull was abnormally swollen at the skull forehead, lacking external occipital protuberance, crooked jaw, characteristic for female adolescents, aged at about 13 -15.

(2) The height – the skeleton retains the length, the characteristic height of modern Chinese. M23 is 169 to 170 cm high. M17 is from 152 to 157 cm.

(3) The race - M23, M17 both have high cheekbones and wide, shovel shaped incisors, like residents of the Yellow River Basin in Neolithic period.

III. Comments:

Throughout the twentieth century, the world humanities influenced by two postulates:

1. Modern East Asian people from Tibet migrated to.

2. The human civilization originated from Mesopotamia, and from there to Europe then via Central Asia spreaded to Chinese, ultimately to Southeast Asia.

The above archaeological finds in the Chinese land created the above views on the other hand also influenced by those misconceptions. Because it was very soon, from the 1920s, the Neolithic Yangshao culture was discovered. Black ceramics distributed on a large area, owners' remains were close to the modern Chinese people. That makes world scholars believed that both humans and Chinese culture were originated from the West and then spreaded to the East. In 1930s, when the Lungshan culture with later age discovered the artifacts similar to Yangshao culture, then people have more reasons to affirm this view. But in spite of human prejudices, scientific facts themselves followed in its stubborn footsteps. Not only is Lungshan, in the 1970s, Hemudu culture, Liangzhu, Fairy Cave etc were discovered, all in the South belonging to the Yangtze River Delta. Not only richer, more advanced, but ages of these Southeast cultures were earlier than age of Yangshao many thousand years.

Before the truth that can not be argued, several Chinese scholars run by treatment methods of "two principles", said, "the Yangtze River Delta is the second cradle of Chinese civilization." "Yangtze River Civilization is the second mother of Chinese civilization."[3] It is a conflict thinking so it is difficult to convince. No way a people, a culture that has two origins, two places arise.

Into the new century, to repair the outdated opinions, rejected by the facts, Zhou Jixu in "Origin in Chinese civilization, the difference between archeology and ancient documents using the same explanation - Learning the Origin of the civilization in the Yellow River basin, "[8] proposed the theory that Chinese ancestors were Indi-Europian nomadic tribes from Europe came. This is the latest opinion typical of modern perceptions of the Chinese people about their own ethnic origin. The author wrote:

"Unlike the Yangshao and Hemudu people who came from Southern China, Yellow Emperor's population came from the West of China, from the Western part of the Eurasian continent. They conquered people of the Yellow River and the Yangtze River, who possessed the developed agricultural cultures.

By combining their own culture with elements of the indigenous culture, the population of Yellow Emperor gradually developed a brilliant new civilization in the Xia, Shang and Zhou dynasties. They replaced the indigenous people holding the leadership roles on the stage of Chinese history. It was thought that the population of the Yellow Emperor is a branch of the Indo - European, is one of the most significant events this known in human history. A large number of Indo-European words in ancient Chinese language clearly confirmed this fact. The remaining ruins of the Yellow Emperor age are relevant to the Lungshan culture with the archaeological evidences and the civilization of the Xia, Shang, Zhou, Qin dynasties as its successors. Evidences for this claim comes from two sources: The first to use the evidences of ancient documents to prove that the people of Zhou dynasty were the people under the Yellow Emperor's reign, started from nomads, and the second evidence that there had a large number of Indo-European languages in the Zhou dynasty, based on the evidence of historical linguistics. The third was the religious similarities between the Yellow Emperor's people and the Pre Indo-European people. "

Thus:

"Chinese civilization had experienced conflicts in ancient time. The Europeans from the Central Asian steppe west brought

new cultural elements to the Yellow River valley about 2300 years BC. They have combined their advanced techniques, such as copper smelting, metal tools, weapons, horse carriages and horses tamed, culturally indigenous agricultural development in the Yellow River basin and Yangtze basin. This combination created the splendid civilization of the Xia, Shang and Zhou. Contrary to public opinion that "Yellow River civilization has its independent history," it was really harmony. The idea that Chinese civilization has an independent history has been very popular, due to the strong influence, especially of the Chinese writing letters system, has been used since the Shang's reign (1600 BC) until today. The Chinese characters with special types make it hard to figure out the relationship between ancient Chinese and other ancient languages. The ancient square characters easily gave people the mistaken illusion that the ancient Chinese language was stable and not change as the square. If that so how are we able to understand this strange language by the method of common language? How can we find the relationship of ancient Chinese language and other languages? In fact, ancient Chinese language is one of the ordinary languages of the people just like other languages, if we strip away the overcoat of the characters from the language.

"There was a prevailing notion to consider that the Chinese history began with Yellow Emperor (about 2300 BC), who defeated all his opponents and dominate the Yellow River area. But not many people know that Yellow Emperor and his people migrated from Western Eurasian continent to and that they and their descendants really had the leading role in the stage of history from the Yellow River valley about 2300 years BC. History was written in the traditional documents that the only considered from the time when Yellow Emperor's people entered the Yellow River valley and developed a civilization there. Those who had previously lived there, and created a prehistory glorious civilization of the two rivers (the Yellow River and Yangtze River) were sunk after the fog of history. They *were excluded from the traditional annals, which covered almost all the history of China, from Shàngshū (上書), Shījīng (詩經), to the chronicles etc. This was a history to bring the tendency to overturn the position between the host and the guest. One reason for this situation was that the oppression and elimination made by the Yellow Emperor's powerful force. The other reason was that, while these other people did not invent their own writing system, the Yellow Emperor's nation had already done; one of which was used by the Chinese people up to now. The ancient Chinese characters were recognized only in the formation and the recession of the Yellow Emperor's ancient nation. That was why there was great disparity between the archaeological area in the Yellow River, Yangtze River and the traditional historical records related only to the early days of agriculture in the region. Concerning to the civilization of the "Two Rivers in East Asia" created by those who came previously. We also found a significant amount of information from historical documents that could last be confirmed by the discovery of archaeological evidence and historical linguistics. The difference in lifestyle, customs and languages among the natives and residents of the Yellow Emperor gave us further evidence that the people of the Yellow Emperor had appropriated an existing culture."*

In the concepts shown above, the idea of the author Zhou Jixu was the latest and also seemed more scientific when he relied on the evidences of archeology and historical linguistics. However, there is the fact that, archeology, despite with the many discoveries about prehistoric humans but because of the randomness in the archaeological findings as well as the inadequacies in deciphering archaeological exhibits, archaeologists in many cases were led to serious mistakes. A typical example was the 70s of last century, when discovered the Homo erectus remains at Neanderthal that was very similar to modern Europeans, the majority of scholars said that it was the European ancestry. This conclusion led to the prevailed position of Multiregional hypothesis, a false assumption about human origins, humanities sciences were led to a disastrously wrong way. Not only that, historical linguistics, a methodology was widely featured in reality, it could only detect the proximity between the two languages without sufficient jurisdiction to determine who was the mother, who was the child! Malay origins of the Vietnamese, one work with much sweat and dedication of Binh Nguyen Loc writer was an example of the wrong direction, causing much harm!

Thus, what the author was proud: "Thought that the population of Yellow Emperor is a branch of the Indo - European people, is one of the most significant events this known in human history" is a serious mistake. In the following section, we will discuss with the author.

References.

1. Wangdong Ling. *China's ethnography*. (Extracted by Kim Dinh –Viet ly to nguyen. An Tiem, Saigon, 1970).

2. Zhougu Chéng. *Chinese General History* (中国通史). (Extracted by Kim Dinh - Viet ly to nguyen. An Tiem, Saigon, 1970).

3. Tangde Yang edited. *Chinese cultural origin* (Original: The formation and development of Chinese culture) Publisher: People Shandong 1993. Translated by Nguyen Thi Thu Hien. Writers' Association Publishing House, 2003.

4. The Peking Man World Heritage Site at Zhoukoudian
   http://www.unesco.org/ext/field/beijing/whc/pkm-site.htm
   http://www-personal.une.edu.au~pbrown3/UpperCave.html
   The Peking Man World Heritage 4. Site at Zhoukoudian
   http://www.unesco.org/ext/field/beijing/whc/pkm-site.htm
   http: //www-personal.une.edu.au~pbrown3/UpperCave .html

5. 仰韶文化 http://baike.baidu.com/view/9771.htm.
   Yangshao culture http://baike.baidu.com/view/9771.htm

6. 龙山文化 http://baike.baidu.com/view/22365.htm.

7. 河姆渡文化 http://baike.baidu.com/view/1567.htm

8. Hemudu culture http://baike.baidu.com/view/1567.htm

9. Zhou Jixu. *The Rise of Agricultural Civilization in China: The Disparity between Archeological Discovery and the Documentary Record and Its Explanation.* SINO-PLATONIC PAPERS Number 175, December, 2006

CHAPTER II

CHINESE ORIGIN
UNDER THE NEW LOOK

Finding the ethnic origin is the work of natural science particular biology and anthropology. From the nineteenth century, by the discoveries of the human skulls in the archaeological relics, anthropological science invented the survey methodology of skull morphology. This is measuring the key indicators of skulls and through the statistical accounting, taking the average index for each category represent for each race. By this approach method, anthropology had succeeded in identifying many human species around the world. But by applying the method of measurement and statistics, the success of the survey is determined by the number of specimens that had been. With cases with so few skull specimens, the survey cannot be performed. The history and culture are the social activities of the human community in time and space so we should be able to go from the survey the history, the culture to discover the culture's owners. This approach is useful; helps to solve many cases in which anthropology is unable to do. However, that is indirect ways, the reliability is low and sometimes caused the serious mistakes. Because now there are enough biological materials to determine the owner of the Chinese land and culture; so here, I go in the opposite direction: surveying the formation of people on China land and from that to understand the Chinese culture through its real owners. For this, we must first identify human origins

I. Beginning from the human origins

Every nation was not born naturally but it had an intimate relationship with human origin. Once it incorrectly identified the origin of the man-kind, the affirmation of any ethnic origin has not yet sufficiently reliable. Chinese people were not beyond this practice. Therefore, first we must agree about human origins.

In the XX century, there were two conflicting theories about human origins. Out of Africa hypothesis said that humanity appeared in Africa, particularly East Africa and from there spreaded to all parts of the world. Multiregional hypothesis stated that, mankind was born from many different centers: Africa born the blacks, Europe born the whites, Mesopotamian highlands born the Sumer people, Asia was the place originated the yellow skin people. Nearly a century, two competing theories were inconclusive and have formed two opposing schools.

But by the '70s, when the Neanderthal remains were discovered in Israel, they were very similar to modern Europeans, many scholars said that the Neanderthals were the ancestors of the European people. Thus, the Multiregional hypothesis prevailed, became the unique, and suppressed the Out of Africa hypothesis, driven most studies in the world.

Applying Multiregional hypothesis in explaining the formation of the Asian population, it said that the Asian population had been developed continuously, from Yuanmou Homo erectus in 1,7 million years ago to become the Peking man over 600,000 years ago then to become the modern Homo sapiens to today.

The idea of two authors, Wangdong Ling and Zhougu Chéng, said that 500,000 years ago, after the last frost, the survivors gathered in the southern Tianshan then immigrated throughout Asia was due to be dominated by the Multiregional hypothesis. Likewise, the authors of Origin of Chinese culture advocated that the Chinese people today were the products of continuous evolution from Yuanmou Homo erectus.

As a result, almost throughout the twentieth century, it was confirmed that humans appeared in the Tibetan Plateau, invaded China then spread to Southeast Asia. Southeast Asia was the standing water in the history, where only received and didnot create any the contributions to the human civilization! But when they couldnot explain why in several archaeological sites in the South China had a higher age than those in the North, and several cultures in the South were in higher development than in the North. That made the way of migration from northwest to southeast were suspected, the Multiregional hypothesis became unconvincing. Therefore, the world humanities science in the half of the previous century fell into crisis, it was unable to lead the human ideology.

It was glad that, in the last years of past century, a new technology and new methodology were invented. It become the magic wand to ultimately solve the urgent problems for thousands of years of the humans. It is the genetic engineering used to map the human genome, and with it, the genetic method used to find the human origins.

We can say, on September 29, 1998 when the group of Professor J.Y. Chu announced the study results of the Genetic Relationship of Populations in China [1], it marked a special milestone in human awareness of its origin. Three discoveries were announced for the first time:

1. Homo sapiens first appeared in East Africa, 160,000-200,000 years ago.

2. 70,000 years ago, the pre-historic people were from Africa, immigrated along the South Asian seaside to Vietnam.

3. About 50,000 years ago, from Vietnam, people migrated to Australia, islands of Southeast Asia, India and 40,000 years ago, when the northern climate improved, they immigrated to China. 30,000 years ago, they passed the Bering Strait entered into the America.

Those announcements published in the Los Angeles Times on September 29 that were a shock to the American scientists. Though being excited, but as the intrinsic nature of true science is skepticism, many leading genetic centers in the world embarked immediately to expertise the conclusions of the Texas research team.

About three years later, many genetic studies were published: Out of Eden Peopling of the World and Journey of Mankind the Peopling in the World of the Stephen Oppenheimer in Oxford University [2] [3]. The Journey of Man: a genetic Odyssey of Spencer Wells. [4]

It was not only to confirm the J.Y. Chu group's discovery, the studies also clarified many important events like the people living on the grasslands of Mongolia were also from the Southeast Asia to go up. People from the Vietnam migrated to make Austronesian people on the South Pacific islands; then chickens, dogs, pigs also from Vietnam and Southern China to be brought down there etc. That was clear that the new genetic discoveries have changed our perceptions, not only about human origins, but also about the origin of East Asian nations. Humans had only one origin. People today are descendants of only ancestors born in Africa 160,000 years ago.

Upright people (Homo erectus) were not our ancestors. This discovery also demonstrates the correctness of the school of African origin: The Homo erectus appeared in Africa two million years ago. About 1,9 million years ago they migrated to Asia, their representatives be the Javanese in Indonesia, the Yuanmou, Peking man in China, as well as the ancient people in Do mountain, Vietnam ... However, in 250,000 years ago, we did not understand why they left Asia, immigrated to Europe where the Neanderthals as the last representatives extincted about 34,000 years ago.

Obviously, the findings of genetics had rejected the old beliefs of the authors said that the Chinese people were continuous evolution from Yuanmou Homo erectus to today. It also rejected the hypothesis that prehistoric man concentrated in south of Tianshan and entered into China. Moreover, the work of W. Ballinger et al. also affirmed Vietnamese people who had the highest genetic diversity in Asian populations. It meant the Vietnamese people were the most ancient people in Asia and Vietnam was the cradle of Asian residents. Due to this reason, if we want to learn the origin of the Chinese nation, we must first understand the process of forming the Vietnamese people.

II. The formation of Vietnamese people

From the DNA survey of Chinese communities today, geneticists discovered, they are the descendants of people came from Vietnam to explore China 40,000 years ago. So, if we want to know origin of Chinese people, we cannot help but begin by understanding human formation process on Vietnam land. Combination of genetic information with knowledge of archeology, anthropology, ethnology, cultural studies etc, I would like to present as following:

Approximately 70,000 years ago, prehistoric men from Africa immigrated along the Indian Ocean coast to Vietnam. It was a breakthrough discovery. But this time, it brought us the question: who they are, which race did they belong to? Only when answering this question, we can follow them on next migration routes to form regional population. Because there was not any genetic research on this issue, we find the answers in archaeology and paleoanthropology.

In 80s of last century, from the survey 70 skulls from stone Age to Bronze Age, discovered in Vietnam, in the work named South East Asian Anthropology, Professor Nguyen Dinh Khoa concluded: "At beginning, in the territory of Vietnam had two big races: The Mongoloid and the Australoid. They mixed blood with each other and born four strains: Indonesien, Melanesien, Vedoid and Negritoid, belonged the Australoid type in which Indonesien was the main strain.

In Bronze – Iron Age, across the whole Southeast Asia, there was a strong transformation of the Australoid type into Southern Mongoloid type. Composition of Australoid narrowed to the maximum in the area, it didn not know it was due to the immigration or the assimilation. "[6]

The discovery of the leading Vietnamese anthropologist opened the door to know the original inhabitant of Vietnam as follows:

People from Africa came to Vietnam included two big races: Mongoloid and Australoid. They mixed blood, born four strains of the ancient Vietnamese: Indonesian, Melanesian, Vedoid and Negritoid. According to genetic theory, the Indonesian must carry the highest rate of Mongoloid blood and it is typical Mongoloid race. However, because the Australoid occupied majority of people so then blood mixing in their offspring; the Australoid element became dominant, the Mongoloid elements became recessive, resulted that the entire Vietnamese population carrying the Australoid genetic code, the latter were classified as Australoid type. What to be said here was that, although they were recessive Mongoloid genes, but in ancient Vietnamese residents, the Indonesian strain (Lac Viet) had the highest proportion of Mongoloid blood.

So, it is understandably that many authors, while surveying and comparing the skull morphology, ranked Indonesians into the Mongoloid race. This mistake lasted almost throughout the twentieth century, caused quite a nuisance for the Vietnamese population study. Just to the 80s, with his talent, Nguyen Dinh Khoa discovered the above secrets.

Genetics also help us to answer the question posed by Nguyen Dinh Khoa: "Why did the Mongoloid disappear from this country?" That was the truth that the Mongoloid disappeared from Southeast Asia during the Stone Age, but they didn't "evaporate" because their precious genetic resources were existing in the Australoid genome.

We can imagine the circumstances that led to the appearance of Vietnamese people as follows:

According to Stephen Oppenheimer [2],

Approximately 85,000 years ago, the immigration out of Africa was carried out. A group crossed the Red Sea (the Gate of Grief), then migrated along the south bank of the Arabian Peninsula to India. From Sri Lanka, they continued to go along the Indian Ocean seaside to Western Indonesia and 70,000 years ago, a group of people along Western Borneo coast to Vietnam.

At that time, it was in the Ice Age, most of the water from the ocean evaporated and formed the ice covering the continentals. Therefore, the sea level was 130 meters lower than that of today. J.Y. Chu's researches said that prehistoric people immigrated to Vietnam. After the arduous journey lasted up to 15,000 years in the direction of sunrise, to Vietnam, people met the good land, according to the Bible, it was a paradise. The small groups of migrants suddenly were overwhelmed by the immense plain, plentiful food, pleasant climate. They soon settled, Australoid race and Mongoloid race met and the blood intermixing took place. During the long migration time, the Sun was such as their Savior, heating and pointing the direction for their journey to the oriental direction. Perhaps this explains why the Sun God was the first god and sacred to the Oriental ethnics!

50,000 years ago, when the number of people became crowded, by their feet and rafts crossing the rivers, the lakes, the Vietnamese people had immigrated to Australia, occupied the islands of Southeast Asia. To the West, they came to India, became natives, later called as the Dravidian.

To read this episodic story, please to note to the events, the genetic studies suggested, perhaps due to the difficult environment, food scarce, so the ancient people immigrated in the small groups. There were also small groups of Mongoloid up to Northwest Vietnam and due to the weather was too cold, they couldn't go forward so they stayed there. Because they didn't meet other people to mix the blood so they kept their pure Mongoloid genetic resources. The remains of Mongoloid Liujiang people with 68,000 years old found in Guangxi can testify to this. Up to 40,000 years ago, Northern climate improved, people from Vietnam gradually immigrated to enter China, dominated the Yangtze basin and then went up to the Yellow River basin. In this time, the Mongoloid was from Northwest Vietnam, went along to the west corridor to Mongol land. Here they maintained the purebred Mongoloid genetic resources, later known as the North Mongoloid. The skulls of the Mongoloid people with 40,000 years old discovered in Mongolia confirm this.

Genetics also said, around 30,000 years ago, the ancient Viet from China migrated to Siberia and crossing Bering Strait to occupy the the America.

Surveying 5,000 fossil teeth found in Europe, the scientists discovered, 40,000 years ago, had an influx of people from East Asia through Central Asia to Europe. Here, they met Europid people just from the Middle East to come to. Two lines of blood were mixed and they born the Euraspian, ancestry of European today [7].

III. The formation of the population on the Chinese land

First of all, to discuss the formation of the population on the Chinese land in a scientific way, please get rid of the the old notions relating to Homo erectus, Yuanmou or Beijing man, we only spoke about the modern Homo sapiens.

Looking paleoanthropological map of East Asia, we saw that, previously, people in Niah Cave Indonesia with 39,600 +/- 1000 years old were the earliest Homo sapiens who were discovered. Then people in Son Vi Vietnam with 32,000 years old. But the 1930s, they discovered the Homo sapiens skulls with the 27,000 years old in Upper Cave of Zhoukoudian sites. Along with Zhoukoudian, Upper Cave has a very important role in East Asian anthropology studies.

It is remarkably that the commentary of the experts surveyed the skulls of Upper Cave: "A surprising fact is that three skulls were discovered with good condition, one male and two females, were representing for the three groups ethnic today scattered literally from the poles to the equator." Weiderich described the male skull as "White" (in general as some of the oldest CroMagnons Perigordian tradition of European contemporary) and two female skulls as "Melanesian" and "Eskimoid", i.e., the Australoid and Northern Mongoloid. After many debates, the age of the relics is extended from $10,175 \pm 360$ BP (ZK-136-0-4) for the upper part of the cave and $33,200 \pm 2000$ BP (OXA-190) for the bottom layer. When discussing race relations, skull 101 was considered a primitive Mongoloid, 102 was a Melanesian and 103 was an Eskimo."

Excavation conducted in 1973 at No. 4 (New Cave). Here they detected the jaw teeth no. 1 of the upper left jaw of an early Homo sapiens, "an intermediate form between Homo erectus position 1 and the later Homo sapiens" in Upper Cave. Along with it, there was the small number of stone tools, ash, burnt stones, burned bones, seeds (Hackberry) and more than 40 fossil mammals. Their absolute ages were about 200,000 to 100,000 years ago, during the late Pleistocene geological age.

Because three Homo sapiens skulls discovered in 1933-1934 in Upper Cave were lost in World War II and molars of the people in the New Cave was not surveyed by the DNA so we couldn't draw the firm conclusions about the anthropologies of these people. However, it was able to believe that, the upper jaw tooth of a New Cave was not belonged to a Homo sapiens, because at the time of 200,000 years ago, the modern humans were not able to immigrate to Asia. It is very likely the above judgement was also on the same fate of the theory that Neanderthals were a form of ancient Europians. The earliest skeleton of a Mongoloid people in Liu Jiang, Guangxi was only 68,000 years old.

The idea that, the male skull (101) in Upper Cave was a white Europid man is dubious, because so far, in ancient skull collection in the East, there has never been Europid. If the classification of Weiderich is true then this is the need to learn more. If the skull 101 was a primitive Mongoloid, 102 was a Melanesian and 103 was an Eskimoid, then situation will be explained as follows:

The world archeologists thought that, from about 250,000 years ago, the Homo erectus left Asia to migrate to Europe that the last representatives were Neanderthals. This explains why human was absent in Asian in that period. There were no traces of Homo erecrus at Zhoukoudian in 250,000 years ago was the evidence of this fact.

In East Asia, Homo sapiens only appeared 70,000 years ago. 40,000 years ago, two strains of ancient Vietnamese people were Indonesian, Melanesian, were all belonged to the group of Australoid types migrated to China. In this time, there were also Mongoloid groups from Northwestern Vietnam went along the West corridor going up Mongolia land.

Try to find out how the ancient Vietnamese people had lived on the vast mainland China? Archeology and genetics suggested that, the exodus from Vietnam to China took place in several stages. First, there was still the way of life of traditional hunting and gathering, they brought old stone tools. But about 20,000 years ago, the Hoabinhian created the new stone tools, those tools were also brought up in The Fairy Cave that we found out.

About 15,000 years ago, when the Hoa Binh People in Vietnam created millet, rice, chicken, dogs, pigs, these plants and animals were also taken up to China by many different paths. By the following the Western corridor led to Northwestern China. By the path following the South China Plain led to the Yangtze basin and the coast to the east of China. The Fairy Cave sites with pottery shards of 20,000 years and 12,400 years old rice grain were the earliest traces of pottery and rice which were discovered in China.

Late than 9,000 years of Jiahu culture with rice agriculture at high level, along with pottery, divination word (符字Fú zì) on turtle plastron. An achieved higher level of development was the Hemudu culture with 7,000 years ago and Liangzhu culture with 5,300 years ago. At the Yellow River Midland, there was Bonfo 2 relic with pottery 6,000 years old and characters. This were the remains of the ancient Viet people too. Throughout the long time, on East Asian land in general and China in particular, only the Australoid lived. But about 7,000 years ago, an event were recorded by the anthropology, which were the Yangshao culture in Yellow River basin appeared new race: Southern Mongoloid. It is a big event of the East Asian population. Because there were no researches on these two phenomenons, I would suggest the following hypothesis:

1. About the Yangshao people

In 1921, archaeologists discovered Yangshao Culture at midlands of Yellow River, aged 5000-3000 years BC. At Bonfo millet planting village in Shanxi Province, Southern Mongoloid people remains, and owner of the Yangshao Culture were detected. Because the Bonfo people were close in morphology with modern Chinese, many argued that they were the Han's ancestors and this place was also the original place of the Han ethnic and the Han culture. From here, the Han culture was transmitted to Lungsan and then to the down to the South. So far, the majority of Chinese scholars still had been following this thought.

I would like to explain about the Yangshao people as followings: As stated before, the Mongols from Vietnam imigrated to Western China and Mongolia land. Here, they lived a long time by hunting-gathering and maintained a pure Mongoloid genetic code, later known as the Northern Mongoloid.

About 10,000 years ago, the last Ice Age ended, the vast ice field of northern China freed from frost, became the grassland. Mongolians domesticated goats, sheep, switched to nomadic existence. Because they were nomadic, so the Yellow River was more important to them. Not just for fishing as before, but it also provided the water, reserved forages, planting cereals ... So, the Yellow River was the survival of the nomadic tribes.

Long time ago, Viet people also lived by hunting, fishing and later began planting millet in southern of the Yellow River. The natural contact between the south people and north people happened, of course, led to the bloodmixing. Halfbreed of Mongolia – Viet were born. Who could they be? Genetics shows that, in the Indonesian body, it still has the potential Mongoloid gene. At present, the intermixing with Mongoloid caused the Mongoloid blood ratio increased in their children [10]. But the more increase was not enough to become the pure Mongoloid. Therefore, the Mongolian-Viet hybrid was a new strain: South Mongoloid.

In other words, the Southern Mongoloid was a product of the intermixing between the Mongoloid and Australoid Viet people. Maybe, for a long time, people on both sides of the Yellow River lived in harmony, mixed race marriages occured: Mongolian-Viet hybrid were born. But nomadic life type inevitably led to the plunder: the Mongols reached the Yellow River and hit the agricultural people, robbed the food, cattle, male and female slave. Along with the robberies, the rape occured.

On the South bank, due to often being suffered by the pillages, the hybrid Southern Mongoloid people were born more. And like a chain reaction, the hybrid blood spread to their fellow, made the number of hybrid people being increased and in about 5.000-3000 BC the Southern Mongoloid became the main owners of the Yangshao culture population. Author Jixu Zhou said, the Yangshao people came up from the southern China. This was a speculation that seemed reasonable but in fact it was not so. Archeology confirms that the New Stone age in the Southern there were no Mongoloid It can be only the Yangshao people who were born in place by Mongolia-Viet bloodmix!

2. About the Lungshan culture's owners [11]

Lungshan Culture was a big culture, played a particularly important role in Chinese history. Most Lungshan cultural sites located in Shandong peninsula, Shaanxi, Shanxi, Henan, Hebei. In the Liaodong Peninsula, Jiangsu, Hubei etc also found similar sites. This culture contains black, thin, hard, glossy potteries, especially black thin ceramics as eggshells (in Rizhao, Zhangqiu) which are extremely unique, so-called as "black ceramic culture." The study of bone's DNA of the owner Shanxi Taozi

(4500 years ago) can ensure that the residents of the Lungshan culture brought the Y chromosome SNP haplotypes : O3-M122, only contains O3 and O3e sub typ. From this, the authors concluded: "The genetic code was consistent with all parts of modern Chinese people. In other words, the ancestors of the modern Han people completely came from Zhongyuan ancient people ie Lungshan people." And "We can be sure, today's Han ethnic in many places in China, from Northeast to Guangdong, from Kèjiā (客家) in Southeast to Lanzhou Northwest, the subjects were the ancient people with 5,000 years ago from Central Highlands. Han people today were direct descendants of the ancient people at Central Highlands, in paternity of Han, chromosome O3 held an absolute dominant position throughout 5,000 years, and it has not changed. "

3. About the Hemudu (河姆渡) people

From the remains of the Northern Mongoloid (skull 101 and 102) found in Upper Cave, we can assume that from ancient times, there were small groups of Mongoloid came to live at the Yangtze River estuary, Shandong Peninsula. They lived by hunting, gathering and fishing. Around 5000-6000 BC, the sea was receding, the Viet people lived by agriculture from the mainland advanced towards the sea.

In Zhejiang estuary encountered between rice farmers and fishermen, led to the intermixing blood between the Australoid and the Mongoloid. The Southern Mongloid hybrid people were born. Until 5000 BC, they became the subjects of Hemudu culture. Just as the Yanshao people in the North, the Hemudu people multiplied rapidly and became the majority population in Eastern China. After 2698 BC, they arrived in Taiwan, Indochina and then went down over the sea to Malaysia, brought the Southern Mongoloid genetic resources to the South, created a revolution of Southeast Asian population, which later called as the Mongoloidization process of Southeast Asian residents.

4. The formation of the Chinese people

Above showing that, from about 5000 BC, on Chinese land, there were two centers appeared the Southern Mongoloid people as Yangshao and Hemudu. The Southern Mongoloid people increased in number, became the majority in the population on Chinese land. According to calculations of British mathematician cum geographer Buckminster Fuller [12], on the coast of East Asia in the fourth-third millennium BC, Viet people occupied 54% of the people in the world. If whole Asia continental included, that number was not less than 65%. On East Asia land, the Viet built a brilliant early developed rice culture in the world.

In 2698 BC years, a major event occurred that changed the history of East Asia. It is the alliance of nomadic tribes led by Xuanyuan clan, opened a big attack in Zhoulu, defeated the Viet people, then occupied the Southern of Yellow River and established the Yellow Emperor's dynasty. Many documents based on the legends showed that Yan Emperor and Yellow Emperor were brothers, in the same tribe alliance. That's just the refraction of events that happened in the past that people wanted to conceal the nature of an invasion. Such a brutal big battle in ancient time, it could not be a war between people in same tribal, it must have been a death fight between two civilizations. Of course, the nomadic civilization won. Here there was an important issue to clarify: Who did invade the Viet people's land? Most Chinese history books wrote that that were Han people: From the Zhoulu Battle, the Han people rushed into the South of Yellow River and evicted Viet people run over the Yangtze River. But the reality was not so. At that time, just in the south of the Yellow River, only on the land of the Viet there were the South Mongoloid people. And the North bank, where the number of the Southern Mongoloid people were not many and they were still slaves in the Mongolia families (women were arrested as housemaids, their children with their fathers were slaves) not lived freely into the tribes!

Scholar Jixu Zhou said they were the Indo – Europe came from the West. But the truth was not so. If Indo - Europe occupied for the Zhongyuan land at that time, then so far, now Chinese must have the other genome. At that time, if the Westerners had enough force to occupy the southern of Yellow River, they could only be the Arian tribe in Persian region, who later occupied India. Scenario would occur; native people were destroyed brutally, were enslaved, and were herded down South. The North China's territory would be directed by the Arian people with Brahmans, Sankrit letters and same cruel caste system like in India.

The corollary would be a constant devastating ethnic war rather than Golden Age of Yao, Shun. And most importantly, the majority of Chinese people today should have Indo-European genetic code rather than Southern Mongoloid as Mr. Zhou admitted. In the regional context of that time, the people who invaded land of Viet people were only the nomadic Mongols. The Zhoulu battle took place in the south bank area of the Yellow River of Hebei Province,

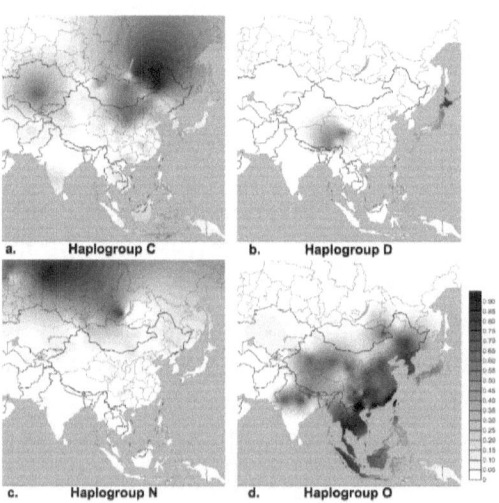

Four groups of people from Vietnam dominated East Asia
Haplogroup C = Melanesian race, D = Negritoid
N = Mongoloid, O = Indonesian
https://investigativegenetics.biomedcentral.com/articles/10.1186/2041-2223-4-11

North of Beijing. Thus, the battle took place in the North of the Yellow River midlands rather than West of China, so that was the land of Mongolia. The most solid evidence was that the Chinese people today have been carryng genes of Southern Mongoloid, the Mongol genome, that are not genes of Indo-European people.

In fact, when the nomads founded the Yellow Emperor's kingdom, in China still remained many strong nations of the Viet people: Ba, Shu in Southwest; Emperor Li in the East and Chiyou in South of the Yangtze River. In fact, the land where the Yellow Emperor gained too small compared to Viet independent nations. The predominant means of Mongol people were horses, could only be promoted in the Loess Plateau.

Out of this area, encountered the muddy plain, the invaders didn't promote such advantages anymore. The persistent resistance war of the Viet people has been written in Qi men dunjia daquan shu (奇門遯甲大全书): "Yesterday Yellow Emperor combatted Chi You (蚩尤), Zhoulu, battle was not ended up to now." Not only that, Thuong thu (Shangshu -上書) also wrote that, until Yao, Shun, they still had to worry about fighting with Sanmiao barbarians. Chronicles records that until the Qin dysnaty, i.e., more than 2000 years later, the Qin people could pass the Yangtze River.

Based on the significant amount of Western vocabulary in language of the North China during the Zhou dysnaty, to say that people who occupied the South of Yellow River at that time were the Westerner was hardly convincing hypothesis! Now science shows the fact that 40,000 years ago, an influx of people from East Asia to the West contributed to the population of Europe. Along with blood, these migrants also contribute a voice to make the European language. That is the reason why there are ancient Viet words in the European language. Those are also words stored in the Chinese language.

In South of Yellow River, the Yellow Emperor's population met a vast land, rich economy and persistent struggle of the crowded Viet people. Unlike Arian people occupyed India killes or captures natives as slaves; Mongols were unable to pacify by military power, they applied a wise policy. They let most Viet people peacefully plowing in their land with taxpaying conditions and the forced labor. On the other hand, they gave up the nomadic life, and learnt the cultivatation, the language, the customs and traditions of the Viet people to facilitate the rule. And of course, due to co-living closesly, there was a mixed blood between the two race. Due to the small number of Mongol people, only several generations later, they were no longer pure Mongolia. Mongolian-Viet hybrid that self-claiming as Huaxia, replaced his Mongol father, to become the social leaders.

The documents on baike.baidu.com based on genetics, are accurate: "The ancestors of the modern Han people completely came from ancient Zhongyuan, ie Lungshan people"; "Han people today are direct descendants of the ancient Zhongyuan people, in Han paternity, chromosome O3 holds an absolute dominant position throughout the 5000 year, and no changed" and "The Lungshan culture, considered as the Han's cultural ancestors of the Huaxia tribe, and the relics excavated from Taozi verified, supported this viewpoint "

Thus, the genetic detection was matching with the concepts that have shaped Chinese history that Huaxia people were descendants of the Yellow Emperor, of the nomadic tribes invaded the Trong Nguồn (Zhongyuan) land in 4698 previous year.

How this event was explained?

Obviously, the Lungshan people did not fall down from the Heaven. Archeology and genetics confirmed that they were descendants of inhabitants of the Yangshao Culture of the Southern Mongoloid race, appeared in around 5000 BC. History confirmed that in 2698 BC there happened the invasion of the

Yellow Emperor tribes and the Huaxia people were descendants of the Yellow Emperor. This proved that there was mixed blood between the Yellow Emperor's people and Lungshan people to born the Huaxia people.

Such events only occured when the genetic code of the Yellow Emperor tribe already was available in Lungshan people's blood, so it could not generate the new race. From here, we can say surely that the people of the Yellow Emperor were the Northern Mongoloid race. Meanwhile, the indigenous Zhongyuan people, Lungshan culture's owner, as have been identified, were bringing the Southern Mongoloid gene. Therefore, when the very few people of the Yellow Emperor mixed with the overcrowded Lungshan people, born the Huaxia Lungshan people who carried the genetic codes of the Southern Mongoloid. A similar event occurred when prehistoric men arrived in Vietnam: The Mongoloid intermixed with the Australoid. But because the Australoid overcrowded, resulting in, all people born in Southeast Asia during the Neolithic were the Australoid!

There are things need to be clarified about the historical truths are: The Huaxia people were descendants of the Yellow Emperor people. But the majority of Lungshan people as well as other Viet ethnic people lived outside Emperor state, including Trong Nguồn plain had no any blood connection with the nomacdic people of the Yellow Emperor! However, due to their history, they also brought the Southern Mongoloid genome, homogeneous with the Huaxia people. So, when the Shang, Zhou and Qin, Han merged the land and residents of other Viet states in their empires, the majority people of the population in the state were called the Huaxia, later called as the Han people. While also the Viet people, but lived outside the Chinese empire, were called as Man, Di, Barbarian. The Yellow Emperor's Mongolian brothers still lived in Mongolia, were called as Enemies!

Once again, this was confirmed when researched the Yelllow Emperor genealogy. Yellow Emperor, and Zhoanxu, Shaohao were the kings named according to the naming of the Mongols. But then there were the kings called in Viet names as: Emperor Ku (帝嚳), Emperor Chi, Emperor Du Vong, Emperor Yao, Shun, Wu, De Yi (Cheng Tang) ... It made us to suspect, that those emperors were Viet people? Many people believed so, but no one has proved to be!

As an insight into the origins of the Shang dysnaty, I found out the truth. In the Shang's History, Sima Qian said: The legend said that, Shang clans descended from Gaoxin shi (高辛氏), from ancient history they lived in the downstream area of the Yellow River. King Shun's age, Shang ethnic people appeared an outstanding military leader - Mr. Tiet (Qì契). Later, people often called "Black King" and considered him as their ancestor. Black Bird Chapter, the Shang praise in Shijing wrote: "The Fate was the Black Bird, born the child named Shang..." (Shijing, the Shang praise, Black Bird Chapter).

Thus, the Shang dynasty's ancestor was usually called as Emperor Gao xin shi (高辛氏), also called as Emperor Khoc or Coc (Di ku 帝嚳). Khoc is ancient Viet pronunciation as Coc - name of the cormorant, black bird, with the "The fate was the Black Bird" in Shijing. Last king of Shang dynasty had the posthumous name was Tru. That was the Du word (copulate) in Viet letters when switching into Tang pronounciation. It is like the King Kiet is Cac (penis) or Muoi Hy is Mu Di (whore) in Viet language.

- The ancestor was Di Ku (帝嚳), called as the Coc bird of the Viet people.

- The Last King had a Viet name: Du (fuck)

- The ancestor was Di Ku (帝嚳), called as the Coc bird of the Viet people.

- The totem figure was the bird (black bird) and on top of many other birds, symbolic of ethnic Viet.

-The genetic characteristic was King Cheng Tang (成湯) had a black skin. Tang was the misreading from the Than (coal). Genetics showed that the Mongolian nomads came down from the northern grasslands, belonged to the North Mongoloid race, with the light skin. Cheng Tang's black skin was the genetic characteristics of Viet people who from Vietnam of the Australoid came up. Despite the Mongolia blood mixed, the ratio of Australoid blood prevailed so Cheng Tang's skin was still darkened. This is another important evidence to confirm that Cheng Tang was a Viet person. Thus, from the ancestor down or from descendants up, it proved that the Shang dynasty's people were Viet people.

Problem with the Zhou dynasty is harder. Extirpated the Shang dynasty, the Zhou received Mr. Ze (則) descendant of the Yellow Emperor, to be as their ancestor, established King of Huaxia system after the Xia, the Shang dynasties. But when reading the records of Zhou dynasty's history, Sima Qian wrote:

"Zhou Hou Ze, named Ze. His mother is from Tai clan, named Jiangyuann (姜原). Jiangyuan is Emperor Ku (帝嚳)'s wife. " Hou Ze (后則) was a child of a woman belonging to Tai clan, a part of the Viet race. Meanwhile, Di Ku (帝嚳), as analyzed above, was the Viet King. Mr. Ze's father was a Viet man, his mother was also a Viet woman, so he should be a Viet. Chronicle also showed that ancestors of the Shang dynasty and Zhou dynasty were two lines of descendants of the Viet king named Di Ku (帝嚳). Reference on many documents, Professor Kim Dinh found that Qin's ancestors were Viet tribes in the west of China, living with nomads so they became courageous. After killing the Six States, Emperor Qin established the Qin dynasty.

Thus, the Qin Dynasty was the Viet's kingdom. Source River Basin was the home of the ancient Yangyue or Yiyue people in En and Western Zhou period were very developed, latter belonged to the Chu (楚) nation. In the Zhou dynasty, Taibo and Zhongyung went down the south and exploited the Yangyue's land. Because Huaxia people couldnot speak the consonant "ng" so the Nguồn river name was pronounced as "Hon, Hòn, Hớn." Hon river or Hòn river became the official name in the Huaxia society. In the revolt against the Qin Dynasty, Liu Bang had a great success. According to custom, Xiang Yu used Liu Bang homeland to name for him is Hon King. Up to the Tang Dynasty, due to the voice changes, it called as Han River or Hanshui river.

Also, from that Hon King transformed into Han King. According to the transformation process of history, the Han dynasty converted into the Han nation, Han people! History also recorde that, Wu Zetian, the only female monarch of China also was a Viet woman. As a girl in the family, she called as Mi Nuong, a commonly used name for the Viet female aristocrat. When became The Female King, in many names, she had two names, Viet Co (Viet ancient): Viet Co Kim Luan Holy Emperor (越古金轮圣神皇帝) and Tu Thi Viet Co Kim Luan Holy Emperor (慈氏越古金轮圣神皇帝). Even in this title also demonstrates the Viet character: She used Viet Co (Viet ancient) as a phrase order in Viet language, not co Viet (ancient Viet) as in the ancient Huaxia parlance.

Qin Emperor, then Liu Bang merged land, the population and culture of the Viet's states as Zhao, Qi, Yan (燕), Chu (楚), Wu, Yue, Ba, Shu ... and a part of the Van Lang nation became the Han nation. One conclusion was drawn: the Han, on the fact, was the country of the Viet's people, Viet land and Viet culture. From the above analysis, it can be inferred Chinese family tree as follows:

Xuanyuan was the leader of the Northern Mongoloid tribe, won the local Viet, then occupied the Southern of Yellow River, established the Yellow Emperor dynasty. Yellow Emperor married a Mongolia woman born a son to carry Mongol genes named Zhuanxu. Zhuanxu married with a Mongol wife and born a son named Shaohao. Due to the number of Mongol people in Southern Yellow River was few and the birth rate was low, so maybe at that time, do not have pure Mongolians anymore. Therefore, Shaohao did not find pure Mongolian women to marry, he forced to marry natives (not exclude the possibility, because discovering certain predominance of indigenous women so the Mongol men married Viet wives?) Shaohao married a Viet wife, born a son named Di Ku (帝嚳, De Khoc), carrying the genetic code of the Southern Mongoloid, with a black skin, was named after the Coc bird totem of the Viet people. Di Ku (帝嚳) married Ms. Jiangyuan, a Tai woman. Her descendant was Mr. Ze, the Zhou dynasty's ancestor. A different line of descendants of Emperor Ku (Emperor Khoc, Diku, 帝嚳) born Mr. Tiet or Khiet – Shang dysnaty's ancestor – Khiet is the Ket bird (black bird) in Viet voice. A Mongolian ancestor, but 4-5 the next descendants were Viet people! Similarly, De Chi, De Du Vong, De Yao ... borned another Viet descendant streams living throughout Zhongyuan. At this point, there could be a need to clarify the original meaning of the Zhongyuan. This land is Nguon River (Source River) basin, located in the left of Yangtze river with approximately 1,532 km in length, 174 300 km² in the catchment area. The river originates from the Southwestern of province of Shaanxi, in the area of Banzhongshan in Ningqiang, then flows to the Hubei province. And then into the Yangtze River in Wuhan, capital of Hubei province. While other rivers receive water from the melting snow of the mountains, the Source river receives water sources from the ground of the Tan Linh or Qín Lǐng (秦嶺) mountain range flows in many streams. In tributaries that make the Nguon river, there is the Tanyang river line with 800 km long, dark blue water, so ancient Viet people called as River Den (Black River), later called as Tanyang by the Chinese voice. But after the river flowing into the Nguon river, the water becomes transparent. Vietnamese people called River Nguồn,

Source or In Source (The devotion of the mother's like the water flowing from the In Source River out). This is Yangyue's land at Zhou dynasty. Latter is considered the originated land of Huaxia. Also change the reading: Trong Nguồn became Trung Nguyên (Zhongyuan) the Central of Yellow River basin. Due to rename during 2000 years, Vietnamese people did not recognize their old land and did not understand that the means of (The devotion of the mother's like water flowing from the In Source river out).

Thus, the Huaxia people certainly were Viet people not only the descendants of the Yellow Emperor, but also the descendants of the other lines in Mongolian invasion in 2698 BC.

From the above analysis, we can conclude: Huaxia people were the Viet people born from the invasion of the Mongols led by Xuan Yuan clan. Huaxia is the "noble" title of the community born in kingdom of Yellow Emperor. In fact, the Huaxia people only exist in short time and then dissolved in the crowded Viet community. Though the Huaxia people did not exist, but Huaxia name was shared among the Han people and the used by the dynasties. A historical mistake has been widely postulated: being just an ancestor of a part of Huaxia but later, the Yellow Emperor was proclaimed as the common ancestor of the whole Chinese nation! From the above analysis shows, there is a part, such as scholar Zhou Jixu remarked, the indigenous people were submerged, disqualified from history and their culture were appropriated. But in fact, the invaded person has assimilated the invader, becoming the subject of the Chinese nation. The so called Huaxia exists only nominally. In fact, Qin, Han was the country of Viet people. Chinese culture was also the culture of the Viet people!

Due to discovering this secret, we can understand why the ancient people of Vietnam always have been towards the Tai mountain, Nguồn River (Source River); understand the meaning of language transmission: Viet–Chinese has same culture and ethnic! Likewise, we can understand why the Chinese people were not only the descendants of the Yan Emperor, the Yellow Emperor but also regconized Suiren (燧人), Fu Xi, Nu Wa to be their ancestors.

References:

1. J.Y. Chu & colleagues: *Genetic relationship of Populations in China.* Proc. Natl. Acad. Sci.USA 1998 95 p. 11763-11768.

2. Stephen Oppenheime. *Out of Eden Peopling of the World* (http://www. bradshawfoundation.com)

3. Stephen Oppenheime. *Journey of Mankind the Peopling of the World* (http://www.bradshawfoundation.com/journey/).

4. Spencer Wells. *The journey of mankind: a genetic odyssey.* National Geographic, January 21, 2003.

5. S.W. Ballinger & colleagues: *Southeast Asian mitochondrial DNA Analysis reveals genetic continuity of ancient Mongoloid migration.* Genetic 1992 130 p.139-45

6.Nguyen Dinh Khoa. *Anthropology of Southeast Asia.* Publishing house: University and vocational schools. H, 1983

7. Who were European ancestors?(http://www.radio-canada.ca/nouvelles/ Science-Sante/2007/08/07/004-europe-colonisation-asie.shtml?ref=rss)

8. Ha Van Thuy. *Journey to find the source.* Literature Publishing House. 2008.

9. Ha Van Thuy. *Find ethnic roots through genetics.* Literature Publishing House. 2011

10. http: //baike.baidu.com/view/22365.htm

11. Citations by Vu Huu San. *North Bay Vietnam.* Reprinted 2004. Tripod. com.

CHAPTER III

BACH VIET (BAIYUE)

This chapter was devoted to research on one of the key problems of Eastern history: Baiyue. But before talking about Baiyue, we need to clarify: What is Yue? Until now, many people thought that, there are many different Yue "races": Ouyue, Luoyue, Jingyue, Nanyue etc ... Naturally, these "Yue" had different origins and different histories. The cultural and anthropological diversity, especially the voices formed the Baiyue, it meant Hundred of Yue ethnics. The Baiyue people, in history, the majority were assimilated by the Han people, only the Louyue kept the race and the state. However, it was a misconception of the past due to unknown origin and history of East Asian populations. Entering new century, from various sources of human knowledge, the science has confirmed: 70,000 years ago, two big races: Australoid and Mongoloid from Africa went along the Indian Ocean coastal and arrived in the Vietnam today.

There, they mixed blood and born four strains: Indonesian, Melanesian, Vedoid and Negritoid. From here then, people spreaded to the islands of Southeast Asia, occupied the land of India and went on exploring the China. About 20,000 years ago, from the region today is called Hoa Binh area, ancient Viet created the new stone tools, in which the most typical ones were the axes, hammers, viet (small battle stone axes), ground breaking tools and the remarkable weapons. Proud of this creation, they used "Viet" name as their symbolic. Since then, our ancestors were called as the Viet people. Viet - who bringing the ax (Yue 戉) may appear before 20,000 years ago. Next, our ancestors domesticated the water rice. To commemorate this great achievement, the Viet people renamed to Viet word with the Rice part (Yue 粵) - owner of rice. This term is now used to call Viet people in the South of the Yangtze River. Viet word with the Running part (Yue, 越) is used as the name of ethnic Viet people in the Bronze Age. Be the first inventor of bronze casting techniques, making drums, and weapons, which is typical long ax (戉- Yue, qua), an impressive image of warriors bringing the bronze long ax (戉- Yue, qua) pursued the enemy, was used as the logo for the Viet people. Thus, despite many ethnicities, many groups with different voices but in the region of East Asia, the Viet people shared the same origins and the origin place was the Vietnam land. Bach Viet (Baiyue) people were merely Viet from Warring States Period

Third century BC, the Qin dynasty merged the land, people and culture of the Viet nations into the Qin empire. Succeeding the Qin, the Han dynasty consolidated and expanded the boundary and enforced the permanent policies of assimilation of ethnic, bringing Viet territories and culture to build a Chinese empire with the Han people were the main population. However, after more than 2000 years, on the land of China, despite an intense assimilation, Viet people, under the name Bach Viet still maintained its own identity, not only about genetic but more remarkable cultural features.

Under current popular notion, Bach Viet name is to refer to ethnics or Viet nations existed on time Qin-Han in the south of the Yangtze River. Bach Viet name first appeared in the book of Lushi chunqiu (呂氏春秋), Chapter Shiguan: "In the Southern of Yang han (揚汉), during the place of the Bach Viet, the Jichi,

Chu Phu, Du My lands, Phoc Lau, Duong Xuat, Hoan Dau nations, many of them had no Kings." [1]

Qu dai ren (区代任), in The Bai yue xian xian zhi (百越先賢志) - The book of Baiyue sages - wrote: "Grandchildren in sixth generations of Goujian was Wujiang (無疆), attacked the Chu (楚) state and he was defeated by King Chu Chuxiong (楚雄倗). Wujiang left Liangjia, went to Tungwu. The Viet nation disappeared. Wujiang's son or next generations resided in South Yangtzu coastal area, to become the clan leaders and the Kings etc, all were under the regime of Chu (楚) dynasty, called the Bach Viet (Baiyue, 百越). Zhou Yang since then disunited (333 BC).

Guiji (Kuaij, 会稽) used the Southern stars such as Shuan (淳) star, Wei (尾) star to decide the boundaries, the Kuaij (会稽) land located in Nanhai. When Qin defeated the Chu dynasty, Wang Xian (王羡) ruled the Yangyue, divided into three Countys: Nanhai, Guilin and Xiang (象). Descendants of Wei Tuo (尉佗) surrendered the Han dynasty. Zhao (趙) ruled that all three counties, and Hepu (合浦), Cangwu (倉吳), Weilin (尉林), Jiaozhi (交趾), Jiuzhen (玖甄), Zhouya(州厓) a total of nine counties.

Now at Nanyue region, North adjacent with Gusi (沽司), to Kuaiji (会稽) is the land of the Viet people. East, Wu Tu put the capital in Dongzhi), to Zhangquan was Minyue. Donghai King is Yao, base in the Yongjia was Ouyue. Tiyu Song's ancient territory, stretching from the Jiang River, Li River, to the south is Xiyue. The Land at Sangka, Xixia, Yong, Sui, Jian was Luoyue "[2] Baiyue people, used to live on the ancient land of China are the historical truth. The Baiyue's descendants, live now in the south of China with its customs, its own voice is also a fact that no one can deny. However, for many reasons, Baiyue has not been researched much, leading to the inaccurate understanding about Baiyue people, its history and culture.

More than half a century ago, scholar Lou Xiang Lin (罗香林) in Taiwan published the百越源流與文化 (The Origin and Culture of Baiyue) [1], studied on the origin, location and culture of Baiyue states. This is one of the rare and valuable research on the Baiyue. Luckily one of my friends donated me a handwritten translation of Mr. Vong Chi Nguyen Chi Vien, I would rely on the author's documentation for presentation on issues related to Baiyue. By the way, I would like to express our gratitude to the Mr. Vong Chi and his family.

In the book Origin and Culture of Baiyue, 百越源流與文化, scholar Lou Xiang Lin (罗香林) wrote: "As according to the geographical situation today, Baiyue was in the Southwest within a few Chinese provinces, as Chuan (川), Tian (田), Zhen (鍼), Guì (桂) etc. At the South it was up to Annam and a part in Thailand, Burma. In the East, it was along the beach as the provinces of Guangdong, Fujian, Zhejiang etc, it also was in the boundary with Wan, (皖), Gan (贛), E (鄂) too." Overview, we can see that, these Viet states were the fragments of the ancient Viet nations such as Ba, Shu, Wu, Yue, Chu, Wenliang (文俍) etc at the end of the Warring States period. The Viet leaders who led the people rebelled, founded the Viet people's independent nations. Here I would like to present the main features of the Baiyue communities in the history.

I. The Viet nations in history

1. U Viet (Yuyue, 於越)

Yuyue (於越) nation also was known as Yuyue (邗越). When Shang-En Dynasty was prevalent, Yuyue (於越) was restrained, there were not many activities. When Zhou dynasty was throne, it did not strengthen the territory yet, at the time, Yuyue raised up. The Chronicles of Yue King - Goujian wrote: "輿地志 – the Maganize of Geography – said the Yue Kings were almost 30 generations, from the En dynasty to the Zhou dynasty. In the age of the King Wang, Yue King was Phu Hon, his son Doan Thuong, expanded the land, and proclaimed himself the King.

In the Spring and Autumn Period, he was demoted to become the tittle "Viscount" with alias name as Yuyue (於越)". In the 竹書紀年 (Zhushu jinian) - The Book of Bamboo Annals stated: "Zhoucheng King's 24th year, the Yuyue (於越) nation to visit. " This shows that, during the early Zhou Dynasty, Viet nation has been existed. In the Huainan Zi in the Qi Su Xun (齐俗訓) wrote: "The King of Viet nation - Goujian cut his hair, drew on his body, not wearing leather hat and the Hu (匜), solemn, humble". Yuyue people used Kuaiji (会稽) as a base, to became a very glorious acclamation Kings in the Spring and Autumn age, maintained the prosperity about 200 years.

Up to the Han Dynasty, although the merged with Han nation, but Yuyue has emerged giving independence. Han letter vol 64, the Yanya wrote, "The Viet people wanted to mutate every boundary in Xiantian, Yugan". Yugan is Raozhou in Jiangxi Province today. Thus, the early Western Han period, the northeastern Gong province remains the Viet. Not only that, because Yuyue was the split up, the Mǐnyuè (闽越), came to cause fights in Xúnyáng (寻阳) in Jiujiang. This shows that the Viet residents had been living from the northeast of the Gong province to the southeast of the Jiujiang.

In the early Han Dynasty, Yuyue (於越) territory was till such large, thus the Spring and Autumn period still covered much larger. In summary, Yuyue nation's territory included seven areas: Qing, Shaoxing, Ningbo, Jinhua, Qu, Wen, Dai. And three areas: Huang, Jia, He were bounded with Wu nation. In The book named National language upper - Viet language said: "Land of Goujian, the south to Juwang, the west to Gumie, was about 100 miles wide."

2. Au Viet (Ouyue甌越)

One line of Yuyue (於越) later changed into Ouyue (甌越), also known as the Dongyue (東越), occupied Oujiang land

- southern Zhejiang today as the center, including three areas: Qing, Wen, Dai and the coastal islands. In the Qin dynasty they didn't follow the Qin dynasty. Minyue's King (闽越) was Wangzhu, Dongyue's King was Yao, also were descendants of Yue King Goujian. When feudatory vassals opposed the Qin dynasty, Wangzhu and Yao led the Viet ethnics to fight the Quin. Ouyue leaders in Emperor Han Hui period, who had been crowned the kings, then fought with Minyue, defeated and led 40,000 people to move into China, lived in Jiang, Huai.

3. Min Viet ((Minyue, 闽越)

Mǐnyuè (闽越) was also a line of Yuyue (於越). Qin's First Emperor occupied the ancient land of Minyue (闽越), Fujian today, commissioned Mǐnyuè as the Central area, and dismissed Minyue leaders to become the tribal leader. After helping the Han, Yanzhu was crowned King of Mǐnyuè, based in Dongya, i.e Fuzhou today. In the Han shu Yanzhu, wrote: "Huainan King submitted the letter to Emperor Han Wu: "Minyue is the foreign country, people painted their bodies and cut their hair, we cannot use military measures to them. In the caves, streams, forests, they train marines, facilities for boat use, land about dark, dangerous river. They paints maps, comment on mountains and rivers, major obstacles. Narrowly close together that seemed a hundred, thousand miles, with rugged jungles, not obvious. If they wanted to go China, they had to go down to Lengshui. The Lengshui River is with the high mountain, rocky underground river. The boat hit the rock will break, the big boats can not be used to transport food. The Viet people have the poor health, they do not have the horse wagon, archery. They are not used to fighting on land, but Chinese unable to entry because they entrenched. I heard that Viet nation's troop had more than 200,000 people, so if we wanted to enter the Viet nation, our troop needs to be more than five times of that number. " Thus, we can see, in the first time of the Han dynasty, the Minyue nation was a quite prosperous country. The Minyue nation, in the early of the Qin Han dynasties, with the East reached to the island of Taiwan, Penghu, Liuqiu; the West reached the northeastern of the Gong province.

The Yanzhu story also wrote: "If the Minyue (闽越) wanted to cause the instability, first among Yu, Gan where the leaders used to burn the Han's long boat in Xúnyáng (寻阳), they were in eastern or northern of the Gong province". In the Huainan zi renjian xun (淮南子人間訓, Teaching people of Huainan zi) wrote: " Emperor Qin Shi sent off 500,000 soldiers devided into 5 troops to fight with Viet people. One troop stationed in Yu Gan River area, northeast of the Gong province". The Qin dynasty fought with Minyue (闽越) not at Min land, but at northeast of the Gong province, so at that time, northeast of the Gong province was still the border of the Minyue (閩越).

In the story on Two Yues of the Chinese books (漢書兩越傳, Yanzhu liangyue) story says, "In Yuanting 5th year, Nanyue protested, Yudan kept the ambivalence implicit and co-operated with Nanyue, then when the Han defeated Fanyong. General Yangpu of the long boat submitted the letter to fight Dongyue (東越). The Emperor said that the soldiers got tired, so he didn't agree to fight. He withdrew the troop and ordered the General stationed at Yuzhang, Mailing to wait for his orders. Yudan ordered his troop to intercept the Han's way, and with the Liulì general to enter Pacha, Wulin, Mailing and killed three Han's captains.

The Han dynasty ordered General Honghai being Hanshuo dispatched the Juzhang troops, sailed away to the East. General Yangpu of the Long boat dispatched the troops to Wulin, Lieutenant Wangwen shu dispatched the troops to Mailing, Viet marquess – General Xialai dispatched to Ruxie, Pacha. In the 1st year of Yuanfeng period's winter, all troop entered the Dongyue (東越). Dongyue sent their soldiers to dangerous areas, ordered General Xunbei to hold the Yulin and defeated the Long Boat's captain and killed the Chief. Tiao King Jugu killed Yudan, surrendered Honghai, and was ordained to be the marquess Citadel East ...The Emperor said that: "Dongyue (東越) is narrow land and dangerous. Minyue often betrays and he ordered the troop moves all the people to Jiang Huai region". At this point, both Minyue and Dongyue (東越) were merged into China.

4. Dong De (Dongti)

Dongti included the islands of Taiwan, Penghu, Liuqiu today, was a division of Mǐnyuè (閩越). While Minyue was merged or entered the China, by the remote sea, Dongti was remained independent, became a tribe of Viet ethnic. In the Book of the Later Han Dynasty (Houhan shu, 後漢書) Dongti story wrote that "Outside the Kuaiji (会稽) sea, there was Dongti people, divided into more than 20 countries." Linhui Qiang in the Taiwan ethnic primitive culture said: "The Dongti was aboriginal in the ancient Taiwan, Liuqiu area. The Ti word (堤) in Dongti and the Tai (台) in Taiwan are the same from the different translations.

In the Duoshu Dongyi story wrote: "The kingdom of Liuqiu is in the middle of the sea, the east is Jianan county, it took five days going by boat on sea to arrive there. There are many caves. Their King named Huansi, called Kachu Diu. Nobody knows when that state was formed. The aboriginal Islander called as Kelao Yang, the wife called as Bacha, lived in three caves, three deep trenches around. They planted thorny fencing. House of the King had 16 rooms, surrounded by carved animal imagines, like the kumquat trees with many leaves, with small branches drooped like the hair. In that country, there were 4 or 5 leaders to dominate the caves; each cave there is an emir.

Usually there were villages like Olieu, Shuai... all chose the warlike men to handle things in the villages ... the King rode the wooden animals, ordered servants to carry it away, escorted by below 10 people. Liuqiu people have the deep eyes, long nose, like Hu people. Women often paint the tattoo of snake images on their arms. Boys and girls together know each other and become the couples. When party festivals come, people hold the glasses; wait to be called their names before drinking.

When bringing the wine to the King also calling the King name, touch their glasses together and drink ... Who nearly died or stopped breathing should to be brought to the courtyard, relatives should cry by the funeral songs. Then bathes the corpse, take the silk to wrap tightly, wrap the outside with mop grass, dig and burry, not use coffins. The flat grave above is not covered with soil higher ... The fields are fertile, before cultivating, they primarily burn the grass and bring water into the field. Use the stone hammers have wide blades (20 cm) with long handled made by bamboo or wooden to plant the rice paddy. Taiwanese aboriginal people today are descendants of the Dongti people.

5. Duong Viet (Yangyue)

The Yangyue or Tiyue resided in the Hanshui area, very flourished in the En dynasty and the Western Zhou dynasty. After the Spring and Autumn period, The Chu dynasty's Chronicle says, "Xiongqu (Chu dynasty's King) was very popular with Jianghan people, brought his troops to fight the Yong nation, Yangyue nation. Went to E land, Xiongqu said: "I am a barbarian, so not the same with Chinese people, and raised the eldest son Háng to become the King Goudan, second son Hong to become the Kinh E, the youngest son Zhi zi to become the King Yuezhang, all in Chu land in the upper stretch. """ The E nation was at Yucang county today. The Yong nation was Zhushan county in Hubei province. Thus Yangyue was at about midland Hanshui. Thus, Chuxiong Qu took over Yong, E and Yangyue - three nations – in the King Yi of the Zhou period. This shows that, in the late Western Zhou time, Yangyue people had gathered in the midlands of Hanshui. The Hanshui Basin later fully belonged to the Chu dynasty from the Spring and Autumn period.

The Zhou dynasty from the King Tai moved the Capital to Qishan land, upstream of the Weishui, the south bordered with the Baoxie the upper land of the Hanshui. Mr. Taibai and Mr. Zhongyong of the Zhou dynasty went along the Hanshui to the south, took the Yangyue land, but followed the Viet people's custom. Later their descendants went along the Jiang Han river to the Eastern area, to the Wu nation's land, King Wu promoted him as the Earl and called him as Wu Taibai.

The Wu Taibai Family 's Chr says: "Mr. Taibai run to Jing man self-called as Gouwu, the Jingman people admired his righteousness, up to more than a thousand houses followed him ... Zhuyu King defeated the Shang dynasty and found Taibai and Zhongyong's descendants, found Zhuzhang who was the the King of Wu nation. On that opportunity, King Yu promoted him." Thus, Mr. Taibai in Jingyue land had cut his hair and painted on his body according to the Viet people's customs.

The Chu Family's Chr says: "The King Chengyuan in early years while was newly enthroned King ordered the delegates to send the tribute to the Emperor. Emperor donated a meat dishes and said: You defends the South, do not let Yiyue causing the chaos, invading China. Because that thousand miles land is belonging to the Chu dynasty. " Called as Yiyue because the Yi (夷) and Yang (佯) was same sound in the ancient time.

Though Yangyue took over the Hanshui basin as the center but sometimes the land also extended more. After being taken over by Xiongqu partially assimilated under the Chu dynasty, a part moved to the South and co-lived with other Viet groups at the boundary of the Ri, Xiang, Jian, Xuan, Gong, Gui, Yue. The Viet people in the region were all self-proclaimed their leaders to hold their own lands.

6. Son Viet (Shan yue)

The Yuyue, Minyue and Yangyue after being invaded by the Chu, Qin, Han, though majority belonged to the Han, a part of Viet descendant were still called as Shanyue. Between of the Three Kingdoms to the Tang time, they appeared in the border intersection areas of Min, She, Xuan, Gong provinces. Though Shan yue people were not strong enough to cut the land and proclaim the King, they suddenly rised in revolt in the Three Kingdoms time, so they could not be underestimated.

In the Three Kingdoms jurnal, the Wushi part, story about Zunfu - (三國志, 吳主传 - 孫權, Sanguozhi, Wuzhuzhuan, Zunfu) – wrote: " Yuanshu enraged Ce very much, secretly ordered his men to bring the seal to promote the Danyang, Lingyang, Zuliang, to agitate the Shanyue people, to plot to attack Ce. Ce became a General himself to defeat Líng". This shows that Shanyue had the control power to the Zunwu regime. In the Luxun story again: "Danyang assailant was Feichan, received Mr. Cao's seal, agitated Shanyue people to be the internal supporters. Quan ordered Zun to fight Chan, such as attack the enemy, brought the troops of three eastern counties with few thousand soldiers." Same time, Shanyue people were respected by the Central Highland's martial artists. It is meant that Shanyue forces was not little, became the worries of the East Wu. However, the East Wu, Cao Zao and Liu Bei also only used the flexible policies for the alliance without negligence using the military. Shanyue used the Danyang county as the center. In the Records of the Three Kingdoms jurnal (三國志, 吳主传 - Sanguozhi, Wuzhi) – the Wushi part, story about Jiaji Ke story, wrote: "Ke thought that the Danyang mountain was craggy, people there were brave, though previously had used the troop, it only could get the ordinary people outside the distric to be the soldiers, while it couldn't get the soldiers from the remote places. They would assume that Danyang county terrain was craggy and dangerour, with four adjacent counties: Wu county,

Kuaiji(会稽), New county, Poyang, around several thousand miles of mountains, caves were very craggy and dangerous.

On the Mountain areas, they produced the iron, bronze items, self-casted the weapons, unceased practising the martial arts, combating with the noble vigor. They climbed and overcame the dangerous mountains, the thorny bushes, such as the fish swimming in the water and the apes climbing the trees; waited for the negligence and suddenly attacked for the robbery. When the troops came, they hidden in the caves, when fighting, they gathered again like bees, when being defeated, they ran to hide like the birds, from ancient times until now, they were not under the control. " Later Sima Ke conquered them."

7. Nam Viet (Nanyue)

Nam Viet (Nanyue) was a division of Yangyue, occupied the land in southern of Yangyue so called as Nanyue. During the Qin, Han, Nanyue had built a great country. Before being occupied by the Qin, (Nanyue) still had relationship with Yuyue. While invading the Baiyue, the So people still didn't change completely the internal organization structure of the Viet people.

After King Tiyu Song of Xiou was killed, Viet people all ran into the jungles, lived along with animals, did not let the Qin catching them. They appointed the outstanding people as the General. Practicing the martial arts in the night time, defeating the Qin army, killing Tushu and several thousands of people, the corpses looked like a mountain, the blood flew like a river and then they built the army camps to defend. In the Hanshu Yanzhu story says, "King Huainan sent a letter to Emperor Wu to discuss about the Qin people to use the military force with Nanyue nation: I heard from the elder people that the Qin ordered Captain Túshu to attacked the Viet people and prepared the camps etc to defend. At that time, there was the shock in and outside, many hundreds of people were worried, the left people didn't return, together went to hide, to become the bandits, so that the Shantui matter arised. "

In the Nanyue Captain Tuo Chronicles: "Nanyue's King was Tuo, was born in Zhending, surnamed Zhao. The Qin to take control of the world, invaded Yangyue, set Guilin, Nanhai and Xiang counties to migrate its residents to co-live with the Viet people. In the Qin period, Tuo was allowed to use the Nanhai Lungchuan order. Up to the 2nd Qin King, Nanhai's Captain was Renao, was seriously sick, before dying, he used the Longchuan order to Zhao tuo and said that: Panyu land was very craggy.

With the Nanhai's thousands of miles from east to west, and they had the Chinese people's help, it as also a county, either to establish the state. And the county chiefs were not worth to consider, so I said clearly to you. "Then, he made a fake order for Tuo to become the Nanhai's Captain. Renao died, Tuo released the announcements to Hongpu, Shanyang, Huangxi that, the enemy was coming, urgently to prepare the troops to self-defend. Then he made the reasons to kill all the Qin's nominated county chiefs, replaced by his retainers. The Qin dynasty was destroyed, Tuo took over the Guilin, Xiang counties, established the independent kingdom and self-go throne as Nanyue Wuwang.

Zhao Tuo and his nephew, King Wen, proclaimed as Emperor, fought back with the Han. When Nanyue was prosperous, the eastern area surrounded with Minyue, the north bordered to Hengyou, the west included the Guangxi, Vietnam today, the south led to Hainan Island, got the Nanhai county, i. e Guangdong to make the base. The Zhao dynasty had the hereditary succession through 5 generations, 93 years.

8. Tay Au (Xiou)

Xiou was a branch of Baiyue, now includes Lejiang in Guangxi province to the East; the Southwest is Hengyang in Hunan Province, down to Cangwu, Fengchuan; the North to Ou and Luo or Luoyue. In the Geography of Yongzhou Yihe county, wrote: "Huanshui county in the North, which is Sangka River, called as Yuzhuang River, i.e., Luoyue River, also known as Wenshui." Wenshui, Luoyue River or Sangka River, according to the local expectations to consider, i.e., within the region of Nanban River in Tian, Jian areas. This river downstream called as the Hungshui River, through the Qianjiang, Laijin counties to Xiang county, Danlung town, along with Lejiang, confluenced to Guiping, along with Xunjiang relatively assembly. Xiou, in the end of the Qin, was very active but because Zhao Tuo proclaimed to be the King, his forces were too strong so Xiou surrendered Zhao Tuo. When the Han destroyed Nam Viet (Nanyue), took over Xiou, commissioned the counties and provinces.

The Tong people in Guangxi now are the descendants of Xiou or the Luoyue. The Chang was from the Tang word of Sangge converted into, but from the Han dynasty later specialized as a river name. Today from Nanban river, to the Hungshui River, to the Lejiang, Xijiang were called Sangge River, originally from the man's name. Chang people also self-proclaimed people as Tonggu, Tonggu lao, also came from the Sangge words.

9. Lac Viet (Luoyue)

It was a branch of Baiyue, Luo yue land was, in the east, from the Southwest of Nanning county, Guangxi, province to Leizhou Peninsula down to the island of Hainan and Guangdong and the northern and central parts of Vietnam.

At first, when prehistoric people from Africa came to Vietnam, the two great races: Australoid and Mongoloid mixed their blood and born four strains of ancient Viet people: Indonesian, Melanesian, Vedoid and Negritod, later the anthropologists placed into the the Australoid group. Inside, majority of Indonesian people spoke Luoyue language and played a leading role on social aspects and the languages.

Luoyue people belonged to the Indonesian strain and widely distributed throughout China. Around 5000 BC, the Luoyue intermixed with the Southern Mongoloid people of the Yangshao Culture to become modern Viet people with the genetic codes of the Southern Mongoloid. Luoyue people were the owners of the Neolithic, Bronze cultures and created the Luoyue drums and the pictograms on the Gansang stone shovels and letters of the Shui tribe.

The Qin and Han dynasty merged the Viet people's lands, Viet populations and Viet ethnic culture into the Chinese empire. While most of Baiyue people on the Chinise land were assimilated, the Luoyue in Vietnam land still keep remained their land, their race and their culture, to become the representatives of the independent Baiyue.

11. Dan nation (Tanguo)

One line of ethnic Viet, used to live in a strip of Burma today, created the Tan Nation. Tan nation's descendants distributed in Vietnam, Laos, Thailand and Burma nowadays. In the Book of the Later Han Dynasty (Houhan shu, 後漢書) stated: "In the 9th year (97) of the Emperor Zhang Yongyuan, Tan nation sent the messengers to offer to the Emperor." This is the earliest documentation of Tan nation. In the Book of the Later Han Dynasty (Nanman Xinanyi story): "In the Yongyuan 6th Year (94), Jiaowai district, Rendun Yi King sent the messengers to offer the rhinoceroses, buffalos and big elephants. In the 9th year Jiaowai and Tan nation's King Yongyou Tiao ordered their servants to offer the precious and rare things. In Yongning first year (120), Tan nation's King Yongyou Tiao ordered to send the messengers to come and offer the music and play the magic tricks that can transform, release the fire by mouth, cut himself his hands and limbs, then reattach hands and limbs, change buffalo head into the horse head . They themselves said they came from the West Sea, which Da Qin ... " Called as the Jiaowai county area, just adjacent to the western border provinces of Yunnan province, also in the Burmese location today.

The East was near to the Chendla nation (i.e., Vietnam's Gian Pho Trai strip). The West was adjacent to East Qianzhu nation, the South was Minghai, the North was through with Xieluo citadel of Nanzhao nation. In the ancient time, Viet clan people took the dragon drawings on their bodies as their features, Tan nation people also had this body drawing customs. In period of the Six dysnaties, Tan nation has changed the political system, it was renamed as the Piao nation. In the Jiu Tang Shu (舊唐書, The Old Tang Book) Nanman story, Piao nation wrote: " Piao nation was far more than 2,000 miles from the southern of old Yongchang county, 14,000 miles from kingdom capital, 3000 miles from the East-west nation area, 3500 miles from the North-South. Vietnam, Laos nowadays still keep that customs. "

According to ancient documents as above mentioned, we can determine that the Tan nation in the past, now it is Burma's Karen land. It was also home of the Viet people from 40-50000 years ago, along with indigenous Dravidian India. Here, they found many drums, kettledrums called Karen, star-shaped drum with many wings, frog-shaped in the edges, similar of Luoyue bronze drums (3)

A toad drum Karen

12. Dang Viet (Tengyue)

Tengyue today is the name of a district in the western province of Yunnan. But this strip of land was adjacent to the Ailao yi of Han Yongchang county. Ailao yi was a member of the Viet ethnic, so Tengyue also had relation with Viet ethnic. In the "Book of the Later Han dynasty" (Houhan shu, 後漢書) Nanman Xinan yi story quoted: "The Ailao yi people, there was a woman named Chayi, lived in Mount Laoshan area, often went fishing in the river. One day she touched the agarwood tree, shivered, then she was pregnant, a full 10 months she gave a birth of 10 sons. Then the agarwood tree become the dragon and appeared on the water surface. Chayi suddenly heard the Dragon saying: "You gave my sons' births, where are my children?" Nine children ran away when seeing a dragon, the smallest child couldn't run, sit on the dragon's back. The Dragon lovingly licked all over his child. The mother called the back as Nine (Cửu), the Dragon as Long, called the baby's name Jiu lung. Through the adolescence, the brothers saw that the youngest child, Jiu lung was clicked entirely by his father, become intelligent, then worshiped him and he became the King. Later, at the foot of Mount Laoshan, other couple gave a birth of 10 girls. Jiu lung brothers married them. Then gradually became flourishing. This gave people draw the dragon images on their bodies."

In Jianyu 27th year (51) King Xian li brought 2770 households; 17,659 inhabitants gone to Yuesui to surrender marrow Zheng Hong. King Guangyu assigned Xian li to be the district's chief. In the Tang dynasty, a strip of Dailì land on the west rised in revolt and established Nanzhao country. After Pilai ge was appointed as the King Yunnan, Nanzhao nation become stronger, inherited throne to his son named Geluo fang then joined forces with Tufan, caused the aggression with the Tang dynasty. The grandchildren, Yimao qin surrendered the Tang. Fengyou period was under the reign of Muzong, betrayed the Tang and fought the Shu nation.

Under the reign of King Xuan zong (847- 859) fought against the government dominated Annam. Then he passed throne to his son, Tanchuo Qiulung, claimed himself as the Emperor, named the national name was Daili, then fought Bazhou (now Guizhou Zunyi county), fought Yongguan now Nanning Guangxi in the south ... Nanzhao had many successors and lasted to until it was destroyed by Kublai Khan.

13. Dien Viet (Tian yue, 盔越)

Tian yue (盔越) first appeared in Hanshu Zhang Qian (the Book of the Han dynasty, Zhang Qian General) story: "... Hearing from the West that there was a country to ride an elephant called Tian yue (盔越), which merchants in Shu jian land or brought goods to sell, then the Han Dynasty found a way down, then abled to connect with the Tian Kingdom. Tian yue i.e., the distinct name of the Tian nation. From the Warring States it had a close tie with (Chu) nation. In "Xinanyi story": There were tens of Xinanyi tribal chief. Yelang was the largest, in the western belonged to eimi), including tens."

Tian was the largest nation ... In the past, the King Chuwei ordered General Zhuangjiao sent army troops to go along the river to occupy the Bashu, Qianzhong to the West. Zhuangjiao was descendant of Chu kingdom. Jiao came to Tianchi with 300 square miles, the fertile plain land with thousands of miles away. Jiao brought the officers and returned Chu to inform, but met the Quin's attack. Because the road was congested so his troop couldn't go anymore, he came back to become the King of Tian nation, and he wore the clothes as in the local customs." Then Tian was eradicated by the Quin dynasty and were merged with the Han under the Emperor Wu's reign, became Yizhou county, China.

14. Tuy Viet (Suiyue)

Nowadays, it is a county in Southwestern of Sichuan but Suiyue in the Western Han Dynasty was a very wide county in the range of Chuan county and Tian county. The south bordered with the Tian nation, the north bordered with the Shu, managed 15 counties. Yue sui county in the Han dynasty in elong) River met the Min River, Jinsha River, which named Pushui. In beginning of the Tang dynasty, it occupied the land then named as Xi pu luo mo county, managed four counties. It was the land of the Pu clan.

15. Bac nation (Fu guo)

In Zhangju Xie Zhengyi book wrote: "Now south Yìzhou, north Rongzhou to Da Jiang River was ancient Fu nation." Where the Bac people built the nation, ie. took the Yisan, Nanxi, Bengshan counties to be the center. In Yude 2nd year (619) split Yu zhou as a county to administrate six districts, then later changed into Bozhou. The county called as Fu; it must have been Fu people's land. Clearly, in ancient time, the Fu people were a genus of Pu clan, a clan nickname of Viet people. Poems written by Chenyu in the Tang Dynasty in The memoir of the Tao family in Shu land (Cao shi Shu zhong kuang ji).

Under the cidtadel heard the Yi people singing

Under the Kien citadel of Kha land
Merchant ships dock scatteredly far
Bright yellow moon in the bottom of the water
Bronze drums sad voice echo of the Di songs.

Yi song and bronze drums were the characteristic of Viet culture. On the Jian wei land, discovered many bronze drums.

16. Da Lang (Yeliang, 夜郎)

Xinan Yi Chro story says, "The Yeliang (夜郎) nation was near the Sangka River, a wide river with more than hundred feet, enough to sail. Nanyue used material resources to buy off Yeliang (夜郎), but it could only make them for assistance, it could not see them as vassals. Yeliang had over 10 thousand of warlike soldiers, many boats on the rivers, suddenly attack, it was a strategy to fight against the Viet people. The Han dynasty ordained Tangmeng to be the Lieutenant General, bought many thousands of people and food, went along the Bashuxi road to meet the Yeliang Marquess Duotong. Tangmeng rewarded very much and used the virtue power to convince, promised to appoint as the mandarin positions and and appoint their sons to become the counties's commanders. The people of Yeliang's small villages were greedy with the Han dynasty's silks, then they listened to the promises of Tangmeng. Meng reported and took the land to allocate as Jianwei county, sent off the Bashu troops to do the roadworks, from Pu's roads to the Sangka River." The Yeliang took the Sangka river basin to be the center, had the tied relation with Nanyue in the south, approached with Pu's roads in the north. Sangka River is the Banjiang River flowing through the Guizhou of Yunnan province. In the Old Tang Geographical Book of Yongzhou "Huanshui River in the northern of the district is the Sangka River, commonly called as Yuzhuang River, i.e., Luoyue River, also known as Wen Shui River, it was Luoyue ancient land."

Xinan yi Chr story: "Nanyue protested. Emperor Wu ordered the Chiyihou Jianwei urged to moved the troop. King Culan was scared and went away, the neighbor nation robbed the elderly, came with treason, murdered the messengers and County head Jianwei. The Han dynasty used to bring the sinners in Bashu land to beat the Nanyue, eight Captains together gathered to ravage Nanyue and that eight captains withdrew the troops, killed the Culan etc. After that, pacify all barbarians, named Sangka county. "

17. Quy Viet (Kuiyue)

Quy Viet (Kuiyue) was also a branch of the Viet people. Kuiyue's land was Bigui strip of Hubei and Fengjie of Sichuan today, also referred to as the Guiyi or Pu. In King Zhouxuan first year (827 BC), the King Chu's son, Shugan took refuge in Pu. Up to early Zhoubeng King (770 BC), King Chuyu, Xiongdong expanded the Pu land. Kuiyue was oppressed. King Zhouxiang 19th year (633 BC) Chuxiang King brought the troop to kill the (Kui) troop. However, in the Southern and Northern dynasties, the Kuiyue's descendants called Nandan or Liao, still hidden in the cross borders of Chuan, E i.e Wushan county at Bigui, Fuxie today.

18. Le (Li) people on the Hainan island

Emperor Han Wu invaded Nanyue nation, divided into nine districts. Two counties: Danni and Zhouya on Hainan Island. The inhabitants of the island were the Diaoti people and Lini people also draw their faces with fish scale paintings, tattoos. In the Zhuqu Pi in Ling wai, wrote: "The history commended that the Luoyue people had much copper and silver. In the Jiaozhou Chr. wrote: The Viet people casted the boats. In Guangzhou Chr. wrote: Old Li man casted the bronze drums." Old Li man was the senior of the Le people. In Doguang Guang dong geographical summary magazine, wrote: "The Li metal drum looks like the bronze drums, small and flat, on three ears. Li people beate the drums for making the signs. "

Qu Dai Jun in Guangdong New letter: "In the Yongle reign (1403-1424), Wanzhou territorial head was Huanghuì, found a bronze drum in Tuohui creek, 3 feet long, 1, 5 feet wide, embossed more than 2 inches. Around, all were Kuadou letters, waist with wide bottom. Wan chang wan zhou also had the Tonggu ling - drums mountain, because they digged the drums so they named the mountain that name."

In the Qiongzhou county geographical book, wrote: "The voice of the Li people was the complement words stand before noun as chicken-meat they said meat-chicken; front - district was said as district – front." This showed that Le people were also as a part of Guangdong, Chaozhou kept that saying "the main element is in front and the sub element is in after: the noun, the verb precedes, the adjective, adverb goes after " in the saying of the ancient Viet people.

19. Nanzhao nation

China's southwest border, from Tang era to the end of the Song dynasty, there was a vassal nation that occupied a large wide land, took Yunnan, Dali today as the capital, Kunming to be the sub-capital. Having accepted the title by the Zhongxia, sometimes betrayed Zhongxia and proclaimed their own emperor's regime. Though having the the same cultural organization affected by Zhongxía, and Zhongxia also had been faced the crash caused by their soldiers. That was Nanzhao nation.

The Nanzhao nation's leader claimed himself as Mengshi, emerged in Menghua county, Yunnan, Lancang Jiang basin and No Jiang basin. In the reign of Xuanzong (712-755), the leader was Pixin Ge, to establish the Taihe citadel, ie. Dali county, Yunnan Province today. In the 26th Year of Kaiyuan (738), the Tang dynasty crowned as the king of Yunnan.

In the reign of King Wenzun (827- 840), Nanzhao nation brought the troops to attack the Shu nation, attacked Annan duhufu. The King proclaimed as Emperor Dali. King Lizun (860-873) ordered Qiaobian to pacify. Nanzhao contributed into the Tang dynasty's collapse. In the Old Tang book (Tangshu) Nanman story: "The Tang lost because of Huang Chao and the crash in Guilin!" From Mengshi, Nanzhao nation passed 22 generations, to Yuanxian zun 3rd year, was defeated by Kublai Khan.

COMMENTARY

First, in order to make clear about the origin of Bach Viet (Baiyue). Throughout the book, Mr. Lou Xiang Lin (罗香林) tried to convince the readers that *"the source of Baiyue derived from the Xiayu's Huaxia race. When the Xia dynasty collapsed, Xiayu's tribe migrated to many places and formed of ethnic Baiyue."* When reading, we have the impression that, perhaps in his mind, the author did not really believe in what he said. Because there was not a sure confidence and the fear of being doubted by the readers so he was forced to repeat too many times, to confirm his idea! The author did not believe he was right because he raised the colour of nationalism and the politics and not based on science.

So far, there was no any study has determined the Xiayu's origin. Generally, it was thought, the Xiayu ethnic was a branch of Huaxia. But the reality was not so simple. According to our research, residents of the Yellow Emperor state came from two sources: mostly local Viet people, owners of Yangshao Culture,

Lungshan Culture, from Southern Mongoloid race. And lesser number of belong the Huaxia people, born after the invasion of the Yellow Emperor in 2698 BC, by intermixing between the North Mongoloid and Viet people carrying the genes of South Mongoloid, so they also belonged to South Mongoloid.

According to our speculations, based on pedigree of the Yellow Emperor then Emperor Ku (帝嚳, Diku), was the descendant of the Yellow Emperor. De Khoc (Emperor Ku, 帝嚳)'s sons were Mr. Xie, Mr. Ze, their descendents were the Shang and Zhou dynasties's originators. Emperor Yao was Emperor Ku (帝嚳)'s son, Yellow Emperor's descendant. Emperor Shun and Emperor Yu were not descendants of the Yellow Emperor. Maybe they were the leaders of the Viet native tribes. Due to their prestige so they got the kingship after Emperor Yao. As known, Xiayu became the King in 2200 BC. Therefore, he could not be the ancestor of the Baiye branch. As above mentioned, to about 4000 BC, the Viet were the owners of the entire land of China. So the ancestors of Baiye lived in China for so long and created the Jiahu, Hemudu, Xanxing tui cultures ... At sites of Cansang, Baigua city Guangxi province, found the ideograms carvings on the stone shovels of the Luoyue from 6000 to 4000 years ago ... The former residents such incidents could not be descendants of clans born after them many thousand years.

The second thing to say clearly that the author (Lou Xiang Lin, 罗香林) didn't know that Wu, Chu people who were also the various branches of Viet ethnic. Because of that, the Viet killed the Wu then the Chu destroyed the Viet state were the internal disputes of the Viet race people that too large and widely distributed throughout China. And author [Lou Xiang Lin] also could not imagine that the Qin dynasty was also a Viet branch also. The Han dynasty was more Viet because the Han lived in localities of the ancient Han Shui region of the Viet race. Above, the part of Yangyue wrote: "Yangyue was at in Han Shui midland. Chuxiong qu occupied three nations

Rong, E, Yangyue (揚越) under the reign of Di King of the Zhou Dynasty. This shows that, in the late Western Zhou, Yangyue people were gathering in the Han Shui midland. Han Shui Basin from the Spring and Autumn period fully belonged to the Kinh Chu." Thus, until the end of the Zhou dynasty, the Viet people of Liu Bang's state on the Han Shui remained independent.

II. The Viet people's body tattoo custom

Vietnam is the cradle of Asia people. The ancestors of all ethnic groups in Asia were all born and resided about 20,000 and 30,000 years on Vietnam land in the ancient Viet community. Due to centralized settlement thus many of the cultural elements of Asia were formed here. First it was the voice. In the richness language of Asia, the Luo Yue languages became the main languages, contributing to the uniting of the majority ancient Asian populations. Next, they had the living habits and practices to form the cultural imprints and then followed the emigration to all parts of Asia. One of the typical traditions of the Viet was the body tattoo custom. Many studies showed that it was a common practice not only in Vietnam but also in China and Malaysia, Indonesia, the faraway islands in the Pacific Ocean as the identification of the Viet people.

Scholar Lou Xiang Lin (罗香林), in The Origin and Culture of Baiyue (百越源流與文化), wrote: ancient Viet clans used their haircuts and body tattoo drawings as the unique characteristics. In the Hanshi waizhuan (韓詩外傳) Outer story of the Han family wrote: "Viet King Goujian sent the Lianxi to devote to Chu (楚) King. Messenger saw Lianxi and said that: "Wearing the hat and you will be welcome by the the ritual." Lianxi replied: "The Viet nation was also crowned king by Zhou Dynasty. Do not reside in on the big nation, but at sea River region, and rank with fish, turtles, paint on body and hair cut, and stay there so.

Now I went to your nation, you told me to wear the hat, so you will welcome me, if so, when your nation's ambassador go to Viet nation, your ambassador must also cut his hair and paint his body so we will welcome him, so is it all right?" Huainan zi in the History of Qi (Qi Su Xun 齐俗訓) state wrote: "The King of Viet nation - Goujian cut his hair, drew on his body, not wearing leather hat, no bring the "hu" (圛), solemn, humble apprearance." In the Yuandaoxun wrote: "In Viet, they produced the Kudzu (cassava peel, soaked to get the fiber for making woven fabric) at the south of Jiuyi, they didn't work much on the mainland, they worked much in the water, so people cut their hair and painted to resemble scaly species. "Bi fa" meant the short hair cut, hair pins were still greenish on the head replacing for the hat without buning the hair and wearing the hat. In the History Qi state book (Qi Su Xun 齐俗訓) wrote "The Hu people knocked on the bone; the Viet engraved on body, China tjue* (an old custom: cutting the blood of two people and then merge to receive their relatives), due to many different reasons that faith was one such. Acupuncturing into the arms, sculpting the skin, painting the body must experience through the pain, but the Viet ancient tribe considered as the honore, it all was related to their traditions. In other words, conscious of their totems remained. "Viet ancient nations had the custom to draw the dragon images, so the descendants of the tribes also had the body tattoo paintings, which kinds of engraving and drawings, as well titles related to the dragon, like the Dongti people i.e., ethnic Taiwanese aborigines, from the old time, also painted their bodies with the famous dragon images.

In the book of Duo state about Dongyi people in Liuqiu island (Duoshu Dongyi Liuqiu) wrote that: "The kingdom of Liuqiu was on the islands, women painted their arms with the ink with serpent images, called as the Liuqiu nation, i.e., Taiwan today. These ethnic people still had the customs to paint and draw tattoo drawings on their bodies up to now". "The legend of the Li people" told: In the ancient time, the sky inclined and the land collapsed, the biological world was flooded and buried, the human beings also met this plague, just left a sister and her younger brother were still alive. But the sentiment between the sister and her younger brother were like limbs so they could not get married each other.

Therefore, she went to look for her husband, her younger brother went to look for his wife, each person went on different directions. They went long time and they still could not find anyone, ultimately, they met again, then again two or three times. Thunderer knew, went down to the earth and said to the younger brother that: "Now I am here, two people can marry each other to become the couple." The younger brother said: "Sister and younger brother can not marry each other, if doing so; we will be killed by the Thunderer God." Thunderer said: "I am Thunderer God, I decided not beating you." The younger brother still determined not listenying, and he went looking for a wife. So, Thunderer God painted a black paint on the sister's face. For a while later, the younger brother met his older sister again, he did not realize her and he immediately proposed her. The sister and her younger brother married; born many children and they were the Li people today". The Li people stipulated:" Woman at 12-13 years paints on her face. 16-17 years old, married, then paints on her chest. 20 years old if being loved by her husband, then she draws on her vulva. Drawing on hands or legs are just extra options, it did not a matter." Meanwhile, with the Fu people, only the men draw on their bodies, while women did not do. They draw themselves to indicate: I am a male who has reached the age of maturity. If up to that ages without the body tattoos, he will be ridiculed as unworthy and the woman will not love him.

Body tattoo painting was an art and also represented the social rankings. The nobles drew/ painted much and more complex tattoos, the commoners drew/ painted simpler tattoos.

Besides that, the body tattoos were also indications of each ethnic. Later it was prohibited so the body tattoo customs gradually disappeared.

III. The Bach Viet (Baiyue) sages

Living long time on the vast land of China, the Viet contributed many great merits of exploration and building China. But due to loss of land, loss of independence the Viet also lost their history. Fortunately, during the Ming dynasty, Mr. Oudairen (歐大任), a native of Viet origins, ever wrote an excellent record named The Bai yue xian xian zhi (百越先賢志)-The book of Baiyue sages - about achievement of those gentle sages of Bach Viet (Baiyue)

The Bai yue xian xian zhi (百越先賢志)-The book of Baiyue sages - is a very large book, including four volumes wrote about 120 Viet gentle sage persons, was written by Outaren (歐大任), a Viet origin author, in the 33rd of Jiajing Ming Dynasty (1554). The Book was considered as the accurate historical documents, for engraving printing and starred in The Arts section and stored in archives in the Siku quanshu (四庫全書, The Four Libraries of the Whole Books). In 1772 year, the King Qing Qianlong ordered to open the Siku quanshu (四庫全書, The Four Libraries of the Whole Books)., the The Bai yue xian xian zhi (百越先賢志)-The book of Baiyue sages found not intact, many stages, many letters were corruptible.

In 1831 wenzì yuhuan qui bookstores carved and printed from originals about the remaining 103 Viet gentle persons. In the 26th year of the Republic of China (1936), The Library of Shanghai Commercial Press (上海商務印書館, Shanghai Cangwu yinshu guan) reprinted the publication of wenzi yuhuan qi. In 2006, Professor Tran Lam Giang translated into Vietnamese and the Vietnamese cultural research center published in California, USA. 610 pages thick book, 13x20,5 cm format.

According to traditional notions, are shaped in Từ Hải, then, the "Bach Viet (越), the name of the race, also written as (粵). According to the geographical and archaeological research of Nanyue: from the Wuling (五岭) to the South, a contemporary of Tang, Yu, Sandai, were the nations of Manyi, that was the land of the Bach Viet (Baiyue). "

But today, with the new discoveries of anthropology, history, we know that, since thousands of years, before the appearance of the Huaxia people, China was a land of ethnic Viet. Viet people from Vietnam had built here early the agricultural civilization that most developed on the planet. Around 2698 BC, Mongolia people from northwestern have reached the Yellow River, invaded the the land of the Viet people. In Central Highlands, the Mongolia people mixed blood with the Viet people and the Huaxia had been born.

With time, the Huaxia people develop the Viet's humans, talents and material based on culture of the Viet nation, built the Chinese nation. Until the third century BC, around China's Zhou Dynasty, there were still the powerful nations of ethnic Viet: Ba, Shu in the West; Wu, Chu in the East; Van Lang in the South. When destroyed the Ba, Shu and Chu, the Qin had merged the land, people and culture of the Viet nations into Qin Empire. The men who revolted against Qin, Xiang Yu and Liu Bang were both the Viet.

As the winner, Liu Bang took the name of his clan named the Ḥan dynasty. After all, the history of a country was the history of the major communities that made up the country. Thus, Chinese history was the history of ethnic Viet had been living on Chinese land.

With such perspective about history, we approached the The Bai yue xian xian zhi (百越先賢志)-The book of Baiyue sages in a new light. Not only 103 persons who had names in the book and looked further, from Fu Xi, Nu Wa, Shennong, to Yao, Shun, Yu, Confucius ... were the first Viet gentle sage persons! Next were the heroes as Fuchai, Goujian ... If it had been published earlier, this book would be worth as the torch to remove the history's darkness, help the Viet people to find back the origin.

Now, even more than ever, history was discovered and became more transparent then as a true work of history, rich in literary quality, (Bai yue xian xian zhi (百越先賢志)-The book of Baiyue sages, currently remain its value. Maybe readers will wonder, why such illustrious names as Fuchai, Goujian, Xiangyu, Liubang, Qiaohe, Hanxin, Caosam, Yingbu, Wenweng, Shaobing ... were not in book? But after reading it, we understood the profound intention of the author. It was not a statistical work on the honored sages, it was the stele in honor of the sages who had ben well-hidden. There were three types of people to be honored: They were people who were talented in politic and economics such as Wenzhong, Jini, Fanlai who supported King Goujian. As Gong shiyu who helped Viet kings to revive the Jiao, Kuang regions, Yan zhu helped Emperor Han Wu.

The second type were those who had outstanding creations as Ou yezi wrought the swords, Chenyin made the shooting arrows become more skillful, Tailun processed and produced the paper, Philosopher Wangsung made of more than twenty thousand words in the Argument Action book, had been studied by the next generations. Shi lu digged the canals to support the food boats down south. In the section of the rivers that was too steep, he dammed to made the the waters rise to help the boats travel easily, and also help for irrigation.

The third types of gentle perhaps more numerous were the loyal, filial, faithful people such as Yanguang, Guangwu's childhood friend. When Guangwu became a king, he changed his surename and his name, went in hiding. Hedan was charitable and loved the populations as children. Chenfeng was the district's chief, respected the law, careful in using the punishment. Gufeng and Gongzuncong respected and used the gentle, literary talents.

As Chanhao, neighbors occupied his land, he did not dispute to claim back. When the neighbors felt ashamed, returned his land, Hao did not receive, he used that land for the village road. As hènghéng, when his Master was condemned unjustly and was killed, His Master's wife and children tortured in captivity. Disciples and relatives avoided. Zhengheng trimmed his hair like the condemned man, carried the knives of the late Master with grievances to the door of king to claim the grievances for his Master. The unjust case was clear, Mr. Heng self mourned and brought his Master's family to his hometown to take care of them...

Obviously, along with honoring the heroes who created the history, the author also was very passionate to praise the sages, wise persons who held the middle road, piety, benevolence, righteousness, courtesy, wisdom, credits. They were typical definitions of the ethnic Viet's culture.

Closing the book, we also bear inside us the gratitude to the sages and the proud on the glorious origins. Although there had a pity sadness because what was not unsatisfactory today, look at this book, we found the warm faith with the hope, as the Pearls (zhou) returned Hepu (合浦), there will be the beautiful days that the old precious values shall be returned to the Viet people!

References:
1. Lou Xiang Lin (罗香林). 百越源流與文化 (The Origin and Culture of Baiyue. China series. Taiwan book shop, 1955. Handwritten translation of Vong Chi Nguyen Chi Vien.
2.Outaren. The Bai yue xian xian zhi (百越先賢志)-The book of Baiyue sages, Vietnamese library, California, Hoa Kỳ, 2006.
3. Sylvia Fraser-Lu. Frog Drums and The Importance in Karen Culture. Arts of Asia September/October 1983 issue http://www.drumpublications.org/karendrum.php

CHAPTER IV

CHINA IN NEOLITHIC ERA

As well as history, culture is the result of the social activity of a residential community that have been taking place during a certain time and in a certain space. Because of such relationships, scientists can follow the cultural identity to trace the owner of that culture, once due to some certain reason, that owner was hidden in history.

Conversely, when the owner was being known, we can follow their footsteps to identify the culture that they had created. To do this, I tracked the extremely rich cultural sites that were explored on Chinese land, first in the Neolithic era. According to the traditional notion, derived from the Western schools, the Neolithic era was a period in the historical development of human technology, beginning around 10,200 BC following the ASPO chronology in several parts of the Middle East, and later in other parts of the world. According to the conventional understanding, this was the last stage of the Stone Era.

The New Stone Age was the next stage of Epipaleolithic in Holocene, beginning with the intensification of animal husbandry and cultivation, creating the "Revolution in the New Stone Age." This period existed between 4500 and 2000 BC when metal tools became popular in the Bronze-Stone Age, or the Bronze Age or developing directly to the Iron Age, depending on the geographic regions. Neolithic period was a step forward in culture and behavior, such as the domestication of plants and wildlife animals [1]. It was a classic statement suggested by Western scholars from very early archaeological findings in the Middle East. However, such a provision did not seem consistent with the East, where the grindstone tools and the domestication of plants, animals had appeared much earlier. In the International Archeology Conference held in Hanoi in 1994, the age of the new stone age found in Hoa Binh culture was determined to be 18,000 years BC [2]. Moreover, at Fairy cave's culture, discovering new rock tools and pottery C14 were 20,000 years old, and domesticated rice plants O. sativa have also been around since 12,400 years BP. In turn, from the new conception for the formation of human and Eastern cultures, the previous golden rule of historical standards must be changed. Several cultures will be presented below to prove this assertion.

Official documents of the Chinese government said, to 2007, on the land of China, they had confirmed 16 fossilized Paleolithic relics and 216 Neolithic cultural relics with more than 3,000 excavation sites. We can not present the all of the giant documents but would give that the most typical ones.

I. The Neolithic typical cultures

1. The Fairy Caves [3]

The Fairy Caves (Xianrendong) located at the foot of Xiaohe (小河) mountain, Wannian district, northeast of Jiangxi Province, China, far from the southern bank of the Yangtze River by 100 km. According to the latest study, published in 2012, The Fairy Cave had the pottery that may be the oldest in the world: ceramic pots, ceramic vases with the ages of 20,000 years ago. Far from the Fairy Caves about 800 meters, it was the Diaotonghuan cave which also contained cultural layers like

The Fairy Caves where several archaeologists believed that it was a residential area.

Four cultural layers were identified in The Fairy Caves including a long process of transition from the Old Stone Age into the first phase of the late Neolithic period. The presence of humans was mainly by the fishing, hunting and gathering, although some evidence of early rice domestication was recorded in the early Neolithic. At least some cultural stories have been reversed resulting that the stratigraphic ages were confused. However, reports in the Science journal in 2012 (Wu et al. 2012), proved a time of 20,000 years ago.

• Neolithic period 3 (9600-8825 RCYBP)
• Neolithic period 2 (11,900 RCYBP -9700)
• Neolithic period 1 (14.000 -11.900 RCYBP) appearance of O. sativa
• Late Palaeolithic period (25.000 to 15.200 RCYBP) only wild Oryza.

Archaeological evidence shows that the transition from the Palaeolithic to the Neolithic (19.780 to 10.870 RCYBP) the owners had lived by hunting, fishing and gathering, with the predominance of deers and wild rice (phytoliths of Oryza nivara). At the beginning of the Neolithic period (12,430 RCYBP), ceramic clay composition was more varied and numerous pieces of pottery decorated with geometric designs. Rice cultivation was a clear evident, with both strains of O. phytoliths nivara and sativa.

Stone tools were polished more skillfully; with the main technology was to process the gravel stones including a perforated plate, adzes and several grinding stones. However, with only a small piece of pottery was discovered, the investigation showed that between 12,400 and 29,300 cal BP was confirmed. The ceramic pieces had beeing bearing the lowest heat level, 2B-2B1, having conceded 10 AMS radiocarbon, with different chronologies, from 19.200 to 20.900 cal BP. This was making ceramics of The Fairly Cave was identified as being the first crafted ceramics in the world.

2. The Steep Cave (Yuchanyan) [4]

The excavation of the Steep Cave (Yuchanyan-玉蟾岩) began performing in the 1980s. Extensive investigations were carried out between 1993-1995 and again between 2004 and 2005. Yuchanyan is a region of limestone caves in south of the Yangtze river basin, in the Yao district (道县), Hunan province. This is one of the caves are very well preserved and known or suspected that there were residents. They were the hunters-gatherers from the Paleolithic to the early Neolithic period, during the late Pleistocene and early Holocene, along with other relics as Xianrendong, Diaotonghuan Jiangxi Province and Miaoyan in Guangxi province.

In the sediments of the Steep Cave (Yuchanyan cave) contained traces of at least two ceramic pots with radiocarbon ages from 18.300 to 15.430 cal BP. Until before discovering the Fairy cave recently, these pieces of pottery represented the oldest ones ever knowned. Yuchanyan cave's floor are 100 square meters wide, 12-15 meters east-west axis and 6-8 meters north to south.

The sediment contained the fragments remaining in the range of 1.2 -1.8 m depth, to the Later Palaeolithic period (late old stone age), between 21,000 and 13,800 years ago. At thetime of the earliest residents, regional climate was warm, humid. Fertile land, with plenty of bamboos and deciduous trees. According residence time, climate was warming, wood trees were replaced with grass. In the final stage, at the young Droughts age (Younger Dryas, about 13.000 to 11.500 cal BP), the seasonal rise.

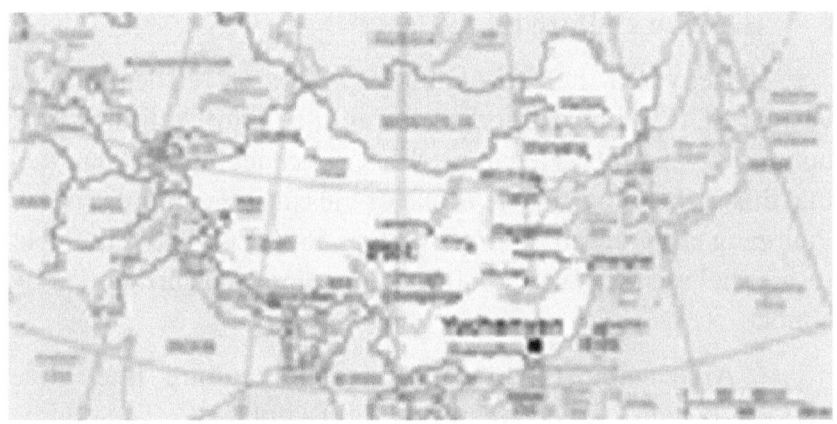
The Steep Cave in the Chinese map

The Steep Cave (Yuchanyan cave) is a combination of rich archaeological bone tools, stones and shell mollusks as well as a variety of organic remnants, including animal bones and plant remains. Plants recovered from the cave's sediments include plums and wild grapes. Phytoliths of rice and husk had been identified. Several scholars suggested that several particles to demonstrate the embryonic stage of the domestication of rice. Animals including bears, wild boar, deer, turtles and 27 different types of birds such as geese, ducks, swans, and five races of fishes. The Steep Cave (Yuchanyan cave) is one of the earliest examples when the pottery had been found. All potteries were dark brown, coarse, the loose clay pottery combined with sand. The clay pots made by hand and were baked at a low degree (400-500 degrees C). Kaolin was the main component of the products. The thickness was uneven, about 2 cm. Both inside and outside of the walls were decorated with text strings. These fragments were recovered to reconstruct a wide mouth pot (31 cm diameter opening round, height 29 cm) with tapered bottom. This pottery style also appeared much later in the cauldrons of China. Stone tools recovered from the Yuchanyan cave included the cutting tools, sharp instruments and hand scrapings. Bone awl was polished, shovel, perforated shells used with tooth jewelry – V notched decoration were also found scattered.

3. Jiahu Culture [5]

Discovered in 1962, Jiahu (贾湖) was a residential area vestige of Neolithic period in the midlands of Yellow River, now is Yuyang city, Henan province. Archaeologists remarked that this archaeological site is one of the earliest examples of the Peiligang culture, settled from 7000 to 5800 BC. The settlement residential area was in 55,000 square meters and surrounded by a moat.

Archaeologists divided the Jiahu culture into three periods. Earliest period was from 7000 - 6600 BC. The middle period was from 6600 - 6200 BC. The last stage was from 6200 to 5800 BC. Two later periods were corresponding with Peiligang culture, while the first period was only just in the Jiahu.

Jiahu residents planted the foxtail millet and the rice paddy. While cultivating millet was popular among Peilicang culture, the Jiahu was the only place to cultivate the rice. Jiahu was one of the first sites of rice cultivation that was found in the north of the Yangtze. More than 300 graves have been excavated, along with the funeral service. Objects were buried include pottery and turtle shells. One of the most important findings was the flute made of bird bones.

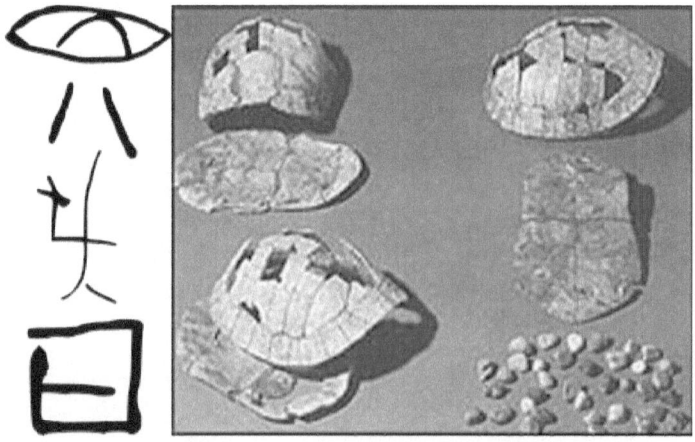

Jiahu shelled turtle carved with the characters

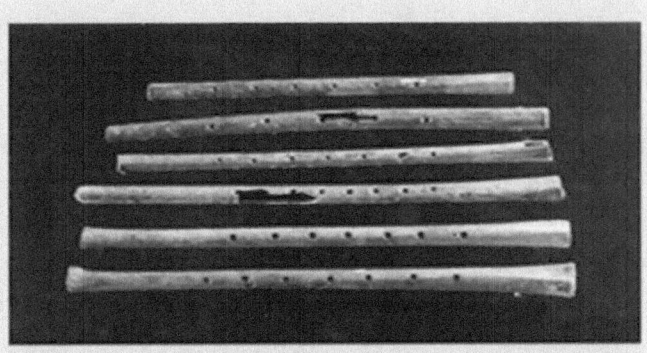

Six complete bone flutes excavated from Jiahu
Institute of Cultural Relics and Archaeology of Henan Province, Zhengzhou, China

Bone flutes in Jiahu

The oldest period of Jiahu contained only two flutes, four holes and five holes types. The middle period contained a pair of six-hole flutes (hexatonic). A flute was broken; the rest seems to be a replica of the first flute, as seen with the adjustment to match the pitch of the other. Innovation in the final period was to use eight-hole flute (heptatonic)...

Jiahu contained some of the first pottery of Neolithic period in China. Scientists from the University of Pennsylvania applied a chemical analysis of ceramic vases' bottom in Jiahu and found evidence of wine fermented from rice, honey and hawthorn. Hypothesis proposed that the wine was fermented with the saccharification process.

At Jiahu also identified 11 signs of the characters, nine on turtle shells and two on the bone, such as possible evidences of the primitive texts. Several signs were similar to the latter characters of China, two of the most compelling signs were similar to the following texts, they were the eye (目) and the sun (日).

4. Pengtoushan (彭头山) culture

The Pengtoushan (彭头山) relics and the Sanshidang (三石宕) relics located in the Mengping (孟萍) village, Taiping City, Li province, may appear around 8,000 years ago. In 1988, they had discovered a lot of cereals and rice husks mixed in pieces of pottery were identified as the first period of the rice cultivation. This finding confirms that in world history, the middle of the Yangtze River is one of those places where rice was planted very early. The Sanshidang was located in Wufu Village (五福 Wufu), town of Mengxi (蒙西) northeast of Liyang delta (溧阳), Li province.

Its history can be started from about 8000 years ago, in parallel with the Second Half of the Pengtoushan culture. The third excavation was conducted from October to November 1995, in which a layer of black sediment was found at a depth of 4.5 meters in the heart of the old channel.

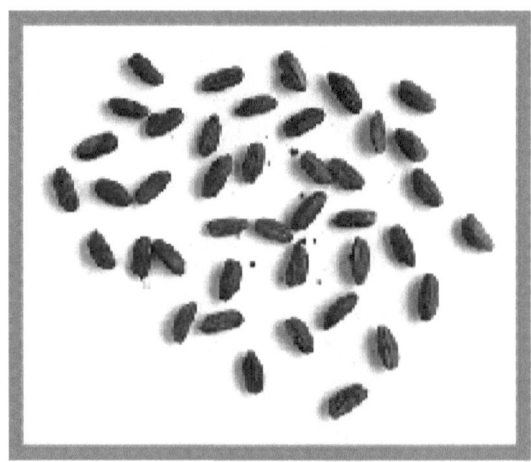

Paddy in Pengtoushan

Discovered a large quantity of organic matters, with more than 100 kinds of plants, dozens of bones of terrestrial animals and aquatic animals, products made of wood, bamboo and bone. Paddy and Rice was collected with more than 15,000 seeds.

Seeds were well preserved and had a great value in the study of agriculture.

5. Hemudu Culture [7]

Was first found in 1973 in Hemudu, Yuyao of Zhejiang Province, the Yangtze River downstream, distributed mainly in the south bank of Hangzhou Bay, Ningbo, Shaoxing plain and Zhoushan Island, with age of 5000 - 3300 BC, Hemudu culture of the Neolithic period, reflected the society in matriarchy.

Hemudu People lived and gathered into the villages formed with different sizes. There were many houses built in these villages. But because the ground was the riparian wetlands, so it formed the architecture and structure here differ significantly from the Central Highlands.

Natural conditions

Hemudu vestiges located in the Yangtze River downstream, with the fertile alluvial soil, providing good conditions for agricultural production. With the big rainfall, the high temperatures, so the there are subtropical broadleaf forests of evergreen, many deers, wild pigs, cattle and other animals. Here they discovered a large number of wild animal bones. The most typical products for agricultural production were "the plows made of bone ", which were made of the scapula of deers and buffalos.

The swamps were the good habitat areas for aquatic and animals, but they also provided the necessary conditions for fishing and hunting and breeding. The appearance of wooden oar proved that boats used for transportation, hunting, fishing, passenger transport. The stilt houses reflected as to adapt to the hot and humid environment in the south.

In 1987, they excavated and found a large quantity of paddy husks from the Hemudu relics. The excavation report showed that, a large paddy barn in the upper part of the fourth cultural layer, along with straws, leaves and saw dusts, reeds conspired to contain the paddy and rice. The average thickness was from 20 to 50 cm, the most thickness was more then 100 cm thick, and over total was more than 150 tons. In the charred husk, the rice was visible. Grain shape was intact excavated, yellow and few particles also showed the tendon lines.

Several husks still remained the pointed tails due to it were still perfectly preserved, which were unprecedented in the history of archeology in the world. Analytical results confirmed that they were the rice grains from 7000 years ago. The paddy cultivation created for society a large number of surplus grains, the separation occurred remarkably between the rich and the poor. The cultural development stepped into a new phase. Agricultural historians repeatedly sampling determined that it is rice planting, including species japonica, indica strains and seeds heterozygotes intermediate of Asian cultivated rice group. This not only provided the valuable materials for the study of the origins of rice cultivation in China, but also to revised the traditional notion that the rice grown in China through from Assam, India. That was strong evidence confirming that China was first country growing rice in the world.

Wood architectural monuments

Hemudu relics had four cultural layers. The second excavation discovered the wooden architectural monuments in the third and fourth layers, especially found the most in the fourth cultural layer, with a total of more than 1,000 items. Mainly piled wood, timber and rectangular, pillars and floor with the crutchs.

Hemudu house built on wooden piles, top with solid beams constituting the floor, then, the roof on the columns, beams. Tenon and mortise wood technology in China existed from 3,000 years ago before the metal age. In the Hemudu excavation, they found 29 products of wooden poles, at least six architectures. By analyzing the arrangement of column showed that in this time the house made following the southeast – northwest directions. The houses were often very long, the longest surface was up to 23 meters. Up to seven meters depth with the eave's corridor was more than one meter wide. The house could be owned by a clan. The door opened in the gable, facing southeast 5 to 10 degrees. It could use a maximum of sunlight for heating in winter, intended to prevent the sunlight in summer. People today inherit this Hemudu housing construction with the reasonable layout, the scientific design, taking advantage of natural geography conditions and creating the convenience to the life.

In addition, up to now, the wells also have been found from the first monuments in the ruins of the second cultural layer. The well built around six meters in diameter, with the pot-shaped bottom, surrounded by a wall inside the square with two meters in length and four rows of piles. The around puddle also had a circle fence, with a protective effect. In the Hemudu culture age, the houses often built surrounding the marshes, however, the lagoon water often linked with the sea water, making the number of salts increase, undrinkable. Thus, the wells appeared as attempts to improve the quality of life.

Original primitive music

At Hemudu, they unearthed a significant number of bone whistle horns, a kind of musical instruments and a type of hunting tools. In Hangzhou, Zhejiang they also found a small pipe made of bamboo, which is kind of whistle that sounds the birdsong, apparently that it is the rest of the bone whistle horn. At Tao Xun relics, they found the empty duck shaped thing with a blowing small hole at one end, that was an ancient instrument. Wine drinking utensils proved that the harvest was richer than before, food was surplus for the distilleries.

Main tools:

Pottery

At the sites of Hemudu, they obtained the largest volume of ceramics of Neolithic period, about 400,000 items, with 1221 items that had been restored fully, about 1/6 of the total number of artifacts were excavated. The most unique ceramics were black ceramics, Hemudu people had known how to mix the clay with the coal in the final stage to reduce the viscosity of the clay and increase productivity.

Many kinds of tools, mainly pots, pans, kettles, pots, plates, bowls ... Cooking equipment can be divided into eating utensils, food storage and water storage. Especially two stoves sao (灶) and he (盉) [the ancient kettles made of land with legs, lid and handling strap, a hose to pour]. The ceramic stove had the ventilation, three nipples inside to help the hold the kettles. The ceramic stove was invented the wood stove fireproof, then they used the jar shaped stoves.

Ceramic teapots he (盉) with the calabash shape, with rising mouth in the front, the steam whistle at behind, flat in the middle, with linked chain earring. Inside and outside of the kettle was polished smoothly, subtle manipulated, up to now, its technical values were still highly valued. Most experts believed that this was a utensil for wine.

Hemudu ceramic pots

Stoneware

In Hemudu culture, stoneware was not rich in terms of variety and quantity, and they unearthed a total of 874 items. Main things were production tools and jewelry. Production tools included hammers, axes, three categories of chisels, smaller shape, rough grinding, still preserved many traces of knocking. These tools were primarily used to cut trees and wood processing into agricultural tools and machining tools of bone, wood. The other stone tools and stone mill stone saddle, football, eventually two of them used to peel the grains and nuts.

Tools made of bones

There were more than 3,000 bone utensils were unearthed, the Hemudu people focused on productivity tools and their tools's functions were divided into plows made of bones, bone arrows, bone chisels, bone awls, needle made of bones, bone whistles/horns, bone spear, needle pipes etc. The bones to make the plough were the most characteristic. The bones to make the plough were the scapula of the large mammal species. Plows maintained the natural shape of the original bones, thick and narrow at the above part, lower part was the form of thin and wide blade.

A shallow vertical groove was in the middle of the bone surface, a lower end of the cylinder was shaped blade, with two parallel rectangular holes on both sides of it, the upper end was rolled square hole. Bone plows designed to fasten in an upright piece of wood. This was a unique method of production of the Hemudu cultural relics. The bone plows were smooth; several plows were cleaved, split into three parts due to the friction with permanent soil. 170 pieces of plough bones were found, corresponding to a large number of hoarding rice, so we could say that Hemudu's agriculture entered the stage of the cultivation by plough land.

Wooden furniture

There was a total of over 300 items, mainly unearthed in the fourth cultural layer dating back to to 7,000 years ago. Wood had been used extensively in the production and life. Wood production technology had reached a very high level. The most important wooden tools were looms and oars. Weaving tools had the wood (ceramic) wheels, teeth-shaped instruments, wood knives, and rollers, round sticks, small trees acuteness, and wooden (bone) knife tip. Tools for getting the fibers were considered the most important parts of textile machinery.

With weaving textile, the Hemudu people came out of the wildlife, entered the infancy of civilization. There was a total of eight wooden paddles, each of which was produced by a single wooden stick, cylindrical holding, willow leaf shaped paddle. There are paddles so it must have boat. As early as 7000 years ago, Hemudu people were sailing travelling between neighboring clans.

Original primitive artwork

At Hemudu, they unearthed the original artwork not only in large numbers, but in the unique shapes and variety contents. Mainly of them were the ivory carvings, decorations on ceramics. In particular, several carved ivory carving works with smooth lines, beautiful shapes, excellent results that were very excellent.

Piles of Hemudu stilts

(a) **Ivory carving arts**.

Eight butterflies's shape, grinding ivory, looked like real butterflies. One of the most outstanding works was the "song bird sunflower" that was the butterfly carved ivory, 16.6 cm long, 5.9 cm wide and 1.1 cm thick, the top half was chipped, the bottom was also slightly missing. Center of the engraved area were the five concentric rings. Between the front incised with concentric circles of different sizes; outside the circle pattern carved a flame, the symbol of the sun's rays. On each side, there was a curved beak to lift the sun, with outer feathers carved motifs. The entire layout artifacts were with strict images, skilled engravings, vivid images and compelling true sense, were the original delicate art works of the Hemudu people. There were four items with round carving of bird imagines. One item was with full length of 15.8 cm, 3.4 cm wide and 0.8 cm thick, ending in the bird's head engravings that looking down, with round eyes, curved beak, like an eagle's beak, between was the body and wings. Flat back surface, negative engraving patterns with short straight lines; both sides of the slash and short crescent created a strong feeling of feathers. Belly was thick, having the ventilation holes to pierce the ropes through. The thin and long tail was bending as the arc. These exquisite works of art were the common property of the clan, but only the chief of the clan had the use rights.

(b) Pottery carving works.

Characterized carving imagines were on the rim and the belly of the ceramics: the sun, the moon, trees and flowers, along with fish, birds, insects, animals ...

Hemudu jasper

simple motifs, stretching, simple style and sense of vitality, reflecting that the Hemudu people loved the life, loved the nature; also showed the desire of the good weather for the good harvest, the people were happy. Many ceramic pots painted fish and algae, an earthen vessel with the rice flower pattern, pork imagine on bowl shape, the five leaves etc ... The art ceramic items basically were still intact when being excavated. Even the fragments, also retained the status quo, so it should be able to recover fully. This showed that Hemudu people appreciated these items, they could be sacrifice items. Maybe it was the sense of religion in the beginning time.

(c) Jewellery:

There were precious stone jade, pipe, pearls, rings, cake etc. Most of the beads, rings and jewelry made of jade and fluorite. Under the sunlight, they were green, with beautiful crystals. There were ornaments made of animal fangs or teeth dogs, fish vertebrae.

6. Liangzhu (良渚) Culture [8], [9]

Discovered in 1936, Liangzhu (良渚) Culture was a culture in the Later Neolithic archeology; existed from 3300 to 2200 in BC, at Liangzhu (良渚) in town, Yuhang District, Hangzhou City, Zhejiang Province. Liangzhu (良渚) culture was mainly distributed in the Taihu, the Yangtze River basin, where the ancient Viet settled and lived there, including Yuhang Liangzhu (良渚), South Jiaxing, East of Shanghai, Suzhou, Changzhou, Nanjing. The relics were extended to the West to Anhui, Jiangxi, North to North of Jiangsu, spreaded to near Shandong and to the south of Shanxi. Liangzhu's power accounted for half of the Chinese mainland. If the economic and cultural level were not high, they could not do that.

The Liangzhu (良渚) culture represented the second wave of jade culture in the Eastern prehistoric age (the first wave of the Hongshan culture jade, Laohe River Basin, Inner Mongolia). There were Tong (cong), Viet (Yue), Royal jades (semicircle jade), crown jewels, trident shape, bracelets, tube shape, Amanda, pendants, cylindrical jade, conical jade, rings. Jade used for Worship (cóng, marble, ax) were highly enhanced, the latter they were inherit by the the Zhongyuan dynasties. Stone tools, there were sickle stone, arrowheads, knives, ax punching, perforating knife, especially rock plow and weeding tools were used, showing that the agriculture entered the ploughing stage.

Polished black pottery was characteristic of Liangzhu (良渚) ceramics. On ceramics and jade appeared a large number of single characters or group of characters bearing the text function, the scholars called as "plain texts." "Original texts" showed the mature stage of hieroglyphic characters. Character was an important sign of a civilized society [10].

The old citadel had a wall, in East-West 1500-1700 m long, North-South direction about 1800-1900 meters, slightly rounded rectangle. Several parts of the remaining wall were 4 meters high, 40 meters of the surface section, 60 m thick (compared to the ancient walls of the Xi'an old city built in the Ming Dynasty, Hongwu years, the foot of the wall was 18 meter, the wide surface 15 m) with pure loess soil, brought from elsewhere, carefully compacted. The west wall was about 1000 m long, cross-sections from 40 to 60 meters, the southern mainland with Fengshan, the north to East Shaohuo

Next, the southern wall, the northern wall and eastern wall, at the foot are the stone foundations, with large volumes of compacted loess soil. Compared with the western wall, the other three sides of the wall are relatively more complex: a lot of rock excavated, the exterior stone walls are relatively large, smaller inside. The wall was covered by loess soil; sometimes adding a layer of black clay, increased the waterproofing.

From the locations, the layout and characteristics of the discovered Liangzhu (良渚) old citadel, the experts believed that there were palaces, where the kings and the nobilities had lived, it was the capital of Liangzhu (良渚) period. Archaeologists believed that the ancient city was "the Liangzhu Ancient State." Monuments of the Liangzhu ancient city could be called as "the first Oriental city", "dawn of civilization" of the Oriental civilization, the mecca of the East, the cradle of Chinese civilization, ranking in the "List of the World Heritage Sites."

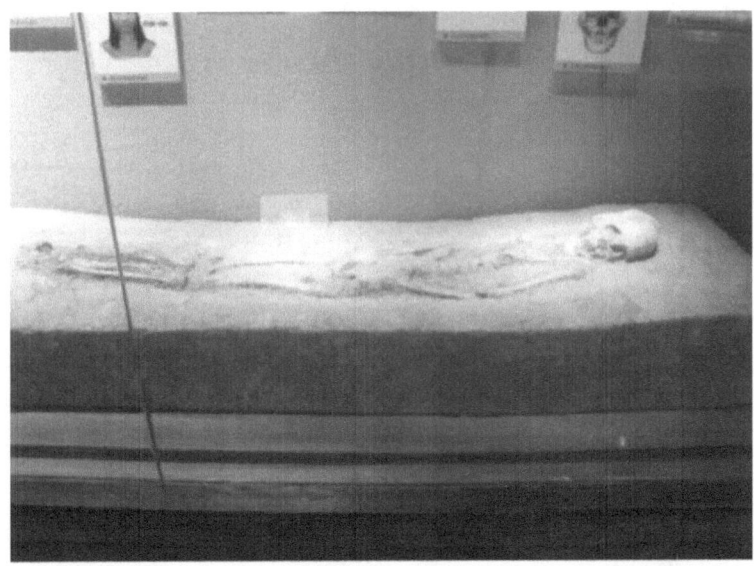

Liangzhu people's skeleton at Liangzhu Culture Museum

The discovery of the Liangzhu ancient city make several people thought that the ages of Chinese dynasties should be rewritten: currently, the Xia, Shang, Zhou dynasties were regarded as the earliest, but this role needed to be delivered to the Liangzhu owners.

In 1986-1987, the Fanshan relics were discovered. 11 large tombs were excavated, collected more than 1,200 pieces of pottery, stones, ivory and jade inlaid lacquer. In recent years, Liangzhu cultural relics were found from 40 to be increased to 135 places, with the villages, cemeteries, altars and other monuments. A large number of objects were excavated from the tombs with more than 90% were jade items, the symbol of wealth and power. Jade ax was a symbol of military power and provided a valuable information.

This was the largest jade collection that was re-determined and re-named in the world; thus, they corrected the initial confusion that those of items was under the Emperor Han Wu Dynasty, pushed history forward 2,000 years. In 1994 they also found the basis of the super giant building, with an area of over

300,000 m2, confirmed the artificial accretion of loess soil, to 10,2 meters thick, its technology and massive scale was rare in the world.

Archaeological studies showed that Liangzhu cultural stage, agriculture has begun to plow period; handicrafts became more professional, jade processing industry were specially developed. The large amount of worship jade appeared that opened the prelude to social etiquette, the distinction between the large tombs of nobles and the tombs of civilians showed that the rise of social stratification. The significance of the rich and poor distinction suggested that it was formed through some kind of social power over-rode the clan society.

The constructions of a large number of graves that required a certain level of guaranteed social order, if not, it was difficult to implement. The construction of a social class differences created the strong links. It could be said, in Liangzhu culture stage, clan and tribe had emerged with the central government leaders; a large amount of labor was organized, formed a large scale of the social structure.

The existence of social power was also fully reflected in the production of jade items. Crafting jade was a multistep complex labor process; therefore, the jade was a handicraft professional product. Handmade ornaments were the nicest, showing that each piece of jade presented much labor result, with the high level. This proved that the division of labor between intellectual work and the manual labor were formed.

In Liangzhu culture, there was a very enigmatic model constantly appeared, a special motive of the fierce battle, could not no help to reminiscent to Chiyu (蚩尤) warriors. Chiyu (蚩尤) was an ancient history figure of the Southeast legendary, fighting and repeated the victory, revered as the god of war. The stone ax culture was developed highly, suggested that Liangzhu people had the elite astute weapons and the mighty in battle.

After Chiyu (蚩尤) was defeated by the Yellow Emperor dynasty, Liangzhu culture entered a period of recession. Legend said several tribal alliances with Chiyu (蚩尤) including East Di, Shandong and the tribes living in the Yangtze River basin. Chiyu (蚩尤) tribal chief had a large tribal alliance called Jiuli (九黎), its scope covered all the cultures of indigenous Liangzhu, Li Liangzhu people are strong so they became the head the Jiuli (九黎). In Jiuli (九黎), there was a branch called Yu (羽) people or Yu residents. They worshipped birds, animals, as their ancestors, and by that faith, worship of birds. Under mysterious patterns on the jade, the birds, the animals, were the totem of Liangzhu people. So, most likely that the Liangzhu people might be the Yu people or Yu residents.

In large vestiges of Oriental prehistoric civilizations, the Liangzhu is the greatest, with the highest level of development. Archaeologists November 29, 2007 in Hangzhou, announced that 5,000 years ago the ancient city of more than 2,900,000 m2 area was found in the core zone of the monument relics. Peking University Professor Yan Wenming and other archaeologists pointed out that this was the city relic of the Liangzhu culture stage was first discovered in the area of the Yangtze River, could be called "the first oriental city". The Ancient City showed that the Liangzhu culture 5,000 years ago has entered a mature development stage of prehistoric civilization. Located in Yu district territory, "Liangzhu relics" were the Liangzhu cultural center. National Heritage Board said that Liangzhu heritage group will become the temple of 5,000 years of Chinese civilization.

From the current knowledge allowed us making following statements:

Until 5000 years ago, in the East Asian continent, the ancient Viet people had created the developed agriculture. Because the plows were used in the cultivation so the labor productivity increased, there was surplus food, promoted the craft and commercial activities. A gem trading networks formed by sea put the gems mined from mines in Taiwan to countries around the East Sea.

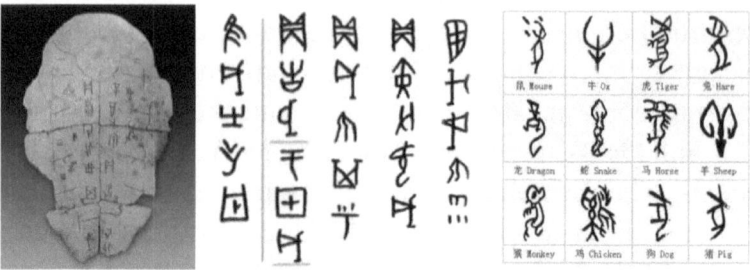

Liangzhu texts

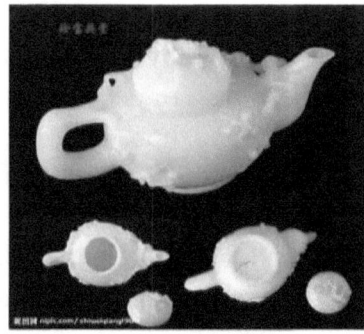

Gem tea set

Dragon shaped gem

Because it was necessary to co-operate to handle the irrigation works of the two rivers: Yellow River and Yangtze River, so agricultural tribes had to ally together and the ancient state formed very soon. In this period, the nomadic peoples of the north bank of the Yellow River and west strengthened their pillage to the rich agricultural population area. Due to requirements against invaders, the alliance between the Viet tribes, same blood, same language and culture became more stringent.

Chiyu dragon head image

Restorated house made of leaves

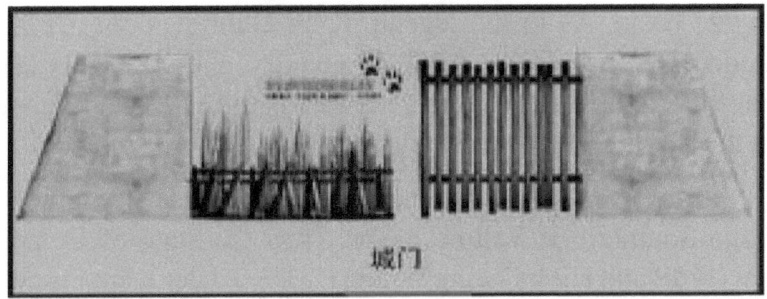

Map of the citadel

Ancient citadel relics   A black ceramic pot

Maybe this time two ancient states were formed: Ba Shu included Ba Shu land in western China and Thailand, Burma, led by the Legen King Cancong. In the rest of the mainland, with Indochina, it was the state ruled by Shennong. Shen Nong's kingdom was vast, including the Yellow River and the Yangtze River.

According to the northward progress of the Viet people, the Yangtze River Basin had the favorable natural conditions and had been exploited early so there was a development before, became a growing center of economic, cultural, political, and military. Due to its special location, so the Taihu Lake region of Liangzhu became the capital of the Shennong dynasty.

Around the year 4879 BC, Emperor Ming (帝明), a descendant of Shennong divided the land, crowned his son Empero Nghi (帝釐) as the King to govern the Yellow River basin and Kinh Duong Vuong King (涇陽王) to govern the Yangtze basin. As in the legend, Kinh Duong Vuong (涇陽王) founded the Xich Quy (赤鬼国家) country; the north boundary from the south of the Yangtze, the east is the East Sea, the west and the south to the Central Vietnam.

In this period, the northern nomadic tribes strengthen to pillage Southern of Yellow River. Thus the state of Emperor Nghi (帝釐) and Kinh Duong Vuong (涇陽王), later were Emperor Li or Dilai (帝哀) and Lac Long Quan (雒龍君) strengthened the arms and allied together to against the enemy.

Around 2698 BC, the coalition of Mongolian tribes led by Xuan Yuan (轩辕) clans to open a big attack to Zhou Lu (涿鹿) in the the south bank of the Yellow River. Viet Coalition of Emperor Li and Lac Long Quan fought courageously but then failed. Emperor De Lai died.

One scenario I've proposed that, after this defeat, Lac Long Quan led the Viet people and troops on boats along the Yellow sea, landed in Nghe An. Here he was welcomed by the local people then they respected his eldest son became the King, called as Hung Vuong (雄王), founded the capital in VietTri, named the Van Lang (文郎国家) country. Based on overlapping boundaries between Van Lang (文郎) and Xich Quy (赤鬼国家), arguably, is the displacement of the capital and changed the country's National Brand of Lac Long Quan dynasty.

At Viet Tri capital, the Hung Vuong kingdom continued leader Van Lang-Xich Quy people building the country and spent a prolonged resistance of the residents in Yellow River basin. About 4300 years ago, due to sea level rise, the Lang Zhu capital was drowned, led to the disintegration of the Lang Zhu state. Liangzhu culture was declined ...

Above was my recokoning thought about the process of formation of the first state in the East, with the capital was Liangzhu. The reckoning was based on the following grounds:

- About the time: The times that Liangzhu culture arose, declined were coincided with the legend of the Shen Nong King appeared the Emperor Ming (帝明) divided land, crowned the King titles for Kinh Duong Vuong to found the Xich Quy (Chigui, 赤鬼) nation. Then it was the formation of Van Lang (Wen Liang) state.

- On the boundary: Liangzhu culture was widely distributed within the boundaries of the Xich Quy (Chigui, 赤鬼) state in legendary

- Legend of the Xich Quy nation was very popular in the Oriental people. This suggested, the only Xich Quy nation appeared here in the past.

- Imagines of Liangzhu gems often engraved "神人獸面" (Animal Face of God) to worship. Today researchers thought this was the Yan Emperor or Chiyu (蚩尤) etc. What people called as "獸面"(animal face), this was the face of the dragon, from the Qin, Han to nowaday, people still meet painted dragons like that.

This was the mark of "Dragon's children and Fairy's grandchilden" in Vietnamese legends. Chinese scholar calls Liangzhu residents as the "Yu people or Yu citizens." Because the Yu belongs to the birds, so it should be able to understand that the people worshiped the Bird and identified themselves as descendants of the Fairy and the dragon, as in the legend of the Hong Bang surname (鴻龐氏).

- Residents of Liangzhu were two strains of the ancient Viet people that were Indonesian and Melanesian. By DNA testing technology, scientists had identified the owners of Liangzhu culture was the Lac Viet people (雒越) based on the mark Y- chromosome mutation – O3 M122. They were the two Viet races who came up from 40,000 year ago to explore China, brought Hoa Binh new stone tools up, created the first pottery and first rice at The Fairy Cave's relics in the southern of Yangtze River.

Through many characters carved on Liangzhu Gems, suggested that, at Liangzhu period, the Viet people's letters had grown. Liangzhu words were more rudimentary than the Enqu Oracle bone scripts and the qualification was equivalent with the inscriptions carved on the Gansang stones, showed that the vast cultural unity in the Xich Quy (赤鬼) nation in the south of the Yangtze. Liangzhu and Gansang's letters, were the predecessor of the Enqu Oracle.

- In the document named "About Heaven tower, place of worshiping Heaven of the Emperor Ming", PhD. Tran Dai Si recodred in his surveys as follows: "Heaven tower was small hill 179m high, with line going round up. On the top there was a small temple, now abandoned etc. At Hunan library I found a very old document, paper tarnished, but writing very nice, consisting of 60 pages. The headline wrote: " Old story of Heaven tower. Dr. Zhouming Wen in Zhenguan era of Tangtai zong king, from 627 to 647 year but we did not know Zhou got his doctorate in what year?

Though the book was composed by Zhouming Wen, but it was not the original. This version copied by later generations in Qing Kangxi period. Contents of the book included three parts. Part of Zhoumíng Wen composed, the next parts, wrote by a nun named Dam Chi, not clearly when it was written. The third part was written the names of the leading monks from to build the temple/ pagoda up to the Kangxi period (1662-1772). Zhouming Wen also reiterated the Emperor Ming went on patrols to the southern, married with a Fairy and Loc Tuc was born. He built an altar on this mountain to worship the Heaven, so tower called as Heaven tower, mountain was also called as Heaven tower mountain. Ming Wen also told more:

«Old time on the mountain there was only a worship to worship the Emperor Ming (帝明), Kinh Duong Vuong (涇陽王). By the time East-Han dynasty, a general named Dao Hien Hieu of the Female King was ordered to withdraw from Spratly. When he withdrew to Que Duong, he and his thousands of soldiers went up to Heaven Tower to worship, listened the temple holder telling the old story of the ancient temple. He and his soldiers decided to fight until the death, so Luu Long's troops were lost many thousands of people to abled to occupy the mountains. The Tang dynasty erased the traces of Viet-Chinese and South North, the officials were sent to dominate Linh-nam to build the temple here."

This document was an evidence that the legendary of Emperor Ming went on patrol the Southern, went to Heaven Tower mountain to build the Altar to worship the Gods of Heaven and Earth appeared from the ancient time and became popular in Jiangnan region. It was also further evidence of the Xich Quy state.

- Shu Shu in the Three Kingdoms magazine wrote that, Xu Qing (许靖) was a person coming from the northern, then taking refuge and going to the southern, serving as an official to write the historiography of Liu Bei, up to the position of Situ

(司徒). Before the battle of Chipi (赤壁之戰, Battle of Red Cliffs), Cao Cao (曹操) sent people to reconnoiter the rear of Liu Bei (刘备) and Sun Quan (孙权). Because respect for messenger of Cao Cao, Xu Qing had wrote a brief for Cao Cao: He had gone from the Huijie (Hanzhou today), through Jiaozhou, Tongou, Minyue, the land of thousands of miles without seeing Han's land.[许靖给曹操的信说：从会稽"南至交州，经历东瓯、闽越之国，行经万里，不见汉地"]

Four letters: without seeing Han's land (不见汉地) of Xu Quing was demonstrate that: The Southern, despite located in the Han nation in hundreds of years but the land was not belonged to the Han, in the fact the land remained to belong to the Viet people! By the end of the Han dynasty, the Jiangnan region remained to belong to the Viet land, so thousands of years ago, that was the land of the Viet. These are more things to talk about the similarities between the Liangzhu Kingdom and the State of Xich Quy but I think, with what happened last 4000-5000 years ago, these evidences were much enough!

7. Peiligang culture [12]

Peiligang culture was first reported in 1977 in the sites in Peiligang, Henan province. It was a society with relatively early culture in the middle and lower of Yellow River. Age of the C14 was defined as 5,000 years BC. In the southern of the Yellow River, Shandong, Shaanxi and Hebei there were also similar findings. Peiligang culture was not only the thing to resolve questions about the Yangshao culture origin, but also resolve the problems of ancient society including aspects like nature, religious consciousness and the breakthrough brought a prominent part of agricultural history.

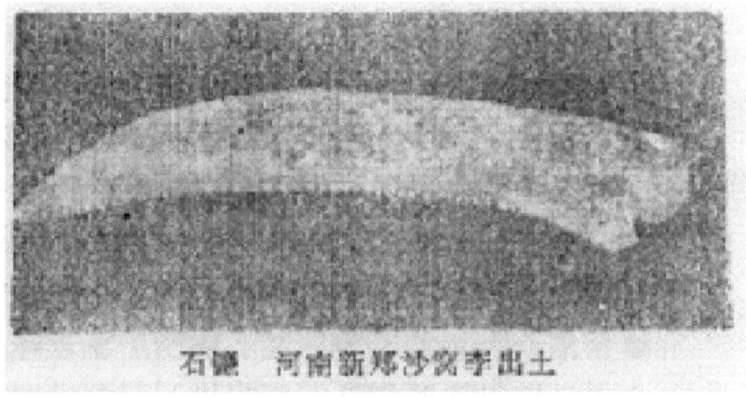

石鐮　河南新鄭沙窩李出土

Figure 1: Peiligang stone sickle

It was not only to confirm the Chinese developed the agriculture since ancient times, but also one of the first places of the world. Peiligang culture showed advanced agricultural history of China.

Four excavations at Peiligang discovered several important tools. Sickle (Figure 1), grindstone etc ... used for agriculture, their technology is not complicated, but the shovels, axes, sickles were popular (Table 2).

The stone tools of Peiligang Culture.

Figure 2 showed the main tools like shovels, axes, sickles and grinding table {metate: A piece of stone with a shallow concave surface, used with a piece of flat rock above, used for grinding grains, relative prior generation to the millstone}, but the knives were less; chisels, knives, hoes, hammers etc were absent. Five types of Peiligang tools were: long flat axes, or trapezoid axes; later than the drills used for cutting trees and breaking the ground (Figure 2: 3,4), with a flat shovel blade to break the ground (Figure 2: 5,6); sickles to harvest like a modern crescent with a concave serrated edge (Figure 2: 1,2); and grinding table was used with a mano for grinding grain, with four columns of legs and one worn thin surface (Figure 2: 7).

All necessary for processing and a minimal basis for the rapid growth of ancient agriculture. 7-8000 years ago, the climate and geography were very different, but initially the farmers with their clumsy stone tools significantly impacted on production. Peiligang culture in the south of

the Yellow River was an agricultural base directly affecting to the agricultural growth in Asia. Because of the geographical location and the climate, the agriculture originated in the south of the Yellow River. Geology of the south Yellow River was a part of the northern China with the vast midland Loess Plateau in the late Pleistocene of the

Quaternary.

Fertile loess soil was ideal for the development of the agriculture and enriches the resources of China. But the climate also affected the formation of the landscape. Soil and climate of Peiligang culture was ideal for ancient habitat, such as rainfall in the north focused on summer. When the north had less rain means the rain falls in the south accordance with millet, a naturally drought-resistant crop.

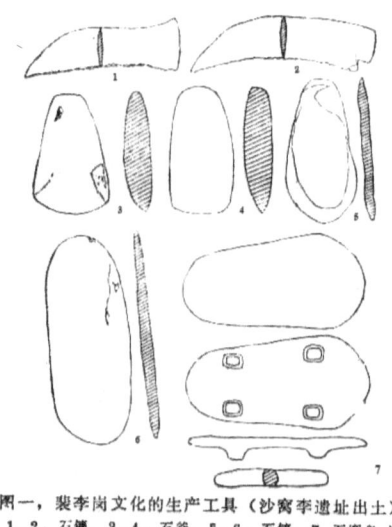

图一，裴李岗文化的生产工具（沙窝李遗址出土）
1、2，石镰，3、4，石斧，5、6，石铲，7、石磨盘、棒

Peiligang stone tools

There was a large quantity of rot Millet in Cishan, Banpo Yangshao culture, Meng village etc. Therefore, the agricultural growth and the economy are dictated by natural conditions, social systems and production methods.

Peiligang people continuously improved the tools. The serration shaped sickle improved the efficiency of the harvest. Improved tools raised the productivity, called people to settle and allowed the development of many types of pottery. Animal breeding reflects and depends on Peiligang agriculture. Pigs, dogs, cattles were raised in earlier implied from a clay pig statue was unearthed. Many people thought that the first animal was the dog because it supported the hunting.

In North America, the first dog was domesticated about 8400 BC in the Jaguar Cave, Idaho. But other people felt that it was the sheep because it grazed the natural grass, while dogs needed meat and cereals. Sheep was raised first in the world from 9000 BC at Zawi Chemi Shanidar, but pigs also appeared early, dating 7000 BC in Cayonu, Turkey. Pig production needed a stable life. Clay pigs certainly could not explain the pig farming, because it could far from that period, making China become a nation with earliest agriculture and animal husbandry.

8. Yangshao Culture [13]

In 1916, the Swede mining engineer, Andersson, while seeking copper ore, accidentally discovered the stone artifacts. This accident discovery changed the life of engineer and turned him to become a famous archaeologist, when in 1921 discovered the Yangshao relics, Sanmenxia City, Henan Province. Yangshao Culture distributed on 3,000,000 m2 area, throughout the provinces of Shaanxi, Shanxi, Gansu, Henan, Hebei, Inner Mongolia, Qinghai, Ningxia ... Existed from 5000 to 3000 BC. Yangshao Neolithic culture left following artifacts:

- Large number of the grinding tools made by pebble stone including axes, hoes, spades, shovels, sowing tools.

- Many finely potteries with brown glaze, red, black,

- Many semi-submersible houses with a large number of jars containing millet shells indoor.

- Many bones of pigs, chickens and dogs.

- In the cemetery found remains of people close to the Han people now.

Yangshao Culture had a great importance, because, with the emergence of highly qualified indigenous culture with the new stone tools, pottery and cereal agriculture, it affirmed the role of Oriental civilization, rejected the old idea that Western civilization spread to the East.

Yangshao painted pottery

With the Chinese, it was more meaningful especially for the first time found the "remains of Chinese ancestry," as the owner of a high civilization. From this, appearing a conception that Chinese civilization was born from Yangshao then spread to the southeast.

About the Puyang tomb in Henan province [14]

In May 1987, Chinese archaeologists discovered the ancient tombs in Xishuí steep, Puyang City of Henan Province. The burial site had 45 the tombs. The tomb No. 45 were excavated by a special survey. By C14 dating, dating from 6500 BP (6460 +/- 135), under the Yangshao Culture period. The head of the tomb was facing to the south, the leg was in the northern, the east was a dragon made of shells, with claws, lifelike; the west of it looking like a tiger made of seashells, the head is quietly, majestically; the tiger's belly made of seashell mosaics shaped like flowers.

In the tomb No. 45, there were three people aged 12 to 16 ages were buried in three directions: east, west, north, according to a certain degree oblique. At the foot of the owner's triangular tomb, there were two tubes of children's tibia bones taken from the Tomb No. 31.

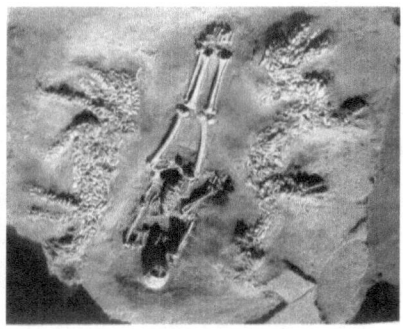

Grave No. 45

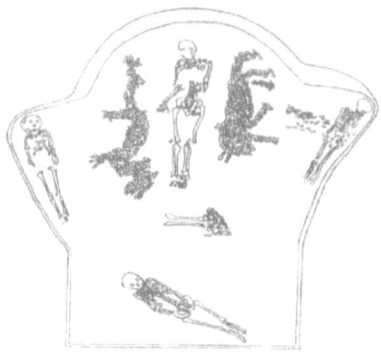

The diagram of the tomb No. 45

Mr. Xushao Can, a feng shui expert had studied each tomb and made the following comments:

* Tomb Puyang 45 had the icon of the green dragon and white tiger and 28 graph places respectively of white tiger-green dragon emblem, (showing) the green dragon-white tiger map of the tomb Puyang map 45 was the "four icon map". According to the shape and size of the dragon and tiger in Puyang tomb 45 showed seven suitable location could be identified 28 locations had been established at the time of burial.

* Farthest to the south in the direction of north-south of the No. 45 tomb was the tomb No. 31. The owner of the tomb No. 31 at the south end was a virgin girl, the Goddess of the summer solstice. Three sacrificial victims in No. 45 tomb, one was a symbol of the God of the Spring Equinox (East, a virgin boy), the Goddess of Autumnal Equinox (West, a virgin girl) and the God of Winter Solstice (North, virgin boy). Here the seasonal cycle was complete. The ancients had a cultural belief is: Winter, Spring was Yang (positive), indicated by Virgin Boy; Summer, Autumn was the Yin (negative) denoted by Virgin Girl.

* Third, in the tiger's belly made of sea shells in the Tomb No. 45, with a variety of seashells scattered. This pile located in the belly of tiger made by sea shelled; the shaped flame in the tiger's belly graph was only to confirm each other. In the scheme of No. 45 tomb with models and reference projects, they reflected exactly the same content, the image was a "star map" (xingtu). In the tiger's belly had an imagined sun as the apricot flowers, it was a Spring Equinox. Generally, the grave was arranged in star icon at sunset of the Spring Equinox.

* Measured by the number of available graves BP'P = B'P'P = 24 ° 00 '. Second, the clamshell with apricot flower shape in the tiger belly was the sun, according to precedent was the star's orbit in the Spring Equinox Day.

* In the night to observe the North Star; in the day to raise

the column heading. At the foot of the No. 45 tomb owner had a small triangle and two tibia bones of a child. Tibia bone was like a handle hilt of the North Star. The North Star was used in astrology by the ancients. To observe the North Star in the night; to raise the column heading to measure the shadow in the day. The measurement method by using the column heading also was the oldest measurement form as the ancients through shadow of human body to change direction but gradually learned how to design, it was to raise the "column heading".

Because the human body, the column heading and the time had a special relationship, so the ancients called it as a "Measuring thigh time", showed the meaning of the human knee. North Star map in Puyang tomb No. 45, the feet and the time reconnected, reflected the ancients through the shadow to measure and monitor the North Star to determine the time.

* In order to put the tibia bones as the handle hilt of the North Star (Polaris), identified four subjects founded on observation of the North Star (Polaris).

* Worship totem of China existed in 6500 years ago. From calculations of the locations from the "four element map " (Cixiangtu), the ancients carried 100,000 minimum astrological observations before started recording.

* This was the first in China detected feng shui of tomb, decided the development direction of feng shui later.

* The No. 45 tomb had the semicircle infront and square behin proves the concept that the round sky and the square earth was formed.

* According to the 28 places and split into the four Gods shows that 6500 years ago people acknowledged the functioning of the year and they invented the astronomical system of sexagenary cycle (Ganzhi - 干支)"

Our Opinions:

First, we must assert, owners of Yangshao Culture 6500 years ago were Viet people went up to explore the ancient China, Viet people brought millet, rice to the the Yellow River basin. At latitude 35, due to the dry climate, the rice could not survive, so the millet became the main food crops.

About 7000 years ago, in the Yellow River midlands, Viet people Indonesian were contact to North Mongoloid people living on the northern shore grasslands, born South Mongoloid race. South Mongoloid people were born by Viet mothers, living in the Viet culture, saying Viet language so they were Viet people. With time, the number of South Mongoloid people increased, becoming the owners of Yangshao millet production culture. Naturally Puyang tomb was that of Viet people.

Puyang tomb No. 45 was particularly significant about the history, culture, showing 6500 years ago that the Viet people had:

i. Knowledge of mature astronomy. The conception, that the sun iss round and the land is square, was formed and explored the North Star and 28 stars in the sky.

ii. Discovered the sexagenary cycle (Ganzhi - 干支)", the extensive calendar with the days in the year.

iii. Had maturity in the fengshui and applied the feng shui in the burial.

iv. Above knowledges proved that Viet people had grasped the principles of change (易理). This is solid evidence confirming the Yi is a creation of Viet ethnic simultaneously showed Yili had been formed before this time.

9. Hongshan Culture [15]

Discovered in 1970, the Hongshan culture located at Liaohe River basin in Xilamulun River's tributary, Laogeha,

Daling with 200,000 square kilometers, Inner Mongolia region, Northeast China. It was a Neolithic culture in 6000 - 7000 years ago, they also found a small number of late Paleolithic Stone Age. Hongshan cultural society was the early heyday of matriarchy, the last period gradually moved to the patriarchy. Economic model was mainly agriculture with livestock production (pigs, cattle, and sheep), fishing, hunting. It had characteristics typical with ceramic painting, ceramics with patterns fonts, rough Neolithic culture and fresh rock (microlithic) coexisted.

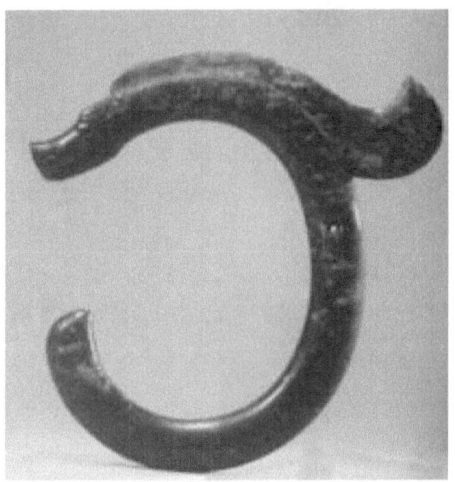

Dragon jades in Hongshan culture

The crafted stone wares were very many while vestiges of both processing methods and hewn stone were on knife sharpening stone two holes, stone plowshares, mattocks play rock, crushed stone countertops, stone and pestle grinding stone arrowhead etc ... The color potteries with incised parallel zigzag lines included the vases, pots, vases, jars ... Special thing was a two-chambered kiln. The gem was highly crafted with dragon-imagined jade with pig head shape, fish, birds made of gem, animal-shaped, cloud shaped, belt shaped jade, rod-shaped gem etc. They also found many fragments of the metal melting crucible that caused from the copper melting. Houses in small or large sizes, square, semi-submersible.

Hongshan culture reflected comprehensively the Neolithic period in China's northern region. Then Chifeng Hongshan relics and vestiges and cultural identity in the region were developed, general known as the Hongshan culture. Hongshan Culture was in the same period of the Yangshao Culture in the Central Highlands.

The Hongshan culture tribes had lived on both sides of the Xilamulun River, with agricultural and economic life was relatively stable, had found relics of clan residence. Daling River, upstream Mangniu of northern Inner Mongolia, Ngao Han Ky Ha (Aohanjihe) Fu Ying village, a tribal clan of the Hongshan culture.

Ceramics industry occupied an important position. At an early stage of Xinglongwa culture, the brick technology was developed strongly. The experienced members of the tribe had been dedicated to this task. A large amount of pottery was mass produced. Productivity and quality pottery significantly improved.

Currently, the majority of scholars have five categories presented comments on the Hongshan cultural backgrounds:

a. Hongshan Culture was a primitive system of Yangshao culture;

b. Hongshan Culture was inherited from Xushan Hebei culture;

c. Hongshan Culture was likely to be a culture of fine stoneware and mutual influence of Yangshao.

d. Hongshan culture period was a unique Neolithic culture to this region. It appeared and developed itself. It was also influenced by other cultures.

e. Hongshan culture likely was a continuation and development of Hemudu culture, ethnic Chinese society from a matriarchal to a turning point in a patriarchal society.

Crude stone tools and fine stone refined; it was a unique characteristic of the Hongshan culture. Dragon topic was the most typical of this culture, such as "national symbols" from the early days of the Hongshan culture was continued later. Leaf-shaped stones, stone plowshares, cinnamon leaf stone knife with two holes, pierced stone, stone knives, stone arrowheads and other artifacts showed the various farming tools. Small delicate, skilled pottery and coarse brown ceramic pots, bowls, vases, top etc each model individually decorated with crosshairs, V, herringbone pattern etc.

Hongshan Culture features decorative ceramics, although impacted by the Central Plains of Yangshao, but still held the similarities and differences. In late Hongshan ceramic type models even the arc point type was out-of-date type, even there was no any in Yangshao pottery. Two cultural similarities, the "red bowl" of the late Hongshan culture and that type of Haucuong Yangshao culture were similar.

Pottery painted with the parallel lines, reduced the types like as ceramic paint Hougang (侯冈) triangles, these different points presented their cultural identity. The similarities between them showed that their ages were closer together, but Hongshan culture was not simply considered as a branch of Yangshao culture, local variations or mixed culture.

There was a viewpoint that in China prehistoric existed two systems of cultures; they were ancient Zhongyuan culture and ancient Northern culture. Ancient culture in the north was mixed by Hongshan culture and Hechao culture. Two cultural systems had both the symbiosis and the specificity. Ancient culture in the north could not simply be defined as a branch or a local variant of the ancient culture of Central Highlands.

To understand the origin of the Hongshan culture, the first task is to find out its earlier existence in the region. In 1983, after the excavation at Xinglongwa sites, clarified that

Xinglongwa culture to support to the discovery of the origin of Hongshan culture, which was the first document to support for the comparisons. In Xinglongwa relics, they found out the earlier Hongshan culture, here the settlement area had been surrounded by the ditches, contained the artifacts that bringing the characteristic of early Neolithic period, with the ages of C14 is 7470 + 80-6895 +/- 250 years ago.

Too early prior to Hongshan culture, it had the cultural relations with the predecessor of Hongshan culture. It should be called "pre-Hongshan culture." The places of distribution of Longwa culture and Hongshan culture were in similarities broadly. Most of the items of pre-Hongshan culture and Xinglongwa culture were the coarse pottery, low level terracotta, less decorative, cylindrical brown ceramic, rough clay bowl (with fine sand) sanded, typical with zig-zag pattern and mesh pattern. Overall, the pre-Hongshan culture showed some progress compared with Xinglongwa culture. Longwa culture had a certain level of agricultural production; there was a size and a number of settlements. There maybe was the thriving Hongshan culture as early agricultural society.

This showed that Xinglongwa culture and Hongshan Culture had the inheritance relationship and perhaps Xinglongwa culture was the origin of the Hongshan culture. The development in the future of the Hongshan culture, had undergone a long period of history. In 1973, they discovered type of Aohanqi xiaoheyan (敖汉旗小河沿, Xiaoheyan culture is Aohanqi Xiaoheyan Xiang Bai Ying srang named sub site of southern taiwan. It is later than Hongshan culture as early as in Xiajiadian ...), and found a strong clue to this relationship.

Type of xiaoheyan culture was a new merger of a cultural type. It and Danyang danhushan both found the Neolithic artifacts, with models of painted pottery, decorative aspects and characteristic of different types of Hongshan Culture but with the dating later. Combining data collected at Aohan

Banner Xiaoheyan Nantaiti and Wengniute Banner Danangou Danfeng shan sites, it was identified as "Xiaoheyan culture". Its distribution was suit with the Hongshan culture; its cultural identity could be summarized in two points:

Reconstructed Statue of Hongshan Goddess

Stoneware

There was the coexistence of the grindstones and small chipped stone tools, with four edges, stone axes with a rectangular cross section polished stone plowshare, stone arrowheads, stone polishing shovel, knife sharp stones rolling bone. Stone blades are polished well. Along with ceramic pigs appeared to reflect economic life combined with livestock and hunting.

Pottery

There were red soil potteries and rough gray potteries, sandy mud and mud potteries manufactured four kinds of black potteries. Rope decoration, incised and additional patterns, delicate rope patten of rope of Trapa began with lightning pattern. Ceramic coatings were mainly black, red and white, decorated with fishbone oblique parallel pattern, folds lines of huiziwen. There was ceramic with inside coating, a typical method of drawing with parallel slashes on white, inside adding three colours of black, red, brown, forming the huizi, three fish, eight fish, reticulated mesh pattern etc ...

A variety of geometric patterns, many drawings by ruddle, its typical artifacts were cylinderal ceramic with sandy ash, bowls, basins, cups, vases with the big mouth and two straps. At the end of the period, there were the big flat-bottomed basins appeared, with the wide mouth and narrow belly shape bowls, their heart part is empty (Dau) and the appearance of painted pottery.

It was notably that, in the Hongshan culture, about 4,000 years ago, many copper smelters appeared.

In anthropology, from a statue of the goddess was reconstructed, indicating the owner of the Hongshan culture was Northern Mongoloid race.

II. Commentary

These above cultures, though little but they also represented the Neolithic culture on Chinese land. On Chinese land there were three regional Neolithic cultures: The Yellow River valley, the Yangtze River basin and Inner Mongolia.

Although there were small differences, these cultures were the Neolithic culture with typical grinding stone tools, pottery, agricultural economics associated with farming and hunting. Chronology and characteristics of "Native cultural production" on Chinese land showed the rule: The Southern culture has the early age with the form, materials, polishing technology of stone tools, potteries, jades or gems etc that bringing the fullest basic characteristics for the Chinese Neolithic culture. This showed that the Chinese culture had been formed from the Southern and gradually had been developed to the Northern.

Under traditional notions formed from the 30s of last century, the origin of the Chinese nation was at the Yellow midlands. From here, the people with Chinese culture spread to the southeast. But since the 70s, when discovered vestiges of the Neolithic culture in the Yangtze River basin, they had suggested that: "Culture in the Yellow River valley was the mother of the Chinese nation." "Basin the Yangtze River was the second mother of Chinese nation. "

When the Hongshan culture was discovered; there was someone said that: China had three cultural centers? Was it that the Inner Mongolia was " third mother of Chinese nation?"

The above viewpoints were a part of the limitations of human knowledge but also the inevitable consequence of the Great Han chauvinism: China was the center of Asia. Everything originated from China and distributed it to the world!

Today, thanked to new discoveries about human origins and the origin of East Asian peoples, we knew that prehistoric men were from Vietnam and went up for exploring not only China but the whole Mongolia and vast Siberia region. Over time, immigrants from Vietnam brought grindstone tools, millet, rices, chickens, dogs up their habitat.

Viet Australoid people dominated the valley of the Yellow River and the Yangtze River basin. Mongoloid people occupied the Mongolia land and made the Hongshan culture. Due to the interconnection that the South Mongoloid were born from about 5000 BC in the Yangshao culture and Hemudu culture. And this connection made the Hongshan culture, Yangshao culture and Hemudu culture had the similarities.

Although the differences might be recognized, they were just the small difference, based on the universality. This was the the common origin of the people and culture of East Asia that was from the Vietnamese cradle, ie. from the Wuling mountain range (五岭) to the Central, the Northern regions of Vietnam.

References

1. Neolithic http://en.wikipedia.org/wiki/Neolithic

2. Hoabinhian http://en.wikipedia.org/wiki/Hoabinhian

3. Xianrendong http://archaeology.about.com/od/xterms/qt/Xianrendong.htm

4. Yuchanyan
   http://archaeology.about.com/od/upperpaleolithic/qt/Yuchanyan-Cave.htm

5. 賈湖遺址
http://zh.wikipedia.org/wiki/%E8%B3%88%E6%B9%96%E9%81%BA%E5%9D%80

6. 河姆渡遺址 http://zh.wikipedia.org/wiki/%E6%B2%B3%E5%A7%86%E6%B8%A1%E9%81%97%E5%9D%80

7. 彭頭山遺址
   http://big5.myxlc.com/Article/dongtinghudxsqsdyzptsyz_129112

8. 良渚文化_互动百科 www.baike.com/wiki/良渚文化

9, 10. Liangzhu (良渚) culture http://en.wikipedia.org/wiki/Liangzhu (良渚)_culture

11. Trần Đại Sĩ. *Về Thiên-đài nơi tế cáo của vua Minh*.
    http://www.vietnamvanhien.net/NuiNguLinh.pdf

12. Wang, Jiehuai. *Peiligang culture*. Chinese Academy of Social Sciences, Institute of Archaeology, 27 Wangfujing St., Beijing, CHINA (Agricultural Archaeology 1985 (2): 81-85). Formatted by G. Leir; edited by Yuping Wu & B. Gordon) http://http-server.carleton.ca/~bgordon/Rice/papers/WANGJH85.htm

13. 仰韶文化 http://baike.baidu.com/view/9771.htm

14. 徐韶杉：从阴宅风水看仰韶天文   http://www.chinahexie.org.cn/a/yishupinsheji/gudongshoucang/shoucangshichang/2011/0106/6043.html

15. 红山文化主人 http://baike.baidu.com/view/56987.htm

CHAPTER V

CHINA IN THE BRONZE AGE

The Bronze Age is the period when people explored the ores and smelt the copper with tin to make copper weapons and tools. These activities required an organized labor force and the skilled craftsmen. In the Bronze Age, humans learnt how to organize the farm to have enough food to feed the other workers - such as miners, copper smelters, weavers, potters and masons, who lived in urban areas - and to support the ruling elite class, the organizers and the leaders of the society. The classic document wrote that the Bronze civilization appeared first in the world at around 3300-2300 BC at Sumeria.

In China, at the Hongshan cultural relics, 4000 years BC, they discovered many copper crucibles. At Majiayao sites in Shaanxi Province, they also discovered bronze knife made in between 3100 - 2700 BC. However, in the formal aspect, the Bronze Age of China began in 1700 BC, in Erlitou culture of the Shang dynasty.

I. The typical bronze cultures

1. Majiaao Culture [1]

Majiaao culture was in the Western of Gansu, the Eastern of Qinghai, the West of Yangshao, belonged to the Neolithic culture. Majiaao had three kinds of culture, early type dated between 5800 to early 4800 years ago, the middle type dated from 4800 and 3800 year ago, and the last type dated from 3800 and 2800 years ago. Majiaao culture had the brilliantly painted pottery, reached the pinnacle of world history. In 1975, in Gansu Dongxiang Lin in the Majiaao culture family (around 3000 BC) they unearthed a bronze knife, which was the first copper artifacts found in China, was a proof to prove the that China entered the Bronze Age.

2. Er litou culture [2]

Erlitou cultural relics were earliest excavated in 1952, at the sites of Yucun Dengfeng Henan Province. In 1956 they excavated the Lac Dat temple ruins in Zhengzhou, named as Lac Dat culture. In 1959, Erlitou was excavated, due to its typical, so the remaining forms of culture renamed Erlitou. Erlitou culture included the cultures in the Earlier Neolithic period and the Bronze Age, from 21 to 17 century BC. Here they were mostly copper worship things, jades, turquoise cards, there were several tools and weapons sites. Yanshi Erlitou site had a large scale never before seen on the Yellow River basin and there was no any archaeological culture like that. Mostly it located in the distribution center area of Erlitou culture, it might be considered as the capital or major city of the Xia Dynasty.

They confirmed two palaces arranged on the urban axis. One palace was little square, lacked the northeast corner, 96.2 meter wide, and 107 meter long, north-south direction, with a total area of 9585 square meters. The main lobby was located in the north with eight rooms, facing south, three times the depth. The palace was surrounded by a wall with inner corridor; the east wall had a series of rooms. Axis palace was facing the southward to open to the south, was divided into three entrances, north, east, there was a side door. Palace II width 58 meters and long 72.8 meters, also north - south, surrounding wall; east, south and west corridor.

Background of the main hall was 3 m thick clay. Both palaces had the drainage channels. Palace II still retained relatively full. Many circular pipelines connected to form a complete drainage. Each segment had a diameter from 16.5 to 22 cm and 52-58 cm long, 2 cm thick, was placed in a trench 1 m deep underground to prevent the water leakage. 5-7 cm above the trench was the paving stone to prevent the clay pipes from breaking. Pipelines in the direction from west to east were used to discharge the rainwater from the palace's courtyard to the hospital. Outside the palace area, across the dirt roads, there were the buildings and the land walls. The total population was estimated at between 240,000-270,000 people.

Erlitou culture was found in approximately 100 locations: Luoyang Donggangou, Zuoli, Dongmagou, Chanxian Qilypu, Linnu meishan, Zhengzhou Luodamiao. In western of Henan, southern of Shanxi etc, Erlitou culture was found in sites of the region and in the Xia Dynasty time, but all found items didn't remain the the bone characters, similar to the Yenqu; therefore, the existence of the Xia Dynasty was not verified. Although many Chinese and abroad historians had argued that archaeological Erlitou of Yanshi city, Henan Province whole period or at least the first stage and second period, there might be the relics of the Xia Dynasty, but it was still looking for concrete evidence to clarify.

Based on the artifacts and relics discovered at the Erlitou site, in the Xia Dynasty, there was a large amount of wood, stone, bone weapons and other things. Specifically, in the third period, they found a few of bronze weapons. Wooden weapons included sticks, many bows, a few of wheel rims etc. Stone weapons included lot of different kinds: rock hammer, stone ax, stone spear, soccer, and stone arrowheads, stone spearhead. Shell was used for arrowheads, as well as being used to reinforce the wooden spear, as the murderous weapons. After the third period, the bronze weapons appeared, though in small quantities, they maybe are the work of the Xia Dynasty, for the generals and upper class in society. There were also grave gifts and bronze weapons and jade buried with them.

At Erlitou, they found shells, cortical bone, stone shells, bronze shells and other things created by men, and they coulg be a kind of currency.

In the Late Neolithic, the society began to form classes, the arts also began to be split. Most of the lower classes used simple and practical tools, with simple aesthetic trends. The king and noble class used the worship things complex decoration, shape things tend to change. Lower classes used the decoration mainly simple geometric patterns, breeding patterns, topics related to fishing and agriculture.

Bronze wine drinking tool

The worship things of the elite class are complex decorated with cloud motifs, thunder, eyes, snakes, animals, and objects associated with spirits. Longshan culture of Henan in last period and pottery of the Erlitou culture in first stage have a very high artistic value. A cup of black ceramic was thin as eggshell, called "eggshell cup," like metal cup. Items were also decorated with carved hole pattern. In Erlitou culture stage II and III of periodic excavation, ceramic was blue surface, decorated with the rope motifs or square mesh motifs, sometimes squamous, circle pattern, geometric patterns. In the period III only, the real practical tools had the art decoration and lacked of the decorative objects with the pure "art for art" objectives.

According to legend, the earliest Chinese texts appeared in the Emperor Cangjie period, but according to archaeologists, Chinese writing letters first appeared after Banging moved the capital into En by discovering the oracle bone script in the Yenqu zone. The oracle bone script was a complete text system. So far found about 5000 words, with one third of them had been explained the meanings. Oracle bone script must have a system for representing the original text but they were not yet found. In China in the Neolithic period the motifs carved on pottery have appeared. The shapes of the little ornaments were more similar to the original of hieroglyphs. Found on a number of engraved potteries "1", "2", "3", "M", "x", "one", "10" were the simple icons that could be used to determine characters. Er litou culture found on pottery there were 24 models that might be a primitive character. Because many single words appeared, not a question, therefore, they could not certainly represent the official documents.

3. Lungshan Culture [3]

The most important characteristic of the culture of this period was the discovery of the location of the sites. Such as in Shandong province, outside the Lungshan Chengzyai, there were vestiges of Yaowang citadel, Shouguang vestiges beside the Yaowang Citadel. At Bengsan they found eight sites, Linzi rural village sites etc ... then they discovered in Henan the vestiges of Pingliang Hoaiyang, Dailu hamlet, Cangzheng relics of the Dengfeng Wang zheng, Yanzheng Hejiatai vestiges, relic Hui distric at Míngzhuangtai etc.

In 1930-1931 they excavated Lungshan Chengzyai vestige, the most prominent representative was the unique shape of these black exquisite handmade pottery, so archaeologists originally called as the black ceramic culture. Shortly thereafter, it was named the Lungshan culture. Earlier, China unearthed a large number of color pottery and red paint pottery. River mud as a raw material in the black pottery could be the unique creation of Dongyi ethnic more than 4,000 years ago. At Chengzyai, they found the black artwork ceramic that was a cup type with only 0.5 mm thick, weighs 50 grams. Not mentioning to 4000 years ago, even now it was also extremely difficult to make such fine ceramics.

Lungshan Cultural Relics

After 1949, the excavations and studies had shown that the so-called original Lungshan culture, was a culture system, it didnot have a single source; it could not be regarded as merely an archeological culture. General characteristics were: Shandong Lungshan culture, or typical Lungshan culture as the sites are named as the Lungshan town, concentrated mainly in the Shandong area, across from the Dawenkou culture on above, under to Yuedan culture, radioactive Carbon after calibration showed that from 2500 to 2000 BC. Two cultural periods, Miaodigou, distributed mainly in the Yuxi, also in Yudong. Henan Lungshan culture had aged 2900 BC to 2800 BC, distributed mainly in a strip of Yuxi, Yubei and Yudong. Two cultures Miaodigou, or equivalent culture in this period still remains. Bronze culture of the early Chinese civilization developed in the Central Highlands, with the dating since 2600 - 2000 BC, and was usually divided into three types: Wangguan with 3 periods, Haugang with 2 periods and Zaoleita with 3 periods.

Shaanxi Lungshan Culture also called two cultures: Kedanzhuang culture, distributed mainly in Jing River, Shaanxi Province to Weihe River Basin Area, dating from 2300 to 2000 BC. Taoshi Lungshan culture with the newly discovered Xiangfen Taoshi relics was typical, mainly distributed in southwest Jinxinan terrane, dating back 2500 to 1900 years BC.

In 1931, at the sites of Houcang Anyang Heinan, first discovered Xiaotun (Shang Dynasty), Lungshan, Yangshao, three kinds of "overlapped" cultural relics, clarified their relative chronology relationship. In the 1930s, said that the Lungshan culture relics, not only in middle and downstream of the Yellow River, but also to the Hangzhou Bay area, at that time, according to the difference in the area, divided into three zones: coastal Shandong province, Yubei and Hangzhou Bay. There were also suggestions that the Lungshan culture was a source in the early history of Chinese civilization, and considered that, Lungshan culture was a direct precursor of Culture in the Shang Dynasty. The common system was Lungshan Shandong culture, namely, culture originally named Lungshan town, followed by Yinshi culture with the Carbon chronology dating before 2000 BC to 2500. Lungshan culture, that was considered as the the ancestor of the Han Chinese culture of the Huaxia tribe, Taoshi relics verified, and supported this view.

Most scholars, based on age of the Lungshan culture, guessed that legendary Yao, Shun and Yu, as well as the Xia Dynasty could be within the Lungshan culture. Especially the Yaowang sites in Rizhao City, Shandong Province, the largest capital cities of contemporary Asia. Ancient papers recorded that Emperor Yao tribe living in this neighborhood. Emperor Yao called as Taotang surname, with the name Taoshi, even thousands of years remains unchanged.

4. Sanxingdui (三星堆) culture [4]

Sanxingdui was the name of the archaeological site and ancient culture in Sichuan, China. Now it believed to be the ruins of an ancient city. Bronze culture was known before, was rediscovered in 1987 when archaeologists unearthed the remarkable artifacts that radiocarbon ages were from 12 -11 century BC. The culture made of the Bronze artifacts, is called Sanxingdui culture, and archaeologists identified it to contact the ancient Shu kingdom.

The discovery in Sanxingdui, as well as discovery of other Xingan (兴安) tombs in Jiangxi, challenges the traditional notions that Chinese civilization spread from midland plain of the Yellow River. The Chinese archaeologists had started talking about "Many centers created the ancient Chinese civilization."

The Sanxingdui archaeological site located in the northeast from the city of Nanxing, Kuanghan Province, the Chengdu area, Sichuan Province about 4 km. It was a walled city under the Sanxingdui culture, founded around 1600 BC. The ancient city had a 2,000 m long wall in the east, a 2,000 m long wall in the south, 1,600 m long wall in the west surrounding the area of 3.6 km2. The city was built on the waterfront Xianhe River and part of Mamu creek. The 40 m long wall and 20 m wall, with a height of 8-10 m, surrounded by 25-20 m wide channel system, depth of 2-3 m. Channel used for irrigation, internal transport, defense and drainage. The city was divided into industrial zones and residential areas and religious centers around the dominant axis. Along this axis, most burial holes were found on four cemeteries. The hall had a rectangular wooden frame; and the largest was a 200 m2 hall.

The Sanxingdui culture was divided into several stages. The Sanxingdui culture was corresponding to the phase II-III of the site, was a mysterious civilization in southern China. This contemporary culture was same age with the Shang Dynasty. But they had developed a method of copper processing different with the Shang Dynasty. The first phase corresponded to the first phase of the Baodun (宝墩) site and final stage (stage IV) merged with Ba and Shu cultures. The Sanxingdui culture ended, might be either due to natural disasters (evidence of the big flood was found), or invasion by a different culture. The Sanxingdui culture marked a strong central theocracy with copper trade from En Dynasty and ivory from South East Asia.

This event demonstrated that, there were independent cultures in various regions of China, despite the traditional theory of the Yellow River was "the only cradle of Chinese civilization." In 1929, a farmer, while digging a well, discovered a large inventory of jade items, the following years, many of them fell into the hands of private collectors. Chinese archaeologists identified the sites but they failed until 1986, when workers accidentally found the sacrificial holes containing thousands of items made of gold, copper, jade, pottery and artifacts that were broken (probably beating ceremony), burned, and buried carefully.

The first hole was found at Lanxing Brick Factory on Monday July 18, 1986. The second hole was found on August 14, 1986, just 20-30 meters from the first hole. The bronze artifacts found in the second hole included men statues, bells, decorative animals like dragons, snakes, chickens, birds, and ax. Cards, masks and belts were artifacts made of gold and many items made of jades as cards, rings, knives and pipes. There were also a large number of ivory and pearl shells. Researchers were surprised to find an art style completely unknown in the history of Chinese art, which was fundamental for the history and artifacts of the Yellow River civilization.

Head figurative of the Sanxingdui culture

The Sanxingdui (三星堆) cultural identity

Many archaeologists identified that the Sanxingdui (三星堆) culture was relevant with the ancient Shu kingdom and associated artifacts found at the sites belonging to the first legendary king of the Shu. There was very few of references on Shu kingdom in the Chinese historical record (mentioned in Chronicles and Shujing as an alliance of Zhou, who defeated the Shang), but the information about the legendary kings of Shu could be found in local chronicles.

According to Huayang nation journal composed in Jin Dynasty (265-420), Shu kingdom was founded by Cancong (蚕丛). Cancong was described with the bulging eyes, a feature found in the the Sanxingdui culture's items and cultural objects. The other eye-shaped objects were also found which suggested the eye worship. The other leaders were mentioned in the Huayang nation journal, were Boguan (柏灌), Yufu (鱼凫), and Duyu (杜宇). Many fish and bird statues, might be the totems of Boguan and Yufu (Yufu name actually means the cormorant), and the clan of Yufu had been proposed as one of many possibilities associated with the Sanxingdui.

Recent finding in Jinsha also assumed to be a move of Shu kingdom and was a continuation of the Sanxingdui culture.

Metallurgy

This ancient culture had made significant progress in casting technology by adding the lead beyond the usual combination of copper with tin, creating a solid substance that could be used to manufacture the bigger and heavier objects. For example, the oldest statue in the world was with human size (260 cm tall, weighs 180 kg), and a copper tree with birds, flowers and decorations (396 cm), which several scholars identified the image of the life tree in Chinese mythology.

The most striking exhibits were dozens of large bronze masks and human gargoyles (at least 6 gold plated masks) with typical angular faces, almond-shaped eyes were exaggerated, with pupils protruding out, and big ears. Many bronze-made faces of the Sanxingdui culture had the traces of paints: black on the eyes and eyebrows too big, lipstick on the lips, nose and ears explained the vermillion that "was not the color but it was something like the ritual for the leader to taste, smell and hear (or something for it the strength to breathe, hear, and talk)."

Based on the design of the head statues, the archaeologists believed they were mounted by the the wooden supports or totems, perhaps were dressed. It concluded that "wearing the ritual mask played an important role in the community life of the ancient in the Sanxingdui". Features of the ritual bronze masks were as something that could have been worn by shi 尸 (literally "dead") "human, player – the ceremonial representative of a deceased loved one." Shi in general was relative, almost young when wearing a costume (which might include a mask) to recreate the characteristics of the dead.

Shi was a stunt, that meant, one who served as a reminder of ancestors that the sacrifice was consecrated. During the ceremony, the stunts were more than the actors in a TV drama. Although there might have been different exact meanings, the Sanxingdui group hid all bronze figures that had the character of a stuntman. It was capable that the masks had been used to impersonate and identify with the spirit to create the good effect.

Other scholars compared the " the bronze gargoyle masks with bulging eyes, big ears" with "idols' eyes" (effigy with big eyes and open mouth was designed to create the illusion) "might be the effigy of South China that wearing the bronze masks to hypnosis, so it might represent the spirit of a dead ancestor with a mask representing a face disguised by a mask". Other artifacts included bronze birds like eagles, tigers, a large snake, animal-shaped masks, bells, and what appeared to be a copper wheel, but more likely the ornaments from an ancient shield. In addition to copper, at the Sanxingdui, they also found the jade artifacts matching with the earlier Neolithic cultures of China.

The cosmology

As long ago from the Stone Age, the Chinese determined the four corners of the sky with animals: The Green Dragon of the East, the Phoenix of the South, the White Tiger of the West, and the Black Tortoise of the North. Each part of the four icons (Chinese constellation) was associated with a constellation that is visible in the relevant season: dragon in the spring, the birds in summer etc... Because the animals - birds, dragons, snakes and tigers were dominated and found in the Sanxingdui, the Bronze objects could represent the universe that were not clear whether they were part of the ritual event were designed to communicate with the spirit of the universe (or ancestral spirits). When there was no written record, it was still very difficult to determine the intended use of the objects found. Several people believed that continuing to describe the animals, especially during the later Han Dynasty, was a human endeavor to "fit their understanding with their world."

The gem items that were found in the Sanxingdui also seemed to correlate with the six known types of furniture ancient Chinese ritual jades, once again showed the linkage with a compass point (N, S, E, W) corresponding to the heavens and the earth.

5. Madame Fu hao (妇好)'s Grave [5]

Madame Fu hao (妇好)'s tomb located in archaeological zone, the old capital of the En Shang Dynasty in Anyang City of Henan Province. Discovered in 1976, it was identified as the final resting place of Queen and General Fu Hao, who died around 1200 BC (likely was killed by an officer), recorded on the oracle bone script as one of the King Yuting's wives. It was the Shang royal tomb found intact so far.

In 1976, the archaeologists explored the surrounding Yenqua area with a long shovel, called Luoyang shovel, and found several items with red lacquer. From there the burial holes were discovered, named graves No. 5, it is a 5.6 m long and 4 m wide tomb, just outside the royal cemetery. The tomb dated back 1,200 years BC. Based on the inscriptions on bronze worship items, it was Madame Fu hao's grave. Inside the hole, there were the remains of a wooden chamber with 5 meters long, 3.5 m wide and 1.3 m high, containing a completely decayed lacquered wooden coffin. Artifacts found include jades in Liangzhu culture; they were possibly the antiques that the deceased used to keep. A number of bronze artifacts might have been used by the dead such as two bronze hammers wrote " Fu hao (妇好) "

The artifacts unearthed in the tomb, included:

755 jade items (including Lungshan, Liangzhou, Hongshan and Shijiahe cultural artifacts), 564 bone objects (including 500 hairpins and 20 arrowheads). 468 bronze objects, including more than 200 worship bronze pots, 130 weapons, 23 bells, 27 knives, 4 mirrors, 4 tiger statues, 63 stone objects, 11 ceramics, 5 ivory objects, 6,900 seashell (used as currency during the Shang Dynasty). Beneath the corpse is a small pit holding the bones of the six sacrificial dogs and along the sides are 16 human skeletons, proof of the sacrifice. There is also ground evidence of a structure built on top of a tomb, perhaps a temple.

Excavating the Madame Fu hao (妇好)'s grave explained what was lacking about the Shang dynasty. Bulk bronze items and weapons and jade bulk were important exhibits to study the ritual system of the Shang Dynasty. This also showed that the prosperity of the Shang Dynasty and the level of development of handicraft industry. The Shang Dynasty's Culture was formed and developed in a long time. It could see that the jades had absorbed the advanced elements of the Neolithic period culture, such as pig dragon jade of Hongshan culture, Liangzhu culture etc express the consecutive growth and innovation.

6. Trieu Van De (Zhaowenti)'s Tomb [6]

In August 1980, while conducting built a building in the north of the Xiangcang (象崗) hill, Guangzhou province, people accidentally found an ancient tomb in the rock mountain. The main grave had an area of about 100 m2; included 7 bedrooms, 2-meter-high ceiling, and the walls were paved with blue stone, wooden floor. The dead was placed in clothes made of jades as the burial ritual of the Western Han kings, wearing ten lumbar iron swords with gold mosaic, the longest bar was 1.46 meter long. Around the middle of the chest and abdomen of the tomb owner, they discovered a gold seal, knob with a dragon images, glistening. Turned over they saw in the bottom is four words engraved " The seal of Emperor Wen" (文帝行璽). Therefore, they could identify the dead in the tomb was Zhaomei, the second king of Zhao Dynasty of the Nanyue state. Artifacts in the tomb included:

Gold seal and juebei ge

Silver items

Circle silver box, 12 cm high, and diameter of largest site 14.9 cm, weighs 572.6 grams found in the tomb of the master's coffin room. In the box there are 10 small boxes containing pills . Besides this box, they also found several other silver accessories like sinks (wash - 洗), drinking cup, belt locks (帶钩) etc are everyday utensils of the Viet king. Among seven belt locks, there were five different shapes: swallow head, turtle head, dragon head, snake head that were the beautiful delicate sculpture. These belt locks's heads were 18.4 cm long, curved, mounted with gems found in the coffin of the tomb room.

Bronze items

The total numbers of bronze items found in Zhaowentí Zhaomei tomb, were more than 500 items, varied and fine with indigenous nature of the Lingnan region. There were 36 copper cauldrons, including three different styles of the Han, the Chu (楚) and the Viet, nine of them engraved the two letters: Panyu (蕃禺), were the products casted in the Nanyue capital (now in Guangxi, China).

Especially there was a big copper cauldron bearing Viet style, 54.5 cm high, inside carved the two words: Daiguan (泰官), a position of a specialized officer in charge of daily food for the King. Therewere nine copper pots (銅提筒), one of them was gold encrusted, 37 cm high, long neck, bulging belly, everywhere sparkling gold mosaic, it was a special technology. There were also nine bronze jars (銅提筒), they were one of the typical items of the Viet people

In addition to the items listed above they also found 39 copper mirrors, sophisticatedly manufactured, casted with floating dragons, clouds, mountains etc and the largest diameter 41 cm was the largest diameter found in Western Han China, regarded as the national treasure.

A bronze item in Zhaomei grave

Brass bells

There were three different kinds of antique bells by names: niuzhong: 14 pcs, products of Nam Viet, the largest was high 24.2 cm, the smallest one was 11.4 cm high. Yongzhong was with a set of 5-ones, and at the cau dieu bronze bell set: 8 pcs. Tonggoudiao largest bell was 64 cm high, squarish shape, full casted shaft, arc-shaped mouth. On the body of the bell was engraved with the sealed words: Made by the Music Department in the Emperor Văn reign's 9th year (文帝九年樂府工造), only from first to eighth items had the apparent dating at this time. They also knocked to test the cau diêu bell, the sound was still good.

Copper spear, bonze sword and tiger imagine motif. Besides 15 steel swords, the other items were all made of brass. The most precious rare item was the Zhang Yi (張儀銅戈) copper spear engraved words "The King's 4th year Zhang Yi" (王四年相邦張儀). This was a weapon item brought from Qin nation into Nam Viet, it was not a local item. A copper sword, with the shape like in Chu nation (楚國) in the Warring States Period, was the only one bronze sword found.

They also found a tiger motif on casting a tiger image, with a lively status in the posture to catch the prey, the head up, the open mouth with the canines, the tail curled back on its body plated gold, it was only one tiger motif that the Chinese people found so far. On this tiger motif, there was also a gold inlaid inscription: "King's order: the wagons must run" (王命車徒). There were three types: tiger image motif; dragon image motif and people image motif were the orders to used in military to command the troop. Only those who held this order then he could mobilize the troops and the tanks.

Bronze growler vase, flowered seal (印花)

The bronze growler vase (Fang, 鈁) was the growler with the square mouth, belly slightly bulging, engraved with the complex contours. These vases' manufacturing technique was sophisticated. Several of the most important artifacts found in the Zhao Mei's tomb were two bronze seals, one big, one small used to assemble together to print on the cloth as the sample of the embroider form. The worker would use these two seals to print on fabric, in place of then were embroider by hand with these available printed samples. Two similar pattern samples were found in the tomb in Ma Wang Hill (馬王堆), Changsha (長沙).

Iron sword, iron spear, iron armor.

In Zhaowenti Zhao Mei tomb, there were over 700 items including various types of iron items used in the cultivation, technology and weapons. 58 cm high armor with totaling 709 square scaly pieces, round corner assembled together, suitable for hot and humid climate of the south, different with the types of armor used in the north for cold and dry climate.

There were totally 5 iron swords, one of them was being worn on one side of the waist strap of the tomb owner, the sword's bag was made of bamboo, the sword's handle was made of wooden with the silk cord wrap. Four swords inlaid with green and gold jades, delicate sculpture, interesting molded animal image. Especially, there was a spear made of iron and copper yellow and gold plated, on it, they carved a beautifully shaped cloud so it was thought that if it was not Zhao Mei's personal weapon, it should be a kind of a stick to symbolize the imperial supremacy.

Jade

Jades in Zhaowenti's Tomb

There were 56 jade items in the Zhaowentí's tomb, only in the coffin room there were 47 of them had to be thought that the tomb owner liked the jades. In these jade items, the best specialties to mention were the dragon sculptured jade items, and a big jade with a 33.4 cm long as the largest jade item, with a fine sculpture. The big jade was named the beauty of "King of Jade" by the archaeologists.

Jade costume

Jade costume was a unique form of wrapping the dead in the Han period. After the Eastern Han period, people no longer found the similar burial way anymore. The costumes were made of jades were specified under the levels: gold, silver, and bronze (the strands to tie the jade pieces together made of gold, silver or copper). The tributaries of the Han often used the gold fiber. Trieu Van De used the silk to connect the jade pieces together. Jade costume was the only one jade costume they could find until now. Jade costume was 1.73 meters in length, with a total of 2291 pieces of jades tied together by red silks into the nice geometric shapes.

Jade seal, gem ornament and jade cup

There were totally nine jade seals including three of them had the etched texts (six others were no words) all were square seals, found on the body of the tomb owner, carved the word Zhao Mei (趙眜), Prince (泰子) and seal of king (帝印). Even from the seals we could determine that Zhao Mei self-proclaimed Emperor, same level with king Han that he did not shrugged and surrendered as Chinese history had often asserted.

Gem ornament

In the tomb of Zhaowenti Zhao Mei, there were more than 130 jade items; many items were very fine and precious such as a horn shaped carved jade block, the jade block carved two very lively dragons, bared their fangs and glared their eyes.

Several of the jade items of the concubines, so it believed that they could be attached together in various ways depending on the circumstances and the initiative of the wearers.

An exquisite gem item

Jade cup

The cup was found right in the coffin room of the tomb owner cup used, 18.4 cm long, tubular mouth, the cup's smallest diameter 5.8 cm, the greatest place 6.7 cm, looked like a horn, looked strangely. This was an item that the experts rated as "unique" in the Han Dynasty's jade items. This jade cup was made of translucent jade, with veins of blue to brown, carved from a block of primitive stone and had to use and different types of techniques to carve, shallow or deep engraving.

Porcelain

They found 371 porcelain items in the tomb, grills for cooking and other kinds of daily use. There were also items as the burial items, manufactured items were cburied with the dead, which imitated the everyday items that the grave owners had used, included the incense burner, the flange (items that the ancient kings held according to their titles), the jar, the cup, the bowl etc. Especially there were a jar and a cauldron with four-letter Changle Palace (長樂宮器) and was a question for the researchers: "Was there the Changle palace in the Zhaoyue dynasty not? ". Changle Palace was the name of a palace in Chang'an, was the residence of the Han's Kings and Queens. The fact that several the existing porcelains in the tomb of Zhao Mei were really remarkable.

Fabrics, silks

In Zhao Mei's tomb, the found fabrics that varied both in quantity and variety. In the western room, they found a lot of cloths, among them including silk (絹), (朱羅), embroidery (綉) and many kinds of the thin cloth etc. These silks were all torn when unearthed, became a dust glass to 20-30 cm high, and roughly calculated not less than 100 sheets of fabrics, stacked of about 700 classes.

A large amount of the grave gifts was also wrapped by the cloths, no different from what we used the wrapping paper to haul the goods to other places. The fabrics were dyed in different colors and showed that in that era, the fabrics were quite popular in the South for use in trade and exchange with other places.

Ivories, pearls

In the tomb, they found the intact ivories, a total of 5 pieces; the longest one was 1,26 m, superimposed high 57cm. According to biological experts, these ivories were not that of the huge Asian elephants, they were like ivories in Africa so they thought that they were not the local items, they might be brought by merchant ships from abroad to Guangzhou. Besides the intact ivories in the tomb, there were also several items and carved ivory items.

In the pillow placed under the jade costume, they also found 470 pearls, diameter 0.1 to 0.4cm, they were natural pearls and were not polished yet. According to several archaeologists deciphered, the pearls perhaps used to exorcise and this was the first time such a pillow was found. Also in a large painted box, they found a large number of other pearls with diameter from 0.3 to 1.1 cm, total weighs 4117 grams.

Being buried together with the dead person

In Zhao Mei's tomb, they found altogether 15 people who were burried together. Being burried while still alive to become the servants to serve the dead in the after life, it was a fairly common custom in ancient period. Fifteen people were divided as follows:

- Front room: a doorman. (景巷令)

- Front of eastern room: a person accompanying musician instrumental, probably he was a musician.

- Eastern room: Zhao Mei's four concubines were buried together with many gem items, bronze items and ceramics. There were four seals as described above.

- West room: seven people with the kitchen tools, perhaps a chef and waiters or waitresses. Here, each person was buried with one or two copper mirrors.

In the tomb, there were other two people, perhaps a bodyguard, and a rickshaw puller. According to the inspectors, then all the people of this grave were hit hard in their chests to be died and burried with the dead. In all these graves dug up in the Han Dynasty in China, outside the tomb of Zhao Mei, we did not see the situation to be buried together with the dead person. This practice was only in China from the Qin Dynasty onwards.

II. Bronze drums

The bronze drum was one of the important archaeological objects ever found in southern China and Southeast Asia. Laos, Cambodia, Thailand, Burma, Malaysia, Indonesia, Cayce Islands, New Guinea molded and used from prehistory to the present. North Vietnam and southwest China are where there were a largest number of bronze drums were discovered. According to a report in 1988, China now has been keeping approximately 1460 bronze drums [7].

Museum of the Guangxi Zhuang autonomous region was proud of the world's largest drum collections. Total bronze drums discovered in Vietnam to 1980 were 360 units, of which about 140 units were Dong Son drums. The earliest historical documents recorded relating bronze drums appeared in the the Book of the Later Han Dynasty (Houhan shu, 後漢書), described that Ma Yuan, in 43th years, collected the bronze drums from Jiaozhi for melting and casting horses.

More than half a century there has been an endless controversy occurred between scholars of the two China and Vietnam countries in many aspects of drums.

Here, we would like to briefly introduce a very elaborated and hearted monograph made by Mr. Han Xiaorong - a doctoral student in the Department of History of the University of Hawaii at Manoa under the title: "The Present Echo of the Ancient Bronze Drum: Nationalism and Archeology in Modern Vietnam and China. "[7]

1. About the classification of the drums:

The classification of the drums was published in 1902 in Alte metalltrommeln book Sudost aus Asien by an Austrian archaeologist F. Heger. From 22 drums collected and records or photographs of other 143 drums, he divided into four categories (I, II, III, IV) and three temporary types (I-II, II-IV I-IV), based on the forms, the distribution, decorations and chemical compositions. He believed that the type I, which was found mainly in northern Vietnam and called as Dong Son drums was the earliest. Vietnamese scholars supported Heger's classification and agreed with the statement that the bronze drums were invented first in the Red River Valley and the Ma River in North Vietnam by the Lac Viet people, Vietnamese's ancient ancestors. Then they spread to other parts of Southeast Asia and Southern China. Meanwhile, the Chinese archaeologists tended to classify drums in contrary with Vietnam scholars. They believed that the classification of Heger was outdated and it should require a complete replacement. They claimed that the Pu (濮) an ancient nation of southern China first manufactured drums in Yunnan. This technique was applied by the peoples living in the surrounding area, including Lac Viet people in Red River Delta. However, the changes in the natural classification of Heger led too many doubts from many Vietnamese scholars because we knew that China had very few drums that Heger classified as Type I at that time, but the majority of the drums were Heger Type II found in Guangxi province, Southern China.

Dong Son Drum

From the mid to late 1970s, China had discovered many drums and they thought that they were Heger type I. Moreover, after excavation of Wanjiabai sites in Yunnan Province in 1975 -1976, the Chinese archaeologists believed that they had found the most ancient forms of Heger type I drums.

As a result, they recognized the Heger classification. However, they had made significant amendments that they added the Wanjiabai drums into the Heger's classification and maintained the previous opinion that Southern China was the first place of origin of the drums. But instead of Guangxi as before, now they said that Yunnan was where the drum originated in Southern China.

Vietnamese scholars declared that that efforts made by Chinese archaeologists to reclassify the drums were completely groundless. The Chinese classification system did not reflect the historical reality; on the contrary, it was a product of the current arrangement. China put the argument that the Wanjiabai drums first appeared due to their forms and decorations were very simple.

Vietnamese scholars have been arguing that the simple forms and simple decorations could also be a sign of degradation, thus implying that the Wanjiabai drums were not the earliest ones, it was the latest. Pham Huy Thong said that the same drum type was found in Vietnam in the 1930s and had long been considered to be rough, but dated back to late age.

Wanjiabai drum

Thus, the Vietnamese classification proposed that Wanjiabai drums were just the 4th sub category of Dong Son drums (Heger Type I). Thuong Nong drums were in same style with Wanjiabai drums found in Vietnam in the 1980s, located in the same sub-type.

Thuong Nong Drum

Other Vietnamese scholars believed that Dong Son drums could be casted early in the 7th century, or the 8th century BC. Later Vietnamese scholars then admitted that it was difficult to determine the exact age of the Dong Son drums because many drums were discovered by chances, and therefore, the relic sites were not protected well. Moreover, it was difficult to find any biological material directly related to the drum could be helpful in making an absolute chronology.

The C14 earliest age that Chinese scholars gave a bronze drum that was unearthed in China was 2640 + / - 90 before 1950, or 690 + / -. 90 BC. From materials coexist with the drums in the tomb, the scholars said that the C14 chronology was the first reliable for any bronze drums. They argued that the Wanjiabai drums were made mostly between the 7th century and the 5th BC, and the Shizhaishan (Dong Son) type was popular among the 6th century BC to the first century. However, according to Vietnamese scholars, this chronology was wrong. The Vietnamese archaeologists had conducted a test on a piece of wood from the coffin that was excavated and found that the difference in age could be 235 years. They believed that the Chinese archaeologists chose that age to support the idea of

Southern Chinese origin of drums. According to Vietnamese scholars, the bronze drums' ages should not rely solely on the C14 test. Instead, other factors should also be considered. They even went so far to give an example: bronze drums were found in an ancient tomb in Viet Khe, C14 indicated that the tomb was from 2480 + / -100 years before 1950 CE, or about 530 BC. However, based on the style of drum, it was decided that only the 3rd century or 4th BC. Until now, scholars of the two countries have not reached consensus on the ages of the bronze drums yet.

2. Debate on decoration

Decoration of the drum was another topic of debate among Vietnamese scholars and Chinese scholars. Decoration was very important because it is thought to reflect the social life and spirit of the inventors and the user of drum, therefore, it could help determine the ethnic and geographic location. The most common motifs on the first drum types (Heger's first two types plus Wanjiabai sub-type) included the birds and other different animals, as well as boats, the lightings, and the geometric lines. A flying bird with a long beak and long legs appear very often in the older drums. Vietnamese scholars believed that it was a stork as appropriate to the reality of the Vietnamese history and culture. Most Chinese scholars also believed that the bird was the stork. However, they did not agree that the stork was a symbol of the ancient Vietnamese farmers. Instead, they interpreted it as a result of Chinese influence. They argued that the stork was considered the drums' spirit of Zhongyuan Plain, China. This motif first spread to Chu nation area in southern China and then to the other ethnic groups living in the southern area of the Chu nation.

Drums excavated from the Chu Xinyang tomb, Henan and Jiangling, Hubei and Zenghouyi tomb in Suixian, Hubei were all decorated with stork image motif. It was a clear evidence to support the idea that the flying stork motif in Shizhaishan drums originated from the stork motif in the Chu nation region.

In addition to the bird images, three small amphibians on several Dong Son drums (Shizhaishan) and the drums that the archaeologists had considered as either the frogs or the toads (see Figure 5). Chinese scholars argued that they were the frogs and explained them as ornaments without special meaning, or something related to the ceremony for rain, or as fetishes of ancient Viet people in Southern China, a population group related to the ancient Viet people. Edward Schafer agreed that the frogs on the drum showed a spirit of the frog - a spirit of water and rain - and the cries of the bullfrogs. Vietnamese scholars initially agreed that the animals were the frogs in the 1970s, but then interpreted them as toads because "in Vietnam we often call the toads as the 'God heaven's uncle' and they forecast the rain, it will certainly rain when toads cry ".

The long boat motif was a very popular decoration on the surface of the Dong Son drums. Typically, both ends of the boat were decorated with the head and tail of a bird. The boat had a lot of fish image decorations under the boat and decorated with birds on the boat. Vietnamese scholars believed that boats carrying souls in the festivals to pray for the cool weather. Feng Hanji, a Chinese archaeologist, disagreed. He believed that the long boat motif was a reflection of popular sailing tradition in southern China. According to Feng, the boat did not have the centerboard (daggerboard), so it could only be used in rivers, small water area such as within Dian Lake. Moreover, the boats decorated with birds were also a tradition in China. He also believed that the motif might indicate some connection with the Chu nation. Ling Shunsheng, a Chinese ethnologist, wrote in 1950 that the long boat motif was a direct reflection of the regatta in the Chu ancient land. Chinese scholars then pointed out that the boats on drums joined four common types of different activities in the ancient southern China, namely, fishing, transportation, regatta, and making an offering to the gods of the river. Vietnamese scholars then accepted the idea of sailing motif. However, they interpreted it as a part of the Viet's ancient ceremony praying for rain and for the celebrating the water.

For light rays located in the center of the drums, several scholars interpreted as a star, while others aw it as the sun. Vietnamese scholars explained that this reflected the sun worship of the ancient Viet people. Meanwhile, Chinese scholars believed that ancient ethnic groups in China, as Shang (En) Dynasty, the Chu nation and the Southern peoples, all worship the sun. Furthermore, there was the rule to regard the sun as a symbol.

The two most common geometric motifs on drums were considered to represent the clouds and the thunder. According to Chinese scholars, similar patterns could be found on ancient pottery carved motifs in southern China, as well as bronze in the Central Plains. Motifs, as had been argued in the book named Ancient Chinese Bronze drums: "Proved the consistency and continuity of the cultural development of ancient southern China and frequent cultural exchanges between the southern China and the Central plains region."

They also reflected the cloud and thunder worship in ancient China. These motifs appeared only occasionally on the Dong Son drums but they could be frequently seen on drums Heger II, most of which were found in southern China, especially Zhuang Autonomous Region in Guangxi. Vietnam scholars had strongly rejected the idea that the culture of the Southern developed under the influence of China and the drums bearing such motifs was the oldest.

In conclusion, Vietnamese scholars tended to see the decorations on the earlier drums, especially Dong Son drums, as a reflection of the cultural characteristics of the ancient Vietnamese people. They believed that the different textures on drums to describe different aspects of the agricultural life of ancient Vietnamese in the Dong Son era. Moreover, they said, the ornaments proofs that Dong Son drums belonged to the ancient Viet people. However, Chinese scholars explained the decorations as a reflection of the cultural exchange between inside China and the borders of China.

They argued that these decorations represented the cultural features of different ethnic groups living in that area, not only Lac Viet. Not deny the relationship between Lac Viet and Dong Son drums, but they believed the same type drums were also used by other ancient ethnic groups - such as Dian, Laojie (老街), Mimo, Yelang and Juding that were said to be relative of the Lac Viet people. Therefore, they thought that the first type of drums was invented in an area of modern China.

According to them, "Dong Son drums were the drums imported form Shizhaishan Yunnan to Vietnam and spread along the Red River." Quote both historical records and archaeological findings, Chinese scholars had tried to prove that the drum was first invented by the Pu-Liao (Liao Boc) on the Yunnan Plateau in the east and then spread to the surrounding areas. Chinese scholars had also suggested Lac Viet also belonged to Pu-Liao group and cited the similarities between Dian culture in Yunnan and the Dong Son culture of Vietnam as evidence.

After 1949, the Chinese government had officially identified a group of southerners as independent group of ethnic Hans. The State encouraged scholars to prove that ethnic minorities had the achievements of their own cultures. History had many interworking between Han Chinese and ethnic minorities in the South. As a result, drums from the places were previous temporary for their "barbarian" origins by Chinese scholars, had been considered one of the great material heritages of the southern ethnic minorities and became a symbol of cultural exchange between the local center with bordering areas.

Chinese archaeologist Wen Ben wrote: "If someone asked, what the important cultural monument of our fellow brothers in ancient China Southern was, we don't hesitate to answer that it was the bronze drum." Bronze drum, he continued to claim, was "the common treasure of all Chinese people." The two authors of an article on drums' owners concluded that their study "reflected a specific aspect of the mixed ethnic and cultural exchange between the ethnic groups of China" and "sufficient to prove that the various ethnic groups in the South of China, along with other ethnic groups in China, had created the ancient culture, the brilliant Chinese nation".

3. Conclusion

Ending his monograph, Han Xiaorong author wrote:

"The core problem was the scholars of Vietnam and China tried to claim the ethnic exclusive right for a product that could be created by the common ancestors of both Vietnam and the ethnic minorities in Southern China. Absolutely there was no boundary between South China and North Vietnam at the time of the bronze drum was invented. Many ethnic groups lived in the vast area had genetic relationships, culture, or both. The inventors of the bronze drums were not aware of the polity. Distinguish "Vietnam" or "China" as we do today is not fair, is the imposition the modern concepts on the ancient peoples. So tried to clarify when, where, and who was the inventor of the drum was meaningless. "

These above words were written in 1998, when the information about the southern road of prehistoric people from Africa to Vietnam had not been announced. Mankind did not know the true origin of the Chinese, Vietnamese and ethnic minorities in southern China. But that commentary was human and matched the historical truth. The time had supported the author when we knew that the ancient Viet people from Vietnam came to explore the China and built the brilliant water rice civilization.

North Vietnam and South China were the cradle of East Asian culture. From here, man, voice, handwriting and Viet-culture were created and then followed the migrants to creat the Chinese culture. Even the Chu people also was a branch of Viet people, independent of ancient Central Highlands until late Zhou Dynasty, China merged only after the invasion of Qin Shihuang. At the last of Stone era, while in Central Highlands, the Huaxia appeared, studied the agricultural culture, while in their vast land, the Viet people continued to build agricultural culture that typical product was the bronze drum. These motifs of storks, boats, frogs, toads, clouds thunder etc on drums were the continuation of Viet culture ever shown on ceramics, on jewels before the Huaxia people born.

III. Commentary

In the Hongshan culture 4000 BC the stove with metallic residue appeared, was considered as the copper melting stove. A thousand years later, at Majiaao relics 3000 BC, found the bronze knife. However the Bronze Age in China officially recognized only from Erlitou culture (二里头文化) , in 1700 BC. Recognition or non-recognition, up tp now, the hitherto was the prerogative of Western scholars. However, partly, it was because of limitations of Carbon marking methods, partly, it was because of dominant opinion "European centered perspective" so the above ideas were only relative.

If we accepted the age of 1700 BC, the China's Bronze Age was later than Go Bong relice of Phung Nguyen culture, Vietnam that had the age of 1850+/- 50 years-old BC. This might explain that the people emigrated from Vietnam to bring new stone tools and animals and plants to China, and then the copper technology also was transferred under that way.

Created from Neolithic culture in China, so the Bronze culture was widely distributed. Bronze item category was abundant but the high achievement consisted three main groups of weapons, worshiping items and daily use items. The weapons started from the axes, copper hammers, and copper arrows, copper swords. This was a technical progress: copper was the better material for weapons and replaced the stone weapons. Daily use tools were mainly used for cooking and drinking. The worship items were more diversity with copper cauldrons, bronze incense burners, bronze drinking cups in Central Highlands, the residence of Huaxia.

Meanwhile, in the Changjiang River basin, where Lac Viet resided, the bronze drums were the representative worship items. This demonstrated the discrimination of the ethnicity and the culture happened in China in the Bronze Age. If the Neolithic culture was unified, it could be said to be uniformity, as only the Viet people as its owner, then to the Bronze Age, it was formed two different cultures. Since 2700 BC, with the Mongolian's Intrusion, Yellow Emperor dynasty was built, a new nomadic culture appeared to make up the gradual differentiation of Chinese culture.

Russian scholar Chesnov, in his refined look, had realized this when he wrote: "Before the Shang, Chinese culture was formed with the sponsorship of the culture of the South and after the Shang, it was due to Western culture." [8]. There was not a material culture from the West, it was the spirit of nomadic civilization, which was implicit in Huaxia blood, up to that time, it had transformed Chinese culture from agriculture to the nomadic civilization.

References:

1. Majiayao Site.
http://www.chinaculture.org/gb/en_artqa/2003-09/24/content_39154.htm

2. 二里頭文化 http://zh.wikipedia.org/wiki/%E4%BA%8C%E9%87%8C%E9%A0%AD%E6%96%87%E5%8C%96

3. 红山文化主人 http://baike.baidu.com/view/56987.htm

4. Sanxingdui http://en.wikipedia.org/wiki/Sanxingdui

5. 妇好墓 http://baike.baidu.com/view/190414.htm

6. Nguyễn Duy Chính. *Trieu Van De tomb in Guangzhou*.
http://www.hungsuviet.us/lichsu/Langmotrieuvande.html

7. Han Xiaorong. *The Present Echoes of the Ancient Bronze Drum: Nationalism and Archeology in Modern Vietnam and China. Southeast Asian Studies* - A Journal of the Southeast Asian Studies Association Vol 2. No. 2Fall 1998 http://www2.hawaii.edu/ ~ seassa/explorations/v2n2/art2/v2n2-frame2.html

8. Chesnov. The origins of the Chinese Civilization. University of California Press, 1977: 133.

CHAPTER VI

THE FORMATION
OF THE CHINESE VOICE

"The Chinese language history was change over time, especially the changes related to the historical study of Chinese language in its various incarnations. Many linguists classified all variants of the Chinese language as a part of the Sino - Tibetan language family. And they believed that there was an original language, called the Proto Sino-Tibetan, similar to the Proto Indo-European, from which the Chinese language and Tibeto-Burman appeared.

The relationship between Chinese and other Sino-Tibetan languages was a field that had been researching and positively debating, as the attempt to reconstruct Proto-Sino-Tibetan language. The main difficulty in this effort was that, while there were very good documentations that allowed for the reconstruction of the ancient sounds of Chinese, there was no written documentation of the point where Chinese split from the rest of the Sino-Tibetan languages. However, before this problem, many linguists thouht that this was actually a common story in historical linguistics, a field which often overcame by using the comparative method.

Unfortunately, up to now, the use of this technique for Sino-Tibetan languages had not achieved the satisfactory results, perhaps because many of the languages that would allow for a more complete reconstruction of Proto Sino-Tibetan were very poorly documents or knowledges. Therefore, despite their affinity, the common ancestry of the Chinese and Tibeto-Burman languages remained an unproven hypothesis.

Categorization of Chinese language was a subject of the scholarly debate. One of the first systems was devised by the Swedish linguist Bernhard Karlgren in the early 1900. The system was much revised, but always relied much on Karlgren's insights and methods.

Old Chinese (上古汉语), sometimes known as "Archaic Chinese," was the language common during the early and middle Zhou Dynasty (1122 BC - 256 BC), texts of which included inscriptions on bronze artifacts of the Shijing (book of Poetry), the Shujing (Books of Documents), and a part of the Yijing (I-ching). The phonetic elements found in the majority of Chinese characters also provided the hints to their Old Chinese pronunciations.

The pronunciation of the Chinese characters was borrowed from Japanese, Vietnamese and Korean also provided valuable insights. Old Chinese did not have the declension. It possessed a rich sound system in which aspiration or rough breathing differentiated the consonants, but it probably was still without tones. Work on reconstructing Old Chinese started with Qing dynasty philologists.

Medieval Chinese language (中古汉语) was the language used during the Sui, Tang, and Song periods (from the sixth century to the tenth century). It could be divided into an early period, reflected by "Qieyun dictionary" (切韵 - AD 601), and a late period in the end of the 10th century, reflected by the "Guangyun dictionary" (广韵).

The evidence for the pronunciation of Medieval Chinese came from several sources: modern dialect variations, phonetic dictionaries, foreign translations, dictionaries constructed by ancient Chinese scholars to summarize the phonetic systems, Chinese translations of foreign words. However, all these studies were during the probe process. For example, scholars had shown that the attemtps to reconstruct ancient Cantonese from the rimes of modern Cantopop should provide a picture of the incorrect language.

The development of Chinese language from early history to the present was very complex. Most Chinese people in Sichuan and in a broad arc from the Northeast (Manchuria) to the Southwest (Yunnan) used various dialects as their home languages. The prevalence of Mandarin throughout Northern China was popular largely due to North China's plains. By contrast, the mountains and rivers of Southern China promoted the linguistic diversity.

Until the mid-20th century, most Southern Chinese only spoke their local languages. However, despite the mix of officials and commoners speaking various dialects, Nanjing Mandarin became dominant at least during the Qing Dynasty. Since the 17th century, the Empire had set up the sound library (正音书院) to make pronunciation conformed to the Qing standard of capital Beijing, but it was not much successful.

During the end of the Qing, the second half of the 19th century, Beijing Mandarin finally replaced Nanjing Mandarin in the royal court. For the common people, although Mandarin had been widely used in China then but there was no any only single standard. Those who did not speak Mandarin in southern China continued using their dialects. Standard Beijing Mandarin was rather limited.

This situation changed with the formation (in both the PRC and the ROC, but not in Hong Kong) of an elementary school education system committed to teaching Mandarin Chinese. As a result, Mandarin now has been being spoken by all people in mainland China and in Taiwan. However, Hong Kong was a British colony, so Mandarin was not used there. In Hong Kong, the language of education, formal speech, and daily life remained the local Cantonese, but Mandarin is increasingly influential. (completed all the citations)

The above text confirmed the fact that, besides Mandarin Beijing became the voice of ordinary Chinese people, all basic researches on Chinese voices did not have any remarkable achievements. The most critical issues were that they did not discover the origin of the Chinese language yet. Therefore, the Chinese language was put into the Sino-Tibetan family, it was not satisfactory!

The reason for this situation was that so far, not only the Chinese people but also the international linguists had the huge misunderstanding about the Chinese language. I hope this study contributed to solve such misunderstanding.

Throughout the twentieth century, due to the lacking of data and being dominated by the concept of " Sinocentrism", so the scholars said that Vietnam's ancestors were from the Tian Shan following the Yangtze River going down the Southern China region. After being chased by the Han, they flooded into Viet's land. Because Chinese people had dominated throughout a millennium, the Viet people were under the influence of China, both in blood and culture.

The historic linguists were influenced by Academician Maspero (1912) considered the Thai language to play a key role in prehistoric East Asia. Then they conducted the comparative linguistic study and brought kanji to be codified through thousands of years to compare with Latinized Vietnamese words a few hundred years old and showed the statistics, that the Vietnamese included up to 60% words borrowed from the Chinese language! The reason for this confusion that the Vietnamese didn't maintain the original scripts, so the reconstruction of Chinese language documents only depended in Chinese characters and then it considered that the voice of Han people existed before that. Thus, any Vietnamese words resembled with the Chinese language to be regarded as being borrowed from the Chinese language!

According to the above concept, many international linguists and Vietnamese linguists (Nguyen Van To, Tran Trong Kim, Nguyen Tai Can) said that Vietnamese language had borrowed up to 70% of Chinese.

Those who disagreed, could only say though there were borrowed words, but not so many! They tried finding the pure Viet words to prove their points. After many debates, they proved the hopeless attempt. Those who had a lesser ancient knowledge should be defeats by the scholars with many qualifications. They cited a lot of European and Chinese books. And so far, our children have still been been stuffed by that dogmatic teaching!

Having been taught but somehow, we never believed that Vietnamese language borrowed too many words from Chinese. A people had to borrow a larger number of foreign words; it was still a nation? Was it worthy to be independent and freedom? Although there was limited understanding, I believed that a nation after thousands of years of slavery became independant will never borrow so many words from a foreign language! Therefore, when feeling that there were many Vietnamese words in Chinese, I put my effort to find Vietnamese language in ancient Chinese bibliography. Then, thanked to the genetics to discover the migration path from Vietnam to China, we had this research.

I. Process of forming the Chinese voice

Today, the idea to reset the origin and the formation of the Chinese language, with many people, is a blasphemy. Like in the old days, Copernicus declared: Earth revolves around the

Sun! Not too hard to prove, but most difficulty is to shake the human prejudices.

From ten thousand of years ago, Lacviet people, from Vietnam came up to settle in the South of the Yangtze. Living in geographic areas with different soils, different climates, the voice gradually divided into Cantonese, Teochew, Yunnan, Hainan ... Then following the footprints of the migrants, Viet language went up to the Hunan, Hubei to become the Wu, Viet, Chu dialects and dominated the plain in the Yellow River basin.

About 20,000 years ago, migrants brought the Hoa Binh new stone tools and millet, rice, chickens, dogs etc built the new rock culture in the Yellow River basin. About 7000 years ago they formed the Yangshao millet culture. Because being lived closely with the Northern Mongolian people, so the mixing blood between Lac Viet and the Mongolian people occured. Until 5000 years BC, an important part of Yangshao culture's population from Australoid became the Southern Mongoloid race. Until 3000 years BC, here, the Viet people developed the agriculture of planting cereal, combined with the livestock breeding. On the basis of the settled agricultural lifestyle, Viet people created a brilliant culture, included a polyphonic language with the words of a wealthy agriculture. Featured in the language of the Viet people was to place the noun and the verb in front of the adjective and the adverb. The parlance that later was called as the main element is front, the auxiliary element is after.

Around 2700 years BC, North Mongoloid people passed Yellow River and occupied on land of the Viet people, to establish Emperor dynasty. State of the Emperor located between Viet countries: Ba, Shu in the southwest, Chigui (赤鬼) in the south. Though being the winner but because of its small poplulation and undeveloped culture, the Mongols were quickly assimilated by the Viet people. The Mongols had to learn the voice of the Lac Viet to adapt to a new life. However, with role of dominance power, the Mongols forced Viet people used Mongol parlance:

the auxiliary element in front of, the main element is in after.

In such contact conditions, of course, the mixing of blood occurred between the North Mongoloid people and the Lac Viet South Mongoloid, Southern Mongoloid people were born, self-called as the Huaxia. After several generations, there were no longer pure Mongolian people. The Huaxia hold leadership positions in the Yellow Emperor's kingdom. Recognizing the voice of the people became more complicated, Zhou dynasty used the voice of southern Guangdong region as the standard voice, called as the Ya (雅, elegant) language - elegant voice. Naturally, being the descendant of Yellow Emperor and also was the tribe lived many generations with the nomads in the West, the Zhou dynasty maintained the Mongol's saying way that the auxiliary element is front of and the main element is after.

Defeated Six nations, founded the Qin dynasty, Qin Shihuang merged the land, the residents and the Viet culture in his empire. When unified the writing, the same type of letters, the Quin used the Ya (雅, elegant) language of the Southern as the standard language but of course, they maintained the Mongol parlance. The Han dynasty still used the Ya language as the national language and used widely the Mongol parlance. But there were still areas, tribes to use the local dialects, that the main element is front of, the auxiliary element is after. At the end of the Han dynasty, China was in the chaos, many millions of Khitan people invaded, brought their voices to mix into, made the Chinese language become more complex.

In Sui Dynasty, many nomadic tribes occupied the land, brought many millions of North Mongoloid people into China. Thus, among other aspects, the Chinese voice had also become complex. Once again, the Tang standarized the language,

The Tang Dynasty used the voice of the Capital Changan as the official language, and called as Tang sound. Later dynasties such as Song, Yuan, Ming etc also took the voice of the capital region as the standard language, called Mandarin [Guānhuà 官话], - the official voice of the authorities. Conquered China, the Manchu Qing brought the Quing voice to mix into Chinese language to created the Mandarin of the Qing empire, called as Beijing Chinese language that has been existed up to today.

In the Mandarin languages appeared in China, the Mandarin of Tang dynasty – Tang sound- had a special meaning. Actually, it was a version of the Lacviet language on Chinese land. That the language was the most mature and standard that the Viet people created in Chinese land. The Tang's sound, with semantically deep and wonderful musicality, had made an important contribution to the most brilliant period of Chinese poetry: Tang's poetry. After the Tang dynasty, Chinese became more chaos. Many Northern minorities clan invaded and seized the power, brought their voices in to China, made the Chinese Language became far from the Viet origin and was closer with the Northern ethnic origins as Khitan, Mongols, Manchu etc.

Tang's sound was sent to teach in Vietnam in the Tang dysnaty and reserved by the Viet society, was an invaluable asset of the Viet language...

Classification of the Chinese language (2)

Name	Abbreviation	Pinyin	Local Romanization	Simp	Trad	Total Speakers
Mandarin Notes: includes Standard Chinese	Guan; 官	Guānhuà Běifānghuà	Pinyin: Guānhuà Pinyin: Běifānghuà	官话 北方 话	官話 北方 話	c. 1.365 billion
Wu Notes: includes Shanghainese	Wu; 吴/吳	Wúyǔ	Long-short: Ng Nyiuor Ghu Nyiu	吴语	吳語	c. 90 million

Yue Notes: includes Cantonese & Taishanese	Yue; 粤/粵	Yuèyǔ	Yale: Yuht Yúh Jyutping: Jyut⁶ Jyu⁵	粤语	粤語	c. 70 million
Min Notes: includes Hokkien, Taiwanese & Teochew	Min; 闽/閩	Mǐnyǔ	POJ: Bân Gú; BUC: Mìng Ngṳ̄	闽语	閩語	c. 50 million
Xiang	Xiang; 湘	Xiāngyǔ	Romanization: Shiāen'ỳ	湘语	湘語	c. 36 million
Hakka	Kejia; 客家	Ke; 客	Hakka Pinyin: Hak-kâ-fa or Hak-kâ-va Hakka Pinyin: Hak-faor Hak-va	客家话 客话	客家話 客話	c. 35 million
Gan	Gan; 贛	Gànyǔ	Romanization: Gon Ua	赣语	105	c. 31 million

Quoting from Chinese language

Looking at the above language classification, we can see: Besides the Mandarin - known as Beijing language today, which was derived from Wu-Yue Viet language, Chinese language was also divided into six dialects:

1. Wu dialect [3]

Wu dialect is the voice of 90 million people, mainly in Zhejiang, Shanghai, southern Jiangsu and Anhui, Jiangxi, Fujian provinces. In particular, Suzhou dialect is considered the most abundant. However due to the size and economic dominance, Wu dialect in Shanghai become the most prestigious, it is also known as Shanghainese. Scholars like using the Wu dialect, derived from the name of the ancient kingdom of Wu Viet existed on the territory of North Jiangsu and Zhejiang.

Since the founding of the People's Republic of China in 1949, people throughout China, including Wu dialect area, were encouraged to speak Mandarin. Wu dialect had been replaced by Mandarin in the media and in schools, and many people from other places migrated to this region. The diversity of Wu dialect was rarely in written language and very few people believed that it was worthwhile to write or develop a written form of standard language. There were several books written to teach Wu dialect in a playful and entertaining manner. There were a number of Wu dialect television programs in each town, however they were not allowed to broadcast in prime time. Wu dialect originally is the Tay Viet dialect.

2. Viet dialect [4]

Yue dialect is the voice of 70 million people, mainly in Guangdong, Guangxi, Hong Kong and Macau. There is also a significant community speaking Viet language in Southeast Asia, Canada, Australia, UK and USA. Yue language also is known as Cantonese. Guangdong and Guangxi people often call their language is Yue language (粤语) or Bai Language (白话). Pronounciation in Yue language as well as its grammatical forms are supposedly closer to ancient Chinese language, especially that of the Tang dynasty (618-907), than Mandarin. For example, many old poems had their rhymes when pronouced in Viet language but did not have rhymes when pronounced in Mandarin. Cantonese originally is Dongyue (東越) language.

3. Min dialect [5]

Min dialect is the voice of 75 million people mainly in Fujian, and a part in Jiangsu, Zhejiang, Jiangxi, Guangdong, Hainan, Guangxi, as well as in Taiwan, Malaysia, Singapore, Indonesia, Thailand, Philippines, Myanmar, the United States, especially in New York City. Ancient name of Fujian is Minyue kingdom's in Fujian province of 334-110 BC. Min is the name of a Viet group had the kingdom in Zhejiang Province in the

Spring and Autumn Period (771-476 BC). Min is divided into 5-9 separate groups. This difference is also seen in the community Min in oversea. Min language originally is Muong Việt language.

4 Hakka dialect [6]

Hakka dialect is spoken in southeastern China, Taiwan and Hong Kong. There are also significiant communities of Hakka speakers in such countries as the USA, French Guiana, Mauritius and the UK. The total Hakka speakers are about 40 million. The name of the Hakka language means "Guest language'. Hakka people have a long history of migration. Hakka history states that their ancestors originated from Shandong (山东) or Shanxi (山西) provinces in northern China. They began their first wave of migration from mid IV and IX centuries, traveling to Henan (河南) and Northern provinces adjacent to the Anhui (安徽) and its vicinity. The second wave of migration took place between the IX and XII centuries. They migrated along the mountains and mountain foothills of East Jiangxi (江西) into Southern Jiangxi and inland Fujian (福建). The last wave of migration took place between the XII and XIII centuries, as Hakka people moved into northeast Guangdong (广东) Province. Hakka people are one of Viet minority ethnic people.

5. Gan or Gong dialect [7]

Gan, Gong or Jiangxi dialect is the voice of about 60 million people, mainly in the provinces of Jiangxi, Hunan east, southeast Hubei, Anhui Southwest and Northwest Fujian. Gong dialect has several points that are close with Mandarin and Wu dialect. Gan (赣) is another name for Jiangxi Province. Gan, Gong dialect is a shared language, the main language used, i.e., the Mandarin in the Pre-Qin dynasty.

6. Xiang dialect [8]

Xiang dialect is also called Hunan dialect, is the voice of

about 36 million people, mainly in Hunan province, especially in the Changsha, Zhuzhou, Xiangtan, Yiyang, Loudi (娄底), Hengyang and Shaoyang (邵阳) cities. There are also in southern Shaanxi, southern Anhui, northeast Guangxi, Sichuan and Guizhou. Xiang dilaect is Viet language of Viet nation in the Goujian time.

Actually, these above-mentioned dialects are all the Viet language:

a. People in Guangxi and Guangdong are also speaking Guang dialect of Liang Guang. The term "Cantonese" by name of Guangdong was forced but it readily accepted because it was understood that Guangdong province people's own voices! In fact, the "Cantonese" is Viet language; Viet (越&粤) is pronounced "Duyt." Liang Guang residents and Vietnam people have similar voices (just different voices of the north and the south) and the grammar is same, the same as the main element is front and the auxiliary element is after:

For example:

- Việt: Tôi về trước = Ngã hồi tiên - 我回先

- Viet: I go back first - 我回先

- Quảng Đông: "Ngọ hùi (quì) sín"- 我回先.

Guangdong: " Ngọ hùi (quì) sín " - 我回先.

- Bắc Kinh: Ngã tiên hồi - "Wò sién hủy- 我先回.

- Beijing: "Wo Sien huy 我先回

b. At Zhuang Autonomous Region, the Choang dialect is similar with Nung dialect. The Nung and Tay have similarities. Tay and Tai are similar. Thailand and Laos remain the same and the same is put in the "Tai" language and divided the south-north. Lao language belongs to "North Thai" language and Zhuang dialect is a branch in the North Thai language. In Zhuang, Yunnan, Guizhou most people prefer using the Thai language and many different ethnic minorities have their own voices as H'mong, Dao, Bo Y, Tay, Nung etc.

c. Hainan has a voice very like language currently being used in Vietnam; many words are same 100% Vietnamese. Hainanese also very similar to the pronunciation of Chaozhou and Fujian and are located in Muong or Min's system, depending on the local parlance. Min (閩) or Minyue (閩越) language had many words that sound like the word called Nom or pure Viet. For example, in Minyue language, they read the words "Mắt (Eye) -目", "Ác (wick)-惡" like the Vietnamese people read.

d. Jiangxi, Zhejiang, Anhui, Jiangsu dialects are Wu language, also called Wu Viet language, or Viet language. This region has the Viet drama (Viet kich), a art of ancient Vietnamese people in China!

e. Peninsula of Shandong and Hebei, Henan, Shaanxi, Beijing used the most Mandarin. Mandarin is the language of the Kings and mandarins; it is the dialect that was "balled" for easy general use for the different regions. Mandarin Chinese is the Viet language version of the Guangdong region, Muong Viet in Hainan, Chaozhou, Fujian and Vietnam Wu in Zhejiang, Shanghai, and Suzhou etc. It is worth noting that the ancient texts and historic books as well as ancient poems only read properly when being read by Viet language (Vietnam, Minyue, Wuyue).

That was clear, to this day, on Chinese land, not only no land named Han, but olso the voice of more than 90% of China's population is origin Viet language!

II. Viet language grammar imprints in Chinese Ancient documents

Language consists of two components; they are vocabulary and grammar. Vocabulary should have to change over time because the exchanges between people in space. Thus, tracing the origin of a word is not easy. With the language in general, it is so, in language relation of Sino – Viet, it is even more complex. Going in this direction, we encountered words like Shennong, Nu Wa, Emperor Ming, Emperor Li, Emeror Du Vong, Diku, Emperor Chi, Emperor Yao, Emperor Shun etc. We could not deny that they were the Viet names. But the reason for the Viet people's names that existed in the Chinese language was a mystery.

Ambition to find the pure Viet words often faces the tremendous protest. A few years ago, several authors suggested that several location names such as Ke, Mo etc in Phu Tho were Viet origin words. But that hypothesis was rejected. They offered the great books like Cihai, Kangxi dictionaries, Sikuquanshu etc to prove that "Ke" is from the Han, the Han words such as "cai", "gioi", "giai" of the Han that the Viet borrowed. Then, when entering Vietnamese, it became the "Ke" in Viet language.

Similarly, "Mo" is also the offspring of "Mai" in Chinese language! A few words seemed most Vietnamese are "pen", "write" etc also be considered "Hundred percent of Han, all are made in China!". In the eyes of these scholars, Viet people are just Han hybrids, Viet culture is very poor, only studied from the Chinese people but the learning is not perfect! Whatever mixing between Han and Viet all are just that Viet learned from Han! Sadly, no any Viet academics could argue. It was a pity for the Viet language!

Not enough ingenuity to find the pure Viet words, I went to the other way: tracing Viet grammar in Kanji (Han language). At this point a question arose: what is the most typical of the Viet grammar? Based on the law " the main element is front and the auxiliary element is after" discovered by a French linguist, Leopold Cadiere, with content: "In a simple sentence, the words stands in the following oders, each word following after shall clarify the meanings of one of the words in front of it», Professor

Cao Xuan Hao made the comment: « Overall, Viet language is very consistent with the word order (the main element is in front of and the auxiliary element is in after), most when compared to the French, English, Han, in which there was not a general statement about the order of words.)

In Viet language, Sino-Viet words make outstanding exceptional case that a person may not learn much but also knows that's a "reverse" order; if not counting the exceptional case as the combination [Modal predicate+ predicate] as the structure begins with the "bất" (不: not) or "vô" (無: none) words that considered as another combination [predicate + modifying phrase] other (the main element is front and the auxiliary element is after). However, there are not rare Han sentences that are wrong in grammar but they have become folklore resources as the mimic of the partridge's cries that "Bat thuc coc Chu gia" (不食穀周家) "Not eating the rice of the Zhou's dynasty" of Ba Di and Thuc Te (if it was correct in Han grammar, it should have been "Bat thuc Chu gia coc" (不食周家穀) . "[9]

From the above rule (the main element is front and the auxiliary element is after), looking into the the Han texts, it is easy to catch grammatical structure: Trung (中, Central) + noun form as the "trung tâm: (中心- center - in the heart), "trung đình" (中庭in the yard): Trung tâm rạng rạng (to feel uneasy inside the heart) Trung tâm dao dao (oscillator of heart), Trung cấu chi ngôn (voices in the words) (Shijing); thứ nhị (Second), thứ tam (Third) (Shijing); Bệ thăng thiên (pedestal skyward), thần thọ (god of trees) ở Lục độ tập kinh (六度集経, Liudujijing). In the above structures, it is true that the order (the main element is front and the auxiliary element is after) is complied. Obviously, that is not the Han grammar structure, it is Viet grammar structure. If only a few cases in a book, then it is random coincidence. But it becomes abnormal when detecting a series of similar cases in many bibliographies:

Shijing (Book of Poetry) [10]:

- Tuc tuc tho ta, thi vu trung lam (in the forest)

- Huoc lang tieu ngao, trung tam thi nieu (Chung phong: to feel uneasy in heart)

- Ho vi ho trung lo (Thuc vi: in fog)

- Trung tam rang rang (Nhi tu thua chu: to feel uneasy in heart)

- Trung tam huu vi (Coc phong: to feel uneasy in heart)

- Di vu trung coc (Cat dam: in the cave)

- Trung tam dao dao (Thu ly: nervous heart is)

- Tai bitrung ha (Bach chau: Between the river)

- Trung cau chi ngon (Tuong huu tu: voice in the sealed chamber)

What did these "pebbles" in languages say something? Were they just by chances? Did the editors when editing, exaplaining the annotation in the Shijing (Book of Poetry) because of the "stupidness" did not see the "wrong" things? Several thousand years no one explained. Through thousands of years of striving to have the axle vehicles had the same size, the same type of letters; though many revisions, annotations, why the Han scholars did not repair, pick these "pebbles" out? Was it true that the words of Shijing time were unstable and different with the Han period and the Tang period? But try to ask what the cause of instability was? According to the shallow opinion, it was in the history of Chinese language formation. The language of Shijing period located in the transformation process from Viet parlance to become the Chinese parlance.

What did the Viet grammar trace in those bibliographies say? It showed that, to the sixth century BC, in Chinese society still coexists both Viet parlance and Chinese parlance. Viet parlance not only circulated in the common class to create the folk compositions in Shijing (Book of Poetry) but also was used by the intellectual aristocracy class. The things mentioned above are irrefutable evidence of the presence of Viet language in the formation of the Chinese language. Even the phrase "不食穀周家Not eating the cereals of the Zhou Family" might be the Viet people parodied the partridge's cry from Spring and Autumn Period to last today?

Not only in Shijing but also in original Vietnamese version, author meticulously cited the sentences having structure of Vietnamese grammar in Shujing, Yijing and Ceremony Jing. However, because of the language barrier, the translator was not be able to translate into English so this section was omitted. We're very sorry.

III. Rediscovering the Viet texts in ancient Chinese documents.

More than 2,000 years, the Chinese people had owned a great cultural heritage created from the Zhuo period. They believed that it was created by Huaxia ancestors and dedicated to them. The Four Books, the Five Classics were the great pride of the Chinese nation not only with the barbarians surrounding but also with the human civilization. But the fact so far that they did not read the Shijing (Book of Poetry) thoroughly yet. With I-ching or Classic of Changes, from initial belief that it was created by the Chinese ancestors, so far, they admitted that they did not know who created it! Even, they could not explain and overcome well the very basic shortcomings of the I-ching or Classic of Changes. Not only that, several ancient texts, were considered as China's national treasure, they also did not read it thoroughly yet! This made people doubted about the role of the masters of the Chinese people with many cultural assets that they owned! Why? From long ago, this question was raised but there was no answer yet.

Up today, in the context of expansion of human knowledge,

we discovered the reason: The classics, documents, texts that initially were the Viet's assets! Firstly, they were created by the Viet people by polysyllabic language and words of mouth through many generations. Then, when the square letters appeared, they were transformed into square literal figurative characters. Two conflicts appeared: too many of voices, and too few of letters/ characters, how having enough letter/ character for each word/ voice? Again, the sounds are polyphonic, the letters/ characters are monophonic, and how could the monosyllabic word "lock" the polyphonic in the monosyllabic? Although it was difficult to find the way going to the heaven, we also had to do because Viet ancestors created the figurative characters, not the ligatures of the rhyme a, b, c! Naturally, the "cutting the feet to fit shoes" were inevitable. Finally, the most important documents were transferred to hieroglyphics. Letters were written on the bamboo cards and then recorded into the books.

Not only because after three times of copy made the original versions lost, but also because the figurative character could only see the drawing itself and then guess the meaning. The result was that people misinterpreted the texts and led the next generations to the wrong ways. Wrote the Dictionary to Explain Word (Shuo Wen Jie Zi: 說文解字) Xu Shen (許慎) gave out two reading ways of the square words, they were fan (反) and jian (借) very helpful in reading. But his reading rules could not encompass all cases so the reading should also depend on each person to guess. Thus, reader often disagreed with one another in the most difficult places.

As a result, there were still a lot of letters were "still being doubtful" that documents couln not be read throughly! Up to now, not only three hundred texts in the Shijing (Book of Poetry), 5000 letters of Morality Jing were in same fate, all unreadable. As a result, until now though there were the great comments of the famous Confucianists in the past, as well as academics in modern time, we still used the failed stuffs! Many people knew this, but the cause was so mysterious!

So far, recently people explained that these classic books were born from polyphonic Viet language. When converting to square monosyllabic words, they were turning both sounds and all meanings so that people could not understand. To understand them, we must first know that they were Viet native language so we also called them as Nom (字喃) script.

So now if we want to understand them, we have to recover them back into ancient Viet words and we must understand the ancient Viet words accurately then we can understand Kanji! Who can understand the ancient Viet word now? Not the scholars who mastered the Sino-Viet. Especially not the famous Chinese Confucianists! It can only be the people who are fluent in Kanji (Han language), fluent in Viet language and understand the ancient dialects, the ancient languages of Chaozhou, Cantonese, Wu Viet, Taiwan, Hainan etc.

We would like to borrow the research posts of the researcher Do Ngoc Thanh as typical examples.

Appendix I

Rediscovered the Yuerenge 越人歌
(the Viet people's song)
Do Ngoc Thanh

The Viet people's song (越人歌, Yuerenge) is very famous. After being put into the film and theater, the movement to research the Viet people's song in the folk singing was emerged, and not only the story of the cultural study experts. It became well-known because it was the first love poem, the earliest folk song recorded completely, about 2800 years ago etc.

A summary of the context of the birth of the Viet people's

song: Liu Xiang (刘向) was the fourth generation of of Liu Jiao (刘交). Liu Jiao (刘交) was Liu Bang's younger brother; Liu Bang was the first Emperor of the Han Dynasty. Liu Xiang (刘向) was author of the book "Stories in royal garden" (Shuo Yuan说苑)". The Book had the chapter to narrate about "the first crowning date of King Xiang Chang Jun (襄成君始封之日). Xiang Chang Jun was King Qingxiang of Chu (楚襄王), named Hung Heng (熊横). In the story, said about Ngac Quan Tu Tich (鄂君子皙) who is King So Hung Ngac (楚熊咢), while sightseeing on the river, a woman was rowing boat and singing the Viet folk song. Ngac Quan Tu Tich (鄂君子皙) asked someone to write and translate into the Chu language. This was the Viet people's song (越人歌).

This original paragraph as follows:

襄成君始封之日，**衣翠衣**，带玉剑，履缟舄，立于游水之上，大夫拥钟锤，县令执桴号令，呼："谁能渡王者于是也？"**楚大夫庄辛**，过而说之，遂造托而拜谒，起立曰：**"臣愿把君之手，其可乎？"** **襄成君忿作色而不言。**庄辛迁延沓手而称曰：**"君独不闻夫鄂君子皙之** 泛舟于新波之中也？乘青翰之舟，极□芘，张翠盖而□犀尾，班丽褂衽，会钟鼓之音，毕榜枻越人拥**楫而歌，歌辞曰：** '滥兮抃草滥予昌栻泽予昌州州饣甚州焉乎秦胥胥缦予乎昭澶秦踰渗惿随河湖。'**鄂君子皙曰：** '吾不知越歌，子试为我楚说之。'**于是乃召越译，乃楚说之曰：** '**今夕何夕搴中洲流，今日何日兮，得与王子同舟。蒙羞被好兮，不訾** 诟耻，心几顽而不绝兮，知得王子。山有木兮木有枝，心说君兮君不知。'**于是鄂君子皙乃□修袂，行而拥之，**举绣被而覆之。鄂君子皙，亲楚王母弟也。官为令尹，爵为执圭，一榜枻越人犹得交欢尽意焉。今君何以踰于鄂君子皙，臣何以独不若榜枻之人，愿把君之手，其不可何也？"**襄成君乃奉手而进之，**曰：**"吾少之时，亦尝以色称于长者** 矣。未尝过僇如此之卒也。自今以后，愿以壮少之礼谨受命。"

Translation:

"The first crowning date of King Xiang Chang Jun (襄成君始封之日), he was wearing nice clothes, carrying a jade sword, bringing high clogs, standing above the water line. The great mandarin was beating the drum and playing music. He ordered that: "Who can take us to the boat?" Great mandarin Zhuang Xin (庄辛) stepped forward, upright, and said: "I voluntarily grip your hand, it is all right?". King Xiangjun became outrage, his face turned colours and he kept silent.

Zhuang Xin (庄辛) lost his face, shaked his hands and said, "Your Majesty, you did not hear about Ngac Quan Tu Tich (鄂君子皙) going sightseeing by the boat? On the Qing Han boat there was the flag, he was wearing a beautiful coat. In the drum sound, Viet boatwoman was singing. The lyric was "" Lạm hề biện thảo biện dư, xương hoàn trạch dư xương châu châu, Thực thẩm châu châu yên hô tần tư tư, mạn dư hô chiêu, thắn tần du sâm, đề tùy hà hồ." Ngac Quan Tu Tich (鄂君子皙) said: "I do not understand Viet song, try to translate into Chu language for me to understand". Then he ordered the interpreters to translated into Chu language, it means: "Kim tịch hà tịch hề, khiên trung châu lưu, kim nhật hà nhật hề, đắc dĩ vương tử đồng chu. Mông tu bi hảo hề, bất hiểm cấu sĩ. Tâm kỷ phiền nhi bất tuyệt hề, tri đắc vương tử. Sơn hữu mộc hề mộc hữu chi, tâm thuyết quân hề quân bất tri." (今夕何夕搴中洲流，今日何日兮，得与王子同舟。蒙羞被好兮，不訾诟耻，心几顽而不绝兮，知得王子。山有木兮木有枝，心说君兮君不知). Hearing this, Ngac Quan Tu Tich (鄂君子皙) folded his sleeves up and came to embrace and used an embroidered blanket covered up Viet boatwoman. Ngac Quan Tư Tich (鄂君子皙) is Chu King's younger brother with same mother, Lingyin (令尹), a high level royal noble title, but he could also be fun along with Viet boatwoman.

Today, why Your Majesty felt hesitated more than Ngac Quan Tu Tich (鄂君子皙), why am I not like the boatwoman, I want to hand the King's hands, why can't I?" King Xiang Changjun stepped forward and reached his hands out and said: "I was well-educated from childhood and was commended by the adults by I never met any situation like this. From now on, I would like to listen to your advice, Master".

It is through this passage that the Viet people's Song

(Yuerenge, 越人歌) still remained to this day. Kanji language text of the song as follows:

今夕何夕兮, 搴舟中流。

今日何日兮, 得与王子同舟。

蒙羞被好兮, 不訾诟耻。心几烦而不绝兮，得知王子。

山有木兮木有枝 ,心悦君兮君不知!

And here is the translation can be regarded as the standard:

Viet people's song

Tonight, what is the night? Sailing on the river

This day what is the day? with the King going along stream.

Ashamed when being loved, don't blame my fate unlucky

The heart is fretting, that does not end, when meet the King

The mountain has the trees, the trees have the branches; I love you; do you know?

(The Vietnamese translation on the Vietnam Study Institute Forum)

Viet people's song now was known as a folk song of Zhuang ethnic group, recorded by phonetic signs by the Chu people in the Spring and Autumn Period *. Several people suggested that the Chu nation's Lingyin, Ngac Quan Tu Tich (鄂君子皙), after listening the Viet people's song, ordered to translate into Chu language. Chu nation was too large so the North Chu often self-proclaimed as Kinh Chu and the South Chu self-proclaimed as Xiang Chu (湘楚).

In ancient history, when the South Chu became independent, it was Duong Viet state. If going back to Spring and Autumn period, Chu nation's Lingyin (令尹), Tu Van (紫云) entered the Zhou dynasty and spoke in Chu language, and the

Zhou dynasty self-proclaimed as Hoa, but nobody understood him. This was written in the Chronicles.

Please consider carefully that the factor in this story, and do not mistake that the Chu language was the Hoa (Chinese) language. Even about the "lingyin" word, Chinese people didn't know its meaning, they just noted that: "Lingyin" was a title equivalent to "宰相" (chancellery) or "丞相" (Prime Minister).

Actually, Linh doan (Lingyin令尹) was from Viet ancient polyphonic ->: quan loan -> quan lang, only existed in Viet language and only Viet people could understand. Viet officials in Hung King period were called quan lang -> quan loan, when being notated in square character, it turned into Linh doan (lingyin令尹). In the Spring and Autumn Period, Hoaxia people still used Viet language as common popular language among small countries in Central Highlands and called Ya (Elegant) language. Ya (Elegant) language was Viet language, which today was also called Hoa / Chinese language, had been being monophonic so many people thought that "Viet", "Hoa" were two different languages.

Now I would like to try for the original Viet song to present to the readers. Viet song's notation recorded as:

滥兮抃草滥予

Lam he bien thao lam du

昌枑泽予昌州州

Xuong hang trach du xuong chau chau

𠄧 甚州焉乎秦胥胥

Thuc tham chau yen ho tan tu tu

缦予乎昭

Man du ho chieu

澶秦逾渗惿随河湖

Thin tan du sam, de tuy ha ho

Comparing the two texts we can see the clear differences. The translation had 54 words, while original version had only 33 words. In translation, the 3rd sentence was missing the word "忄", that was the word 食 – to eat. Meanwhile the translation was added the last sentence, nonsense "the mountain had the trees, the trees had the branches."

There are issues that need to be noted that the formation of the two texts: The song in Viet language of the Viet people. Chu people listened but they did not understand so they requested to translate into Chu language. Then the Chu version was notated by the square Kanji words. If the translation was the destruction, then this was a typical example. The ancient Viet language of more than 2,800 years ago was polyphonic language, "being" transformed into monophonic kanji 2,000 years ago, it was a loss. Losing the letters led to loss of the meaning.

Through the process of such translation, all were changed. Objective view, there were two almost entirely different texts on writing. Perhaps they were same together only in river landscapes, the attachment of the boatwoman and the King or Prince, that was all! More than two thousand years, the anecdote still lied in the book.

Many generations had read and praised and were satisfied with the translation version but no one had studied the original text of the song that was the Viet version! Was it a language that eroded through by years because it was unable to understand, so many amateur literati classes were pleased with the shadow, the imagine! Very difficult to determine between the original and the translation, which one was better!

Maybe due to translation version with the lyrical rhythm of the song was impressive to thousands of people being lured into another song that was not the Viet's song? Therefore, the research, reconstruction of the original text of Viet song (越人歌,

Yuerenge) becomes meaningful.

Translated into Sino-Viet an ancient hieroglyph used to "transliteration" of the Viet language, it was very difficult because the words were not used anymore; they were not in the dictionaries. Even looking up in the dictionaries, they might not be correct because the speeches in different localities were different. Furthermore, many thousand years ago, the voice and the writing ways of several letters might be changed and the sounds were changed in language of each region etc. This phonetic version so far had been being considered as the transliteration to record the "Zhuang" language, i.e the "Thai" language of the Zhuang minority.

I would like to re-represent and classify according to me:

滥兮抃草滥予昌柇泽予昌州州飤 甚州焉乎秦胥胥缦

予乎昭澶秦踰渗愄随

...河湖。

I would like to arrange it again, because it is important, to correct 6-8: (note two hyphenated word is a word polyphonic)

滥兮抃 - **草**滥予

Lam he bien-thao lam du

昌柇泽 - **予昌州州**飤

Xuong hoang trach-du xuong chau chau thuc

甚州焉乎 - **秦胥胥**

Tham chau yen ho-tan tu tu

缦予乎 - **昭澶秦踰渗**愄-随

Man du ho-chieu thin tan du sam đe-tuy.

...河湖。

Ha Ho.

The author, by the genius and wisdom in language by living with the Southern residents, had explained the phonetic signs and turned into the modern Vietnamese as follows:

Năm nầy bảo năm xưa
Thương hoàng tử thương chiều chiều xưa
Sớm chiều em hận tương tư
 Mà ai hiểu đặng tình yêu sâu đầy.
 ....Hò Hớ.

This year, said about old year
Loving the prince, loving in old afternoon
Morning and afternoon, I am in lovesick
Who could understand fully the deep love....Hò hớ

According to my research, the Viet people's song was the poem comprising 6- 8 syllables in Viet language, matching with Viet folk lullabies. If being expressed in six-eight syllable song by today, it would be:

... Hò Hớ.
This year, said about old year
Loving the prince, loving in old afternoon
Morning and afternoon, I am in lovesick
Who could understand fully the deep love....Hò hớ

The search and the decryption of the secret of Viet people's song, for me it was very easy because I knew the hieroglyphs, that used by the Chinese people, were the Viet origin words. When studying the ancient history, I often read in many different dialects such as Beijing, Guangdong, Chaozhou, Sino- iet.

So, we can say, look at Viet people's song (Yuerenge, 越人歌), it will be immediately visible as a Viet poem! With the details of 2,800 years ago, the Viet language had used "biện-thảo" as "bảo" (say), "nầy" kia (other), "nầy" xưa (other old) "thương chiều chiều xưa" (loving in old afternoon) "em hận tương tự" (I am lovesick) etc. But there were things I did not know, what "Hò ... hớ" meant and I has never thought about going to learn what "Hò ..hớ ..." was!

But the original version of Viet people's song (Yuerenge, 越人歌) made me amazed and "enlightened" that "Hò ..hớ …" was the Viet people's folk song while sticking to rivers and lakes, with boats, sailing: ... it means "Hà 河" (River) ... "Hồ 湖" (Lake)

Appendix II

Reconstructions of Wei Jia Ling ("维甲"令) , the Order of Viet King Goujian (越国名王句践"维甲"令)

Do Ngoc Thanh

Along with Viet people's song, Wei Jia Ling ("维甲令, The Order of Goujian) was also a special phenomenon of Chinese culture, attracted many mind power and hearts of the research world. The great Confucianist Guo Moruo (郭沫若); in XX century talked about this.

In modern time, the language specialist Zhengzhang Shangfang (郑张尚芳) of Research Institute of Social Sciences of China was considered a leading scholar. However, his lectures were not satisfied the readers, so the story has not ended!

I feel that, when researching Wei Jia Ling ("维甲"令, The Order of Goujian), scholars followed a wrong methodology. Knowing that the Wei Jia Ling ("维甲令") was a order of Goujian, the Viet king, but while studying, they had not returned to the original language of the Goujian was Viet language, Viet letters. They explained by Kanji with Mandarin pronunciation. Doing so is like climbing trees to find the fish?

I have been living in the folk culture, learnt Kanji but I was imbued with the language, culture of Min Viet, Bach Viet (Baiyue) so when looking at Viet people's song (Yuerenge, 越人

歌), Viet tuyet thu (越绝书), Wei Jia Ling ("维甲"令, The Order of Goujian) etc I easily recognized the Viet soul in ancient words. Unable to let those faded out, withered roots in books and misinterpreted, distorted, I took the venture to write here.

The Wei Jia Ling ("维甲"令) (The Order) was under the current understanding.

"Wei Jia Ling ("维甲"令, The Order of Goujian)" was extracted from the third book in Viet tuyet thu (越绝书, Yue jue shu) , the story about the Internal Wu (吳内傳).

Viet tuyet thu (越绝书, Yue jue shu) was recorded what happened in Spring and Autumn - Warring States Period by several people, in which, most of it was wrote by Wu Zixu in about 484 BC, before Chr of Sima Qian half a millennium. The paragraph as follows:

越絕書•吳内傳維甲令

越王句踐反國六年，皆得士民之眾，而欲伐吳，於是乃使之維甲。維甲者，治甲系斷。修內矛，赤雞稽繇者也，越人謂入铩也。方舟航買儀塵者，越人往如江也。治須慮者，越人謂船為須慮。亟怒紛紛者，怒貌也，怒至。士击高文者，躍勇士也。習之于夷，夷、海也；宿之于萊，萊，野也；致之于單，單者堵也。

Transliteration:

Việt vương Câu Tiễn phản quốc lục niên, giai đắc sĩ dân chi chúng, nhi dục phạt Ngô, vu thị nãi sử chi duy giáp. Duy giáp giả, trị giáp hệ đoạn. Tu nội mao, xích kê kê chựu giả dã, Việt nhân vị nhập sát dã. Phương châu hàng mãi nghi trần giả, Việt nhân văn như giang dã. Trị tu lự giả, Việt nhân vị thuyền vi tu lự. Cực nộ phân phân giả, nộ mạo dã, nộ chí. Sĩ kích cao văn giả, diệu dũng sĩ dã.Tập chi vu di.Di, hải dã; túc chi vu lai, lai, dã dã; chí chi ư đan, đan giả đồ dã.

Viet King Goujian came back six years, supported by the people who wanted to revenge the Wu nation, so he gave out the "Wei Jia Ling ("维甲"令, The Order of Goujian)"

To this day, "Wei Jia Ling ("维甲"令, The Order of Goujian)" is construed as follows:

維甲修內矛 Duy giáp tu nội mao

方舟航治須慮 phương châu hàng trị tu lự

*亟怒紛紛者, cực nộ phân phân giả *　　　　　　　*
士击高文者　 sĩ kích cao văn giả **

習之于夷.　 Tập chi vu di

宿之于萊.　 Túc chi vu la

致之于單.　　 Chí chi vu đan

Note: * and ** are the words that the official historians were forced to write into the Order.

Mr. Zhengzhang Shangfang (郑张尚芳) interpreted as follows:

维甲，修内矛（赤鸡稽緣）= 连结好犀牛甲，快整修好枪矛刀剑！

 Link together the team, prepare the swords and the spears

方舟航（买仪尘),治须虑 = 要想抬起头来航行，快整治战船
Must raise your head u to launch the ship, prepare the war ships.

亟怒纷纷，士击高文 = 激起冲天怒火，勇士们坚定地迈步向前！ Stirred up the extreme anger, warriors, please take steps consistently.

习之于夷 = 让勇士们在海上苦练，

 Let the warriors take the hard training on sea

宿之于莱 = 让勇士们在野地宿营

Let the warriors sleep in the wild campsite

致之于单 = 勇士们到前线致胜攻关！

Let the warriors to the front and win the battle!

Reviews:

The above paragraph was the narrative, accompanied with the presentation of the command's content (维甲"令). In the text, the author did not, as we today did, use the double quotes to distinguish Viet king's order with his narrative, so that the readers easily misunderstood. When Mr. Zhengzhang Shangfang (郑张尚芳) added two sentences: extreme anger (亟怒紛紛者) and warriors please take steps consistently (士击高文者) into the command: Wei Jia ling (维甲"令), I thought that was not right!

Actually, this was just a note of the views of the historians, who wrote the "burning spirit" of troops in maneuvers when hearing the King Goujian's order and gathered together. Because, in an order of "general mobilization" which had two sentences: "Extreme anger" and "warriors please take steps consistently ", it might seem strange? Ridiculous! In fact history had shown that 10 years after having The Wei Jia Ling ("维甲"令)", the Order/ command of Goujian, the Viet nation could conquer the Wu nation.

Before restoring successfully, the nation, the Viet nation was invaded by Wu nation. Under the Wu domination, how could a general mobilization order being launched publicity accompanying the words "Extreme anger" and "warriors please take steps consistently "?

- The meaning explaination of Mr. Zhengzhang Shangfang (郑张尚芳) was completely absurd and obscure. Due to knowing the context of preparing for the war of the Wei Jia Linh ("维甲"令", The order/command of Goujian), he deduced: Jia (甲) was armor! Meanwhile, Goujian's Min Viet language also read Jia "甲" was "cả", "nội", "lại" ... He also forgot that in the Wu Viet time, the language was polyphonic existed upto today: "trị tu lự" composed of two words: "trị" and "tu + lự" = trị tự is "trật tự" ("order, here means neatly and methodically arranged ")!

- The explaination of Mr. Zheng is too elaborately and too long to with too many references from ancient documents such as "the National Language-Viet language", Dictionary to Explain Word of Shuo Wen Jie Zi (說文解字,) " , "Chronicles" by Sima Qian, "Shuijing zhu" and the dictionary of interpretation such as "guangyin" , "xiyin" etc to use or explain the similar words in The Wei Jia Ling ("维甲"令", the Order/command of Goujian) and compared the homophones in Thai language and Zhoang language ...

Due to the absolutely wrong interpretation so I did not interpret that section in this article. If someone wants to study the full article to explain the Wei Jia Ling (维甲令, The Order/ command of Goujian) of author Zheng Zhang, then please refer in www.eastling.org/paper/zhengzhang/zhengzhang_Weijialing.doc

- Whether all this interpretation of this Wei Jia Ling (" 维甲"令"),   I and several Chinese bloggers thought that it was wrong, but currently it was being seen as "exemplary", "official", "value", "documentation for teaching in Universities " etc. Therefore, as anyone loves the truth, we should contribute to discussion to point out the errors and find the right.

Restore the Wei Jia Ling ("维甲"令", the Order/ command of Goujian)

- Traditionally, people used two first letters of the order to name the king command, so the command, that we discussed, was Wei Jia Ling ("维甲"令", the Order/ command of Goujian)! The original Wei Jia Ling ("维甲"令", the Order/ command of Goujian) was in a short paragraph quoted and preserved in ancient Viet language to keep the original character and truthfulness of the "command" by the official historians in many generations.

It was a very valuable work, but they accompanied by explanations that accidentally made its meaning became more obscure! When they added in Nom - Viet, sometimes they added more in Kanji language, the historians had caused more misunderstanding to the next generations.

Some people alleged that and said "The command of Viet King but the word used when in Kanji, when in the Viet word"! Such means that the ordinary people used Viet language while the King and nobles were assimilated by the "Huaxia" so they were so familiar with Chinese and they were afraid that the Viet people did not understand so that it should be accompanied by Viet language! Several people said that "Viet people at that time were assimilated by the Chinese language, so the King ordered to add Mandarin for the people to understand people!"

Until now it was based on the wrong ones of subjective spirit, not reality, not understanding Viet language but interpreting the Viet language and then interpreting the Wei Jia Ling ("维甲"令", the Order/ command of Goujian) was completely wrong! While, the true of the ancient official historians, no one understood, it was ignored and understood in other meanings!

We recorded verbatim of Wei Jia Ling ("维甲"令", the Order/ command of Goujian) as followings:

維甲修內矛　Duy giáp tu nội mao

方舟航治須慮　Phương châu hàng trị tu lự

習之于夷．Tập chi vu di

宿之于萊．Túc chi vu lai

致之于單．Chí chi vu đan

Thus, the order / command of King Viet Goujian was very brief, merely 23 words. But it had been the challenge during 25 centuries. If we wanted to interpret its meaning, it needed looking for the following words' meanings:

- The word: Tuyệt (絕, Absolutely), today read as Tuyệt (絕, Absolutely), but ancient reading was Chép (絕, Copy, Write). The book "Việt chép" (越絕, Writing about Viet), now became

"Việt tuyệt thư" (越絕書).

- The word: Đôi堆, means the pile (eg pile of earth), The Min Viet - Chaozhou dialect read as "Túi 堆" and also meant "Tất cả" (All). Originally a group of people then they said "Túi 堆" ("pile 堆"), it meant many people.

- The word: Wei 維 today we read that Wei 維 but in the " Wei Jia Ling ("维甲"令", the Order/ command of Goujian), its ancicent reading might be "Túi堆" (All) and "túi 堆 cả 甲" (All) wrongly written as "Wei 維 Jia 甲" as the case of the Chép絕 (Copy, write) now read as "Tuyệt絕", they were too different!

Thence inferred:

1. In ancient time, writing as "堆甲 Túi cả = Tất cả" (All).

2. In ancient time, used the word "Wei 維" was read as "Tất" (All), so "Wei Jia 維甲" were also "Tất cả 維甲" (All).

If you do know Chaozhou people who can read the word "vuông" (square) in Chaozhou language and you will find that the Min Viet language is different:

- "Jia 甲": read as "Cả" (All)

- Nội 內: read as "lại" .

- Lai 萊: read as "lái".

- Châu 舟: read as "chuấn"

Only people who know both Chaozhou language and Vietnamese, they can easily see the similarities and the clear meaning of example, "Nội 內" (Inside) somewhere read as "Lội" and Cantonese pronounced as "nồi" or "lồi", then they are not far from sound of "Lại 內" in Min Viet-Chaozhou. And also, it will be easier to understand from the word "Tu 修 lại 內mau矛" i.e., "Tụ lại mau" (Gather together fast) rather than "Sửa xoạn (Prepare), bên trong (inside), giáo mác (spears)" as Chinese linguistic specialists have explained!

I would like to explain each word of The Wei Jia Ling ("维甲"令) according to Min Viet language (Chaozhou):

維: now read as "Wei", its ancient reading might be "Tất" (All)!

甲 Jia read as "Ca, Cà Cả" (All).

修 Tu.

內 Nội read as "lai, lài, lại".

矛 Mao read as "Mao", "Mau".

方 Phương.

舟 Châu read as "Chuẩn".

航 Hàng. 治 Trị read as "Tia".

須 Tu. 慮 Lự. 習 Tập.

之 Chi read as "Chua" pronounced like as "Cho".

于 Vu. 夷 Di.

This word is Di of "Đông Di" but notes that the ancient historians noted in the Wei Jia Ling ("维甲"令) explained this "Di" read as "Hỗi海", Hải (Sea) according pronounced in Chaozhou now as "Hái 海 ", Cantonese people today still read Hải 海 as "Hỗi". "夷 Di" in the Wei Jia Ling ("维甲"令)" was "Hỗi 海".

宿 Túc read as "Sok".

萊 Lai read as "láy".

致 This Chí is "chí 致 mạng 命" meant "to dead", in "Việt tuyệt thư" when using "chí 至" means "đến" (come) the other writing and wrote as "Chí 至". 單 Đan (or đơn). Note: in Mân Việt- Chaozhou the following words will be:

Duy 維 in this text must be "Đôi" read in Mân Việt as "Túi", means "tất" (tất cả) (all).

Phương 方 Chuẩn 舟 today is "Phuẩn" = Phóng.

Tu 須 Lự 慮 is a polyphonic word, today as is the "tự" word.

Vu 于 hổi 夷 is a polyphonic word, is the "vổi" word, today is the "giỏi" (good).

Vu 于 lái 萊 is a polyphonic word, is the "vái" word today is the "vẻ" word

Vu 于 Đan 單 is a polyphonic word, is the "van" word, today is the "vang" word.

After comparing Sino- Viet - The "Vuông" (Square) word / ancient word – Viet/Min Viet / Chaozhuo, Vietnamese today, I would like to present the reconstructions of Viet King Goujian's Order/ command (Wei Jia Ling, "维甲"令)" as follows:

Duy giáp tu nội mao 維甲修內矛 Tất (Túi) cả tu lại mau - Tất cả tụ lại mau (All gather quickly)

Phương châu hàng trị tu lự 方舟航治須慮 Phuấn hàng trị tự - Phóng hàng trật tự (Queue in order)

Tập chi vu di 習之于夷 Tập cho vu hỏi -> Tập cho giỏi (Train until become good, skillful)

Túc chi vu lai 宿之于萊 Sóc cho vu-láy -> Sống cho vẻ (Live gloriously),

Chí chi vu đan 致之于單 Chí cho vu-đan -> Chết cho vang (Die gloriously)

- In ancient times Viet King-Goujian said, "All gather quickly ..." Now, thanks to Vietnamese and Minyue language (Minyue ancient language was different with today, but more similar to current Vietnamese language. Today though the sound had been changed because of the influence of Chinese-Mandarin, but not far much from the "origin"), so I've been restore The Order/ command ("维甲"令)".

Compared with the notes - interpretation of the ancient

historians recorded in Wei Jia Ling ("维甲"令)" , then it can be seen that my reconstruct is correct. Here is an explanation why the ancient historians wrote in the Wei Jia Ling ("维甲"令") could not interprete correctly because they did not know that many words are the ancient words of the Viet language

The restoration of the Wei Jia Ling (The Order/ command: "维甲"令") was not difficult if we mastered the rules of polyphonic and monophonic in ancient time and today, together with the Vietnamese dialect. But in order to clearly present, it was not easy! "Việt nhân ca" 越人歌 (Viet people's song) with the Wei Jia Ling (The Order/ command: "维甲"令") were two ancient documents indicated that about 2,500 years to 3,000 years ago, the Viet people had the "Nom" already!

This was matching with my "Reasoning under the rational inference" was that the "Nôm" words appeared before and the "Sino-Viet" or the "Chinese" appeared after! Because the word of "Hoa" (Chinese) or "Sino-Viet" were all monosyllabic! Were the ancient people to "wait" until the language became all monosyllabic and invented the writing? According to my reasoning, the ancient people did not wait and they invented writing while still using polyphonic voices.

That was the "Nom"! Certainly not only there was only one person who created the language, because no one lived long enough and lived during thousands of years to do so! That was entire ordinary people who invented the writing "Nom". Nom should therefore become no consistency. Later, the royal's documents called "elegant language" that replaced and made the "Nôm" to be lost.

So later people did not understand and misinterpreted the "Yuerenge, 越人歌" (the Viet people's song) and " Wei Jia ling (The Order/ command: "维甲"令")! There were many traces left to see that the words "Nom" appeared before. Hopefully in the 21st century this will be proved.

IV Conclusion

These above presentations led to the conclusion:

1. When the majority of the Viet population became the residents of China, then of course, Viet language became the voice of the Chinese people.

2. Due to prolonged contact with the Mongols, a voice part of Viet people in the Yangshao cultural had mixed with Mongolian voice and other ethnic groups' voices in the West. When invading the Loess Plateau to establish the Yellow Emperor's dynasty, the Mongols had imposed the Mongol parlance for the Kingdom.

Later, when establishing the empire, enforcing the national unified strategy to use only one texts. Elegant language - as the standard language maintained by the Qin Dynasty and imposed the Mongol parlance for the newly invaded areas.

Continue the Qin Dynasty, the Han Dynasty used Ya (Elegant) language. Now the Mongol parlance became practice of the majority population. However, in the area of residence in the South, the Viet parlance was still maintained. Even that many places still have maintained up today.

3. Tang sound was the standard language of the Changan Capital that formed in the Tang Dynasty, following a special historical process. With deep meaning and great tone, it was the creation of Viet people in China land and played an important contribution to create the most brilliant periods of Chinese poetry.

From Tang sound showed that, up to the Tang Dynasty, Chinese language had six bars as well as Viet language. This also proved, at the latest from the Tang period, Viet language had six bars already.

4. After the Tang period, many peoples of the North occupied or migrated to, made Chinese go far from its Viet origin. Yuan Dynasty combined Yuan language with Beijing voice to create the Mandarin of the Yuan Dynasty. The Qing mixed the Manchu voice with Beijing language became the Mandarin of the Qing Dynasty.

Consequently, the Chinese people more and more were far from the Viet pronunciation. Today the Chinese people could not read correctly many letters in the ancient texts in Shijing (Book of Poetry), Jing Ethics, Poem of Chu and China also lost the transcendent poetry arts of the Tang Dynasty.

5. We believed that, in early twentieth century, when arranged the Chinese language into the Sino-Tibetan family, scholar Bernhard Karlgren did not grasp the nature of the Chinese language. He based on the language of Qing Dynasty and detected that in the Chinese language had little or more from Tibet. On the other hand, he also relied on dominant rule notion when the Chinese ancestors were the prehistoric people migrated from Tebet. But the fact was on the contrary.

They were not the people from Tibet migrated into China, in contrary, they were from China to Tibet. This historical reality with practical language showed that the situation was more complex. Based on the pronunciation of modern mandarin and some Tibetan words in Chinese, they arranged Chinese language into the Han Tang family. However, they could not find the so-called Proto-Sino-Tibetan language: a language never appeared on life.

In our opinion, the Chinese language formed on the basis of ancient Viet vocabulary was spoken by Mongol parlance. The reason for the use of folk Cantonese language to search Guangdong original language failed because, the folk Cantonese sound although was ancient but not it was not the origin of the Cantonese language.

To find the original language of Cantonisee people and also the original language of China, we must seek in the language of Muong, Thai, Tay and regional dialects in Nghe Tinh, Vietnam.

6. The biggest problem of Chinese Linguistics today was not trying to prove its Proto-Sino-Tibetan origin, they must with Vietnam academics, scholars who speaks Viet language, Wu language, Min language etc focus efforts and wisdom to restore the Lac Viet language. First of all, to decipher the ancient texts so far had not been read, to help the readers enjoy the essence of the Shijing (Book of Poetry), Jing Ethics, Chu poetry etc.

On the basis of words rediscovered, to make the big Lac Viet Dictionary to reconstruct our Viet ancestors' voices. From here we also discovered, made the statistical of the Viet origin words which our ancestors left in Western languages.

References.

1. History of the Chnese language http://en.wikipedia.org/wiki/History_of_the_Chinese_language

2. Chinese language http://en.wikipedia.org/wiki/Chinese_language

3. 吴语 http://zh.wikipedia.org/wiki/%E5%90%B4%E8%AF%AD

4. 粤语 http://zh.wikipedia.org/wiki/%E7%B2%A4%E8%AF%AD

5. 闽语 http://zh.wikipedia.org/wiki/%E9%97%BD%E8%AF%AD

6. 湘语 http://zh.wikipedia.org/wiki/%E6%B9%98%E8%AF%AD

7. 客家话 http://zh.wikipedia.org/wiki/%E5%AE%A2%E5%AE%B6%E8%AF%9D

8. 贛語 http://zh.wikipedia.org/zh-hant/%E8%B4%9B%E8%AA%9E

9. Cadiere R.P Leopole (1877-1948) *Souvenirs d un annamitisant vien. Indochine*, Hanoi, N143, Julliet 8 1945. According to Cao Xuan Hao: "The legend of the four letters that the main is front and the auxiliary is after in the the Viet language study." (Separate document)

10. Shijing. Ho Chi Minh city Publishing House, in 1990

11. Shujing (Book of Documents). Translated by Tham Quynh, Learning Resource Center of Ministry of Education. Saigon 1973

12. Yiching (I-ching or Classic of Changes), Phan Boi Chau, Culture and Information Pulishing house in 1996

13. Le Manh That. *The collection of Vietnamese Buddhist literature*. Volume I. Quangduc.com

CHAPTER VII

THE FORMATION OF THE CHINESE WRITING LETTER

Chinese nation acquired the rich and highly developed cultures, because they had writing very early. Additionally, Chinese hieroglyphics contained extremely deep meanings, not just the characters, they were also great cultural products. Thus, study Chinese writing history was our priority subject.

From the current situation of the data, we surveyed the process of forming Chinese writing is based on three sources: 1. Unearthed scripts. 2. Living fossils scripts and 3. Modern Chinese.

I. Unearthed scripts

There were many legends about the origin of Kanji characters. A few old books wrote they were invented by Mr. Cangjie. Seeing a god, with special appearance, the face looked like a picture in words, Cangjie imitated the above images, and invested the characters. There are old books again said after Cangjie invented the secret of heaven, a small rice grain fell down from the sky, the spirits cried every night.

There was other Legend saying, Cangjie observed the birds and animals' feet marked in the soil roads, created the inspiration for him to invent the writing letters etc. All the kinds of legends were based on groping, groundless saying. Writing was invented and developed gradually by many people based on the actual needs of life, during the social activities in long time.

From Autumn 1954 to Summer 1957, archaeologists excavated Bonpo site (now the North Bonpo village, eastern suburbs of Xian City) many times, discovered that about 6,000 years ago, people in Bonpo had the long production life and created scripts, the symbol of the sexes, accused badges and art paintings, sculptures, decorations. Many badges engraved on paint ceramic were retained, they can be viewed as the first characters on China land [1]. In recent years, at the Dawenkou cultural relics in Lingyang Henan, Ju district of Shandong province they excavated several tombs dating back about 4500 years, discovered many items. Among the ceramic carving statues, there was an iconic painting with the letter symbols with a total of more than 10 singular words. The characters fit the shapes of the items should be described, so they should be called "hieroglyphics". Self-structured format was very similar to the text on the Oracle bone scripts but they were sooner more than 1000 years than the oracle bone scripts.

However, they were not the earliest characters. On Chinese land, archaeologists had found sites of more ancient letters as following:

a. At the Jia Hu culture [2]

In 24 tombs excavated in Jiahu village, the relics dated from 6,600 to 6,200 years BC in Henan province, Dr. Garman Harbottle of Brookhaven National Laboratory, New York, USA and archaeological team of the Science and Technology University in Anhui province identified 11 special symbols carved on tortoise shells.

Harbottle said: It is significant that these symbols have intimacy with ancient Chinese characters. In the notation, including symbols of "eyes" and "window", number eight and 20, similar to the characters used for thousands of years later during the Shang Dynasty (1700 to 1100 BC). They were earlier more than 2000 years than the characters discovered in Mesopotamia.

At the top, it is the word: "eye" (目), the under one is the word: "八" (No. 8), third letter is the torchbearer's image, it is the word: 火　(fire) and final one is the word: 日 (sun, day)

Jiahu characters

b. In Gansang relics, Guangxi Province [3]

In November 2011, in Guangxi they had detected the Lac Viet people's writing letters, according to Li Er Chan newsletter posted on website news.xinhuanet.com on January 03, 2012 as follows:

"Yesterday, the Council of Lac Viet cultural studies - Guangxi Province broadcasted the news that Lac Viet people in China had created the writing letters at four thousand years ago, demolished the notion about ethnic Zhuang ancestors were the Lac Viet people didn't have writing letters. The detection of the Lac Viet writing this time will rewrite the history of writing in China and proved that the Lac Viet culture was one of the essential origin roots of Chinese culture.

Before this time, Chinese historians had said that the ancestors of the ethnic Zhuang did not have the writing. President of the Council of Lac Viet cultural studies, Xie shouqiu introduced: Experts of the study had collected a large number of evidences to attest that the ancient Lac Viet people created the ideographic scripts four thousand years ago. Lac Viet scripts were first created at the time of the Neolithic, formed at the height of the characters of 'large stone shovel culture' (4000-6000 years ago), and surely had the deep root with Oracle bone scripts with the "Shui letters (水语)" of the Shui ethnic.

In October this year, at the Gansang large stone ritual site, Matou town, Beng guo district, Baise City, experts of the Council of Lac Viet cultural studies in Guangxi Province discovered dozens of mass fragments of large stone shovels and stone sheets engraved and filled with ancient writings. On December 19, experts went to the scene to conduct the survey, research findings, the writing letters engraved largest rock 103 cm long, 55 cm wide, on its surfaces engraved with hundreds of engravings, mostly letters and words of divination ritual. According to the brief statistics, on these rocks there were more than 1000 letters.

Experts rely on the distribution of large complete stone shovels beside the engraved stones and speculated that, the period of rocks appear similar engraved stone with big shovel period. It showed immediate words of the ancient Lac Viet people in the Gansang big stone shovel ritual relic was one of the ancient formed texts discovered in China.

According to information, in November last year, the experts of the research council discovered a large ritual altar of ancient Lac Viet people on Daming Mountain, Guangxi Province, on the ritual altar, they detected the signs and drawings. The head of the Guangxi Museum, Chairman of Guangxi cultural item appraisal committee, Jiang tingyu said that the signs and insignia drawings were engraved ritual signs of the ancient Lac Viet people in the Neolithic period.

A stone engraved Lac Viet Letters

After that, specialists of the study council also found a large number of ancient writings engraved badges on bone fragments, jade items, stone wares in the ritual vestige areas of the Lac Viet people, such as Wuming, Lungan district of Nanning City, Diantung district, Baise City of Guangxi. These badges (the amulets) were clearly a single sentences or special sentences, the experts considered as the early writings." (Completed the citation)

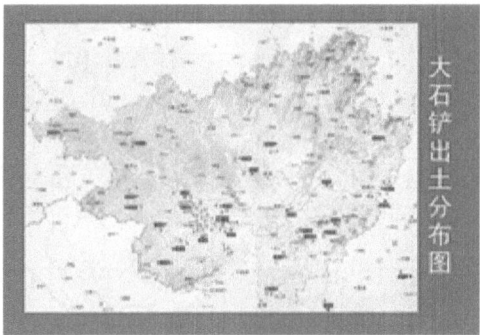

Map of the shovel large stone distribution

[www.luoyue.net]

c. Enxu oracle bone script [4]

Wang Yirong (王懿荣) was the last academician of the Quing Dynasty, a scholar has a deep understanding of ancient and modern literature. In Guangxu 24th year (1898), he accidentally met the turtle shells that people called "dragon remains" sold for healing. Found on tortoise shells inscribed ancient seal scripts, kind of precious antiques in the En Shang Dynasty, he began looking for buying. To the Spring of Guangxu 26th (1900), he got 1500 pieces of left and right sides. But Wang Yirong didn't pay a deep research on these texts yet because July of that year, the coalition of eight countries attacked Beijing.

Oracle bone scripts

In August 1928, under the leadership of archaeologist Tong Suoxin, the first time, Enxu vestige in Xiaotun village, Anyang District, Henan Province, the former capital of En dynasty, the Shang dynasty's end, was conducted a scientific excavation. Until 1937 before the outbreak of war, they collected 24,918 pieces of items.

So far, they had unearthed about 154,000 pieces of bones with engraved letters, in which mainland China kept more than 100,000 pieaces, Taiwan kept more than 30,000 pieces, Hong Kong kept more than 100 pieces, 12 other countries, including Japan, England, Sweden etc kept approximately 27,000 pieces. From 1954, they also found about 300 pieces of bones in Shanxi, Beijing, Chuyuan sites. 4,500 single words were identified, including more than 2,500 readable words and 4,000 different graphics. Pictogram, onomatopoeia words occupied about 27%, suggesting that oracle bone scripts were a quite mature writing system.

The contents of the oracle bone scripts were extremely abundant with many aspects of social life in the Shang Dynasty. They not only included the politics, military, cultures and social practices, but they also included the astronomy, calendar, medicine, science and technology. In oracle bone scripts, there were the method to create the "hieroglyphs, huiyi (會意), xingsheng (型声), zhishi (旨事), chāo (抄), jiajie (仮借)", revealed the unique charm of the characters. In the Shang dynasty and begining of the Western Zhou period (sixteenth century to the tenth century BC), they used the turtle plastrons, animal bones to convey the culture and letters. The inscriptions on turtle shells were previously known as contract documents, oracle bone inscriptions, boci (卜), guibenwen (龟本文), Enxu scripts etc. Finally, they collectively were known as oracle bone scripts.

Contents recorded the word divination boci (卜), from Banquing moved the capital to En land to En King Monarch within 270 years. The Kings of Shang and Zhou dynasties were very superstitious, everything was provided by using turtle plastron or bones (beef shoulder bone) conducted the divination. Then, divination related events (such as fortune-telling about the time, fortune telling about the people, divination work, depending on the results, verify the work ...) then carved on tortoise shells to store documents. Apart from the questions of divination, in the oracle bone scripts, there were few chronicle articles.

The contents referred to astronomy, calendar, geography, countries, generations, families, characters, officials, conquer, dungeons, agriculture, livestock, hunting, communication, religion, ceremonies, sickness, maternity, humanities, natural disasters etc were as a leading precious material in historical research, culture, language, texts in ancient society, especially in Shang dynasty.

The quantity survey and structural methods of the texts revealed that the oracle bone scripts had developed a close writing system. Principle of "record letter" of Kanji, was reflected in the oracle bone scripts. However, trace of the original hieroglyphic text was quite clear. Its main features were:

i. In terms of the composition of the word, several hieroglyphics extraordinarily focused on features of the real items, and more or fewer strokes, the reaction was not unified.

ii. Several words of oracle bone scripts were huiyi (會意) words, required only the combination to make sense of verifiability without requiring the fixed ones.

iii. Pictures of the oracle bone scripts often expressed the simple or complex to decide the size of the objects. Because the characters were carved up with knives on the solid animal bones, smaller graphics and sharp definition squarer.

Because the oracle bone scripts carved by a knife so the knife had to be sharp or blunt, the bone was thick or thin, with soft or hard, so the thickness of the graffiti was different, even as hair-thin lines, sometimes cracked strokes, became coarse. In terms of structures, short-term, small and large ones were not identified, or sparse, very different; or thick layers, very carefully solemn, might appear very fancy shaped outlines.

Oracle bone scripts, although were small or large forms, complex metamorphosis, but were very symmetrical, in a steady pattern. The reason people thought that Chinese calligraphy, was born from the oracle bone scripts, precisely because of oracle bone script had created three elements of calligraphy: pressing the pen (即用笔), mixing of words (结字) and the methods of chapters (章法).

In Shang dynasty they had the good ink, the books were engraved with sharp writings, and there were subtle sharp knives. Clearly seeing that the writing style was influenced by the rise and fall (rise and fall influences the stylistic originality), roughly, they could be divided into five periods:

- Majestic period: from Banguing to Wuting, estimated at 100 years, influenced by the Wuting prosperous period, the calligraphy was abundant, magnificent, majestic, so the oracle bone scripts calligraphy was very skillful. Generally, starting with more circles, collecting the pens spearhead more and curved, straight mixed, with many transformations, regardless of being dark or thin, were very powerful.

- Period of engraved on jewelry:

From Zuguing to Zujia was about 40 years. Two people could be seen as Virtue goalkeepers, at this stage the calligraphy was careful and jewelry, perhaps inherited from the previous period, complied with the regulations, the new style was rare, but there was no the mighty generous of previous periods anymore.

- The decadent and luxurious period:

From Linxin to Kangting was about 40 years. This period could be said that the En dinasty's literature style came to the decline, although there were a lot of neat books, however, the article segments were scattered mixed.

- The hard and high period

From Wuyi to Wen Wuting was about 70 years. Wen Wuting decided to restore, so he tried restoring the majestic style of Wuting period, the strong style of calligraphy in the hard and high period, showing the will of restoration, but with thinner strokes and the brave style.

- Strictly serious period

From Diyi to Dixin was about 89 years. Calligraphic styles tended to be serious, little close to the second stage; the books are longer, more serious, not degenerated and ill, and lack of the powerful strokes.

The think strokes on oracle bone fragments were as well as the impact of carving knives. Divination often used the "shì" or "fou" carved up along the both sides, from the midline toward the left and right of the text, making both sides harmoniously make up the beautiful symmetry of the lines. The carved inscriptions were after the Zuxie, the size of letters filled with black or red ink, or the positive, negative points filled with red and black ink, the more arts's meaningful, called as the miracle of the history books.

II. From living fossil texts

Outside the characters inside the ground were discovered, in China there were ancient texts, as a dead language, dead texts exist only in the minority people. Moreover, these types of letters or books that only a few people could read them, thanks to the teaching of the family or clan. Thus, experts called them as the living fossil texts. Letters and books of Shui tribe were the typical examples.

The Shui people are a minority, mainly distributed in Guizhou province with 340,000 people, say the Shui language, in the Zhuang language family, had ancient ties with Lac Viet origin.

The Shui text [5] was the writing and language of the Shui minority, called as "Lesui (泐睢)", left by the Shui ancestors and passed down from the previous generation to next generations, the shapes look like the Oracle bone scripts, inscriptions on copper mainly used to record the Shui ethnic's notions of astronomy, geography, religion, ethnic customs, moral, philosophy and cultural information.

The teachers of the Shui books had read and understood the book ultimately and thoroughly, made the archaeologists to respect and admire them. In March 2002, Shui book was put on a "list of Chinese carved inscriptions."

Shui book also was known as a "Devil book", "Treason book", firstly, due to its structure, but there are the adapted kanji words but they were written down, reverse, or modified the Chinese self-image method. The Shui letters (水语) were unlike with the Kanji in shape while writing way was in the contrast, today very few people can read. Currently, in the world, Shui book and Kanji are the only kind of non pinyin characters.

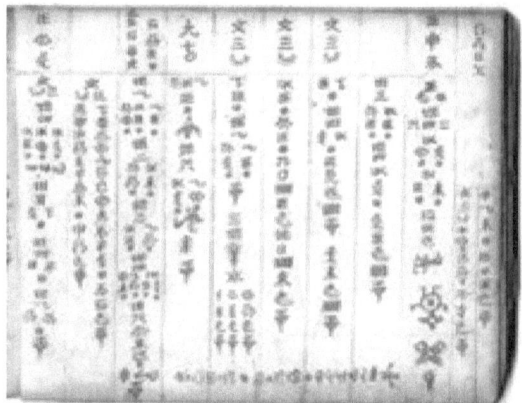

The Shui book

There were many different opinions on a number of letters of the Shui book. "Shui ethnic people's folk history" published in 1986 with about 400 letters. "China Shui ethnic culture research" had about 500 words. Experts said there were more than 2000 research letters, letters heterogeneous detected mainly at 12 Ganzhi (Chinese zodiac), Spring, Summer, Fall, Winter, 9 stars, with single digits, exceptions. They discovered the "Tiger, Cat" and 30 heterogeneous letters. For heterogeneous letters in ethnic Shui ancient texts, it was suggested that each word has at least one variation, the total number of Shui letters (水语) about 1600 letters.

Chinese academicians thought that might be the Oracle bone scripts, inscriptions on copper, had a "predestined relationship" with Shui letters (水语), in which the "father" was the oracle bone script. PhD Wang Yirong discovered the oracle bone script in 1898, to date, only 105 years. Ming Dynasty discovered two steles carved with the Shui ethnic's book. In

Huangzhi period, they discovered Shui letter carved wooden book. So, it did not mean that only after discovery the oracle bone script the Shui book were found. Archaeologists had struggled for more than 40 years of surveying 24 badges on the Xia Dynasty's pottery, and then Henan Province authorities considered a report on Shui book of Guizhou and compared with the other woodblocks, found more than ten badges of corresponding icons. The Shui ethnic's ancient letters and the cultural Shui insignia of Xia dynasty had a correlation

The Shui book recorded a large part of days in the primitive religious beliefs, azimuth, and luck or unluck, statues to dispel evil drive out demons as the shamans's tools to be implemented in order to exorcists.

Shui book

Because Shui minority people believed the spirits, so the Shui book was used widely. Shui book had a special function, boost the Shui people to cult the spirits. In Shui community who could read and knew how to use the Shui book (all are men) were very respected, known as "Devil Master" (Devil Teacher). In folk, they had a very high status, were worshiped. Shui book with the "devil master" was an inheritor, was a precious treasure, just inherit to men only, not to women. Absolutely no inherit to the outside people. Shui book was a textbook, Devil Master was the Professor. Devil Master and Shui book were a combination of primitive religious belief systems of the Shui tribe. The linkage of the spirits world, was the physical factor inherit from the the magic cultural lineage and sustained a mystical world.

Besides the religious content primitive beliefs, Shui book also contained a lot of information about natural objects, calendar information, and ancient texts, was an invaluable cultural history heritage of Shui ethnic. Several of which were present theories as Nine stars, twenty-eight mansions, Bagua jiugong (八卦九宫), Thiangan tizhi (天干地支), Riyue wuxing (日月五星), Yin Yang Five Elements, Liushi jiazi (六十甲子) four times five directions. Regulation of qi yuan li (七原历) mentioned in the Zhengyue jiaxu (正月見戌) of Shui lunar calendar, showed that Shui ethnic ancestors had concluded the high intelligence and high arts, encompassed the philosophical moral science and perspective of dialectical historical materialism. In Chinese culture, it was considered as the brightest pages.

The structure of Shui ancient writing belonged to three types: The first was hieroglyphic, like Orale bone scripts and inscriptions on copper; The second was adapted from Chinese language word, i.e., how to write backwards, conversely or modified the Kanji letter; The third was religious texts, ie the badges signify the passwords of traditional religions. The book was written in the form from right to left, from top to bottom, with no punctuation. Shui texts handed down by three major forms: oral, written on paper, embroidery, writing on leather, carved on wooden planks, write on ceramic and terracotta and burnt etc. Shui book depended mainly on hand-writting, oral and handed down up to now, so the professional scholars praised as the "living fossil" hieroglyphics. Due to the symbolic structures, mostly they depicted flowers, birds, insects, fish and other things in the natural world, as well as some totems like dragons and in written descriptions but still retained its ancient civilizations.

III. From the modern Chinese characters

These above documents written from the unearthed scripts, living fossil were the evidences that difficult to refute, showed that Viet language was the subject to make the Chinese language. However, it could not ignore the goings find Chinese characters through the research of Kanji, writing characters that Chinese people today have been using.

The Chinese characters were born from the Orale bone scripts of the Shang Dynasty. But over 2000 years, people did not know where Orale bone scripts original text came from. Only in the new century, thanks to archaeological discoveries, do we know that hieroglyphs were invented by the Lac Viet people at the earliest in the Jiahu culture 9000 years ago. Not only at Jiahu, square letters are engraved on bones, on turtle covers and on stone also appear in many other archaeological cultures such as Bonfo Shanxi, Liangzhu Zhejiang, Gansang Guangxi ... Can be speculated without fear of mistake, the word Gansang Guangxi was posted to Anyang Henan. When occupying the Anyang land of the Viet people, the Shang Dynasty realized the value of this type of writing and concentrated their efforts on upgrading the word used in divination, sacrifice, and incantation into a common word in life. Following the Shang dynasties, the Chu dynasty improved the Orale bone scripts the text into writing on bamboo cards, on silk ... making writing more and more popular. When was unified the country, the Qin dynasty standardized the writing and popular in the country. During 400 years of existence, thanks to hieroglyphics, the Han dynasty brought Chinese culture to flourish. The outstanding mark showing the shaping of Chinese writing is the book Shuōwén Jiězì (說文解字) of Heshen (鄐慎) drafted in the early Han Dynasty. The book has been lost but is widely cited, so by the Song dynasty, people have restored almost the original one, although there are modifications to suit the reading style that has changed over time. The title Shuōwén Jiězì (說文解字) means the reading and interpretation of Chinese characters. From the original and unmodified parts, it shows that it is a book that teaches how to read ancient Viet, which was used in China to the Han Dynasty. Comparing this book with the Chinese read way today, it is realized that all Chinese, when it is only read in the ancient Viet read way and its interpretation of the old Viet word is correct.

We would like to borrow the article of Do Ngoc Thanh scholar, an outstanding work in the traceability of Chinese characters

Words of the translator:

In the original Vietnamese, the author borrowed the article "Finding the source of Nom word" of Do Ngoc Thanh scholar. A meticulous research work, unique, with plenty of solid evidences showed that in the modern letters that Chinese people have been using, there were many traces of the Nom letters of the Viet people.

However, because the author used many ancient words from Lac Viet, Chaozhou that it was not able to translate into English, the translator had omitted, we sincerely apologize to readers.

IV. Commentary

Above presentation showed that, on the land of China, the texts were formed very early and continuously. From the most ancient characters found in Banpo until Jia Hu scripts, Shui clan's letters, Gansang letters, Enxu oracle bone script etc from simple to complex, but they were in the the rigorous consistency. Due to the magic consistency, from the oracle bone script structure, experts had deciphered the Jiahu letters, Gansang oration letters. The great consistency proved that they were created by only an owner.

The question arose: who was the owner of these hieroglyphic writing scripts?

In his documents, scholar Zhou Jixu confirmed:

"History was written in the traditional documents that only to consider the Yellow Emperor's people went into the Yellow River valley and developed the civilization there. Those who had previously lived and created the prehistoric glorious civilization of the two rivers (the Yellow and Yangtze) were sunk after the fog of history. They were excluded from the traditional historic annals, which included almost all of China's history, from the Upper Letters (Shangshu), Classic of Poerty (Shijing) to Chr etc"

"*This is a historical is bearing the reverse position between host and guest. One of the reasons for this situation is the oppression and exclusion of Yellow Emperor's powerful party. The other reason is that, while other people had not invented their writing systems, the nations of the Yellow Emperor had done. One of which was used by the Chinese people so far. The ancient Chinese characters are recognized only being formed and degraded in the Yellow Emperor's nation in ancient time*" (HVT wrote in italic letters). That was why there was great disparity between the archaeological areas in the Yellow, the Yangtze basin and the traditional historical records related only to the beginning of the agricultural sector in the region. Concerning to the civilization of "Two Rivers in East Asia," was created by who came before. We also found a significant amount of information from historical documents that could be confirmed by the discovery of archaeological evidence and historical linguistic evidence. The difference in lifestyle, customs and language among the natives and residents of the Yellow Emperor gave us further evidences that the people of the Yellow Emperor had appropriated an existing culture".

Thus, scholar Jixu Zhou said: "While other people had not invented their writing systems, the nations of the Yellow Emperor had done; one of which was used by the Chinese people so far. The ancient Chinese characters are recognized only being formed and degraded in the Yellow Emperor's nation in ancient time"

Was that exactly?

The badges on the Xia pottery were not written letters. Following Xia Dynasty, for more than 360 years, from the Chengtang to the Zuyi, over half the time of the dynasty, the Shang did not have the writing scripts. So, why when moving the capital to the En land and suddenly appeared the volume of such many and complete writing letters? If the writing was invested by Cangjie by order of the Yellow Emperor, so why until the En dysnaty they appreared? Writing letters was not created by a person in just a day; it was by a labor process and the creation of thousands of people in thousands of years. Thus, the hieroglyphs on Chinese land were not born at the Shang Dynasty period, they were the results of the long-time creation of the cultural owners of Banpo, Jiahu, Gansang etc. It meant, the Viet people, the preceded owner of China, created the writing letters, from simple to complex, but the Enxu writing letters were the highest development! When moving to the eastward to occupy the En land, the Shang dynasty not only occupied the land but also appropriated the texts, a great innovation of the Viet people.

We assumed the ancient Viet scripts was beginning to take as follows:

Making writing to record the thoughts was desire of human. As the people had a long history, as master of stone tools and invented the rice agriculture, more than anyone else, the ancient Viet acknowledged that they needed to record their thoughts to transfer the great mass of experience for the next generations. As it was said in the Shijing, the Viet ancestors were from the natural phenomena of sky and the earth to invent the knotted letters, letters with foot shapes of the birds on soil, tadpole shaped letters etc. On the rocks in Sapa, along with the pictures drawing their daily activities, the Viet people had sketched the hieroglyphic characters. The first hieroglyphic characters were brought by the Viet migrants by northwest road to Banpo area. Also, from Sapa, the hieroglyphic characters were brought up to the south Yangtze, Guangxi and Jiahu. Here, the writing characters had been evolved and carved in stone shovels, stone axes. Next, the letters were brought to the Henan region, became the inscriptions on animal bones and tortoise plastron.

Invaded Central Highlands in 2698 BC, the nomads had to face two problems: the annual flooding of the Yellow River and the persistent fight of indigenous people. So, the first dynastic reigns remained the capital on the North side and tried to suppress the uprisings. Of course, they had to learn the Viet culture and the farming. Also, at this time, happening mixed blood between Mongolia and Lac Viet born the Huaxia people. Gradually the Huaxia replaced their fathers to take the dynastic leadership. Up to the Shang Dynasty, the Huaxia had been Viet-localized thoroughly, between the Huaxia and the Viet was almost sociable. Not only King Chengtang was the Viet, but the Shang residents also were instilled the Viet culture, including Viet language, worshiping spirits, divination customs. The divination must have appeared before the time of King Yao with the story that the lungma bringing Hetu and God turtle with calendar on his back offered by Yuezhang surname family. Due to powerful force, Banging occupied En land of indigenous people. Here they met many noble families used the Orable bone scripts, and the divination, the En dynasty learned and strongly developed in the kingdom.

Such large number of Oracle bone scripts in the Enxu was more likely they collected and bought back, for learning the history, culture, customs of the newly-occupied areas.

Obviously, unlike Mr. Jixu Zhou said: "The ancient Chinese characters were recognized only being formed and degraded in the Yellow Emperor's nation in ancient time."

In fact, the so-called "ancient Chinese characters" had been created by the indigenous peoples in many places, from very long time before the invasions of the nomads. A part of the Enxu Oracle bone script was the continuos creativity of the Viet with the Huaxia intellectuals.

On the basis of economic and cultural development of the Shang, the Zhou Dynasty opened the most brilliant period of ancient Chinese culture. Zhou Dynasty still used the Oracle bone scripts for some time. But then they switched to use the bamboo cards. This was the period when the great classics in the Oriental history had been summarized.

An issue that needed being clarified: Was it when the Shui letter and the Shui book appeared?

Many books wrote that:

"At the time of the Xia, Shang, in Huaxia ethnic populations included the Shui ethnic ancestors". "But the earliest period is the Shang En, there were writing letters of the Shui ethnic people. Since then, as a result of the two numerous national migration times, it caused the cultural language of the Shui ethnic appeared, due to divergence from a mutual source, then absorbed the gradual integration of this phenomenon". "The central dynasty confirmed the Shui ethnic from the begining, as well as took the Shui ethnic minority as the only witness of the events in history."

The word Lesui (泐睢) in Shui letters (水语) were explained as: "Lac, former ancient Chinese language; However, since ancient time, appeared from the Sui (睢) River Basin. "

[水语称水书为"泐睢"。泐，源于古汉语，是母语遗存；睢，是水族从古至今的自称读音，是发祥于睢水流域的烙印}.　　　(Shui language called Shui letter was "Lesui (泐睢)." "Le泐" was old Chinese, a mother letter. "Sui睢" was named of Shui clan (水族) from ancient to nowaday, lived in Sui (睢) River basin)

It was the orthodox notion of majority Chinese scholars relied on contemporary Chinese chauvinism: Huaxia was the center of the universe, everything started from Huaxia! So far, this confirmation became too simple because just by testing DNA of the few Shui people, we will know exactly who their ancestors are, where they come from. While there is no such material, we would like to explain as follows:

The ethnographic material showed that Shui ethnic people were the Lac Viet people's descendants. Traceability, they were "Banana" tribe, in ancient Viet scripts, the "Banana" also meant "water " (Shui). So later on, according to Tang sound, they were called as "Shui" (Water, 水). They were the same ethnic with the owner of Gansang relics. While the Gansang people brought the hieroglyphs and retained on the stone axes, shovels, the Shui people created the Shui book to pass down to their descendants. From the Qin and Han's invasion, while the majority of their fellows were under the rule of foreign invaders that gradually changed into "Han" people, the independent willpower plus natural conditions, they lived in isolated forests, gradually turned into minority but they still could keep their culture in which there were their letters and books. The phenomenon of reducing the Viet population on the land of China occurred in the mountains south of the Yellow River started from the Xuan Yuan clan's invasion. Right from that time, many Viet tribes could not stand of the invader's oppression; they went into the forest, gradually turned into the minorities. Meanwhile, several tribes in Guangxi, Guizhou, thanked to the long-time isolated life, they could have kept their ancestral culture, including the voice and the scripts.

Therefore, it is able to believe that Shui ethnic people were the Lac Viet ethnic indigenous people that were minimized from the post-Han time, not from the Zhongyuan down. The Shui letters (水语) were the Viet letters, also with the same origin with the texts on Gansang stone shovels.

Things presented above showed, that from the "unearthed texts" in Banpo, Jiahu, Gansang, Enxu to "living fossil texts" of ethnic Shui were all the products of the Lac Viet people from Vietnam to go up and lived many thousands of years in China land. Moreover, the modern Chinese writing had more than a basis to prove that, it was created by the Viet people to record the Viet sound

References

1. Origin of the Chinese Script http://www.chinavista.com/experience/hanzi/hanzi.htm

2. Archaeology of Writing .www.geocities.com/cvas.geo/china.html:

3. According to the information that Li Er Chan posted on the website news.xinhuanet.com January 03, 2012

4. 甲骨文 http://baike.baidu.com/view/8170.htm6.

5. 水口 http://baike.baidu.com/view/95537.htm

CHAPTER VIII

THE FORMATION OF ANCIENT STATES IN EAST ASIA

How the ancient states in East Asia were born like? That was the major concern of the international academic scholars. But although spending much mind power, so far there was no satisfactory answer. There were two reasons led to this issue. First it was the insufficiency of the credible historical evidences. The second reason which was also very important, that there was not any adequate conception of "the ancient oriental states." Western scholars, following the tradition from Prolemee, identified two conditions for the ancient state formation were societies that had the food surpluses and considerable slave force. Also, from this influence, the Marxist conception governed the oriental history background and considered that the states that appeared from the class struggles, the ruling class used to implement its political power. Until now the world history had existed four types of state: slavery state, feudal state, state capitalism and state socialism. However, the reality showed that, such concept was suitable only for the West, where society formed by nomadic economic methods.

Meanwhile, the Orient had other typical characteristics. The Oriental civilization was agricultural civilization, formed from the basin of major rivers. In the agricultural economy, the water handling was a job to be well organized effort to mobilize people's power. Moreover, due to depending on the nature, the ethnic communities always tended to scramble the good land and water resources, so the wars often occured. Demand for water handling and against foreign aggression was a matter of survival. Both tasks required a unity power of the population. So, the group of people had to gather together. When gathered together, the role of the leader, the head was very important. The leader became the supreme power. People worshipped and obeyed him. That was the "king". In addition to the spiritual strength from religion and belief, the position of the "King" was increasingly high, and set out the ruling apparatus, from which the state formed.

The ancient oriental states were born very early, at about Millennium IV - III BC. In ancient Egypt, the ally of the communes (known as the "Nom") was formed between the fourth millennium BC. Around 3200 BC, a powerful nobleman named Menet had conquered all the "Nom" in the Nile basin, Egypt and established the unified state. Around this time, in the Mesopotamian basin, dozens of small states of the Sumerians were formed. In India, the first ancient Dravidian state was founded on the Indus basin between the third millennium BC. Here, they have found the remains of two ancient cities of Harappa and Mohengio Daro with the wide, straight, stone paved streets, flanked by rows of two-story brick houses. By the beginning of the second millennium BC, when the Arian invaded India, they built their state in the Ganges River basin. That was what was widely known.

In the traditional concept, international scholars thought that first state appeared in East Asia was the Shang dynasty (1766-1122 BC). The Shang Dynasty began to emerge from the West Delta Area of the Wei River. By force, King Cheng Tang unified Northern China, built an empire style of the conquerors: left behind a garrison force, to control the local population. Turned the local king to become the dependent. Allowed him governing and collecting the taxes in his territory. Chinese history began to be recorded from this period. The Shang dynasty's land included the provinces of Shanxi, Shandong, Hebei, Henan today. The Shang dynasty's civilization had reached a high level of the Bronze Age. At the beginning, the Kingdom capital located in Bo (亳) area, after being invaded by the west nomadic ethnic, the Capital had been displaced several times. Finally, the capital was moved to Énxū, near Anyang, named the country as the En Dynasty. The Shang's history wrote that it had a thousand vassals. Perhaps only few near the capital were the Shang's dependents, in the farther areas, they were the independent states. That was the origin of decentralized feudalism developed in the early of the Zhou (周) Dynasty.

From the above "resume data", we can see, firstly, the Shang dynasty did not build on slavery but on the basis of the agricultural community to join hands to against nature and against the robbery enemy. Thanks to agricultural development that they had the food surpluses. The State existed mainly based on taxes and the civil service. This fact demonstrates that the Oriental history had gone on its separate way. Thus, the application of the criteria of significantly slavery forces as a prerequisite to the formation of a nation was unsuitable. The second thing was, the Shang Dynasty had developed a high level. The feudal monarchy formed, with strong army, advanced copper industry, mature writing letters. The question must be raised: was it normal when a first state that had formed that had such progress? We could only find the answer if we know what happened before.

I. The formation of the Eastern states

The Xia dynasty (21st -16th century BC), described in the ancient records as Chr, the Bamboo annals (竹書紀年; Zhushu jinian;) the Shijing (Book of Poetry). This dynasty founded by

King Dayu (大禹) after Shun, one of the Five Emperors ceded the throne to him. Most Chinese archaeologists thought that Erlitou early Bronze culture was also the place of the Xia's origin. However, Western scholars were still skeptical because in fact, the first Chinese letters were written after this dynasty over a thousand year. Moreover, Western archaeologists also disagreed about the relationship between Xia Dynasty with Erlitou culture.

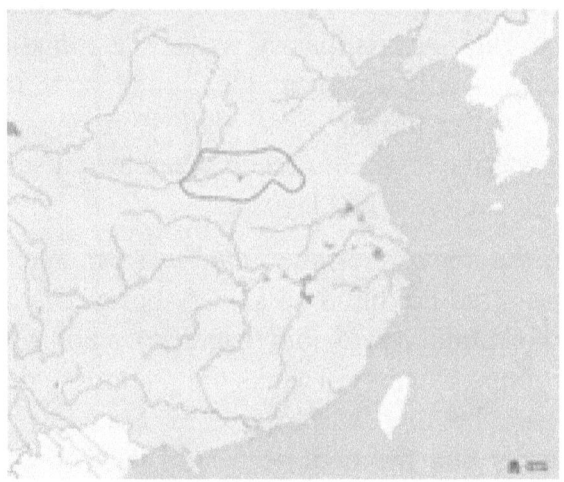

Xia state

Western scholars, the traditional rationalists, they did not believe it was normal. But Easterners, felt by their hearts, that the sentences and the words in the Upper Book (Shangshu, 上书) and the things stored in human memory were true. Nont only just believed in the true existence of the Xia Dynasty, but following the flow of history, they believed in the the real existence of the Shun Dynasty, Yao then Yellow Emperor.

However, all the above classic knowledge was just the tip of the iceberg of the complex Eastern history.

From archaeological discoveries of the twentieth century showed that from the fourth millennium BC, at the end of the Neolithic period, the Viet people with about approximately 60%

of the world's population [1], built in East Asia a developed agricultural civilization. Plouging the land by cattle was common. Pottery and jade processing became exquisite. Fishing and trade were developed. Pearl trade networks spread across the South China Sea. Not only food, but excess in every way, life became rich. Besides, the intangible culture reached its peak. From the tomb in Puyang, Henan in 6,500 years ago with the imagines of dragon, white tiger, twenty-eight stars, the weather in years ... demonstrated the Viet people's proficiency in calendar, feng shui, astrology and mastering the Y-ching (changes) [2]. From the sites such as Gansang, Liangzhu, and Bonpo showed that the writing in the form of consistent self-forming, orations ... The highly economic achievements of such culture could only be achieved when there was a high concentration of human resources and well organized, as a prerequisite for state formation.

From the latest data published in 2016, after 80 years of discoveries and research of Liangzhu (良渚) culture in Taihu region, Chinese scholars concluded: "The traditional view stated that the Shang dysnaty was a state to appear early in the history of China has to be changed to make the space for Liangzhu, because the Liangzhu state appeared since about 3,300 years BC, before the Shang Dynasty almost 2,000 years ago". And "The Liangzhu culture is the origin of the Chinese civilization."

Discoveries of the Liangzhu culture inverted traditional notions of oriental history and opened the true picture of the well-hidden history. Surveying the archaeological site on the East Asian mainland associated with legends and ancient history, showed the ancient Eastern state is formed as follows.

1. State of Shennong:

East Asia included the Yellow River, Yangtze basins and Southeast Asian mailand was the locations inhabited by the Viet community. Because of the same origin, culture and language, earlier East Asian populations formed the tribal alliances to manage the water irrigations and protect the villages resisted the raids outside. From Liangzhu archaeological culture, it showed that, around 3300 BC, the earliest state in the East was born. As in the previous section, when speaking of Liangzhu culture, it showed that, with an area equal to half of China at the time, Liangzhu state was not only the earliest but also the largest and most deveyloped nation at the time. Due to the discovery of the heart of this state located in the modern land Liangzhu, so people named the capital with the country's name was Liangzhu. But surely that was not the original name when the state was founded. Thus, what was the state's name? Answering this question is to look to the end of history. However, this was not easy.

The truth was, the discovery of the state of Liangzhu state is completely unexpected for not only researchers but also the Chinese people for thousands of years. Because in the folk as well as in the books of China have not any suggestions on such state. There were only legends about the Hong Bang surname (鴻龐氏) and the Xich Quy (Chigui, 赤鬼) state of the Vietnamese that saying:

"In the Dog Year, grandchildren of Yan Emperor's three generations, Shennong surname, named Emperor Ming born Emperor Nghi. Emperor Ming went on patrol to the South, coming to Wuling (五岭) Mountain, he got married the daughter of Vu Tien, born the King [Kinh Duong Vuong]. King was a holy intelligence, De Ming loved him, wanted to give him the throne. King tried to give the throne to his older brother, not to follow the order. Emperor Ming passed the throne to De Nghi, ruled the Northern, Kinh Duong Vuong became a King, ruled the Southern, known as the Xich Quy (赤鬼) state ... " "... Au Co (嫗姬) and fifty sons arrived in Phong Chau (Bach Hac district now), respected the elder brother to become a king, named Hung Vuong, named the country Van Lang. That nation was next to in the east, Ba Shu in the west, north to Dongting Lake and south to Ho Ton state (Champa nation now). "

From ancient times, not only passed each other about ancestor Kinh Duong Vuong established Xich Quy (赤鬼) state, the Viet mothers also have had the lullabies:

The father's sacrifice is as high as Thai mountain

The devotion of the mother's like the water flowing from the In Source River out

And

Wind of Dongting, the mother sings the lullabies for the child to sleep

The Moon of Tien Duong (Qiantang) is waking whole night

Bổng bồng bông, bổng bồng bông

On the pink hammocks, the mother is holding the child of the dragon and the fairy.

Taishan, Dongting Lake, Xich Quy (赤鬼), Kinh Duong Vuong with Hong Bang surname, the Dragon father and the Fairy mother as the the The North Star up in the to guide the Vietnamese generations leads to our origins.

Fortunately, in this moment, Liangzhu culture was brought to light. So, there was any connection between the Xich Quy and the Liangzhu?

Let us consider the following criteria:

a. About the time.

Archaeology determined Liangzhu culture appeared from 3300 BC. Meanwhile legend said Shen Nong lived around 3320-3080 BC. This showed that the coincidence to say the magic between legend and archaeological materials. I-ching wrote: "Fuxi surname faded, Shennong surname appeared", Therefore, Shenong wasnot the first King of the South Yangtze. State of Shennong formed on the state of Fuxi and had since grown up.

The legend recorded that when Kinh Duong Vuong crowned, he established Xich Quy (赤鬼)' state in 2879 BC - 400 years after the formation of the state of Liangzhu - showed Xich Quy (赤鬼) was born right at the time of Liangzhu's most prosperity.

b. About territory:

Archaeology showed that Liangzhu State territory occupied fully of Yangtze River basin. Northwest to Shanxi reach. Northeastern reached the Sandong area, crossing the Yangtze River to the northern bank. Meanwhile the legend said that the Xich Quy state: north to Dongting Lake, east to East Sea, west to Bashu, and south to Ho Ton state. Thus, the boundaries of the Xich Quy (赤鬼) were almost identical to the boundaries of the Liangzhu (良渚) State. Of course, national boundaries in legend and boundaries according to the Archaeology were only relatively because there often were the cultural overlaps and so the cultural boundaries were often not same as the national boundaries. Despite these, we also see the fact that, the boundaries of the Liangzhu State in archeology were nearly matching with the boundaries of the Xich Quy state in legend.

c. The Capital

While archaeologists discovered the Liangzhu capital, in the legend of the Xich Quy state hardly said about Taihu Lake, it also said about Dongting Lake where Kinh Duong Vuong was going on a boat and met Long Nu - daughter of Dong Dinh Quan. There were also here the Tuong (Xiang) River and Tuong (Xiang) Field, the places where the sons of Lac Long Quan met again. But the folk lullaby mentioned about the moon of Qiantang. Qiantang River is the biggest river of Zhejiang Province, is derived from the boundary between the two provinces of Anhui and Jiangxi, flows southwest-northeast through Hangzhou, capital of Zhejiang Province, which flows into the Hangzhou Gulf.

The above things were the little light from the star that

sent us the rare traces of ancestors who used to live near the Qiantang River, weren't they?

d. Who were the Liangzhu people?

With the DNA evidences, the Chinese scholars acknowledged that the Liangzhu culture's owner was the Lac Viet people! It was specific that Lac Viet people, but who were they?

Since the imagines of "the god with the beast's face" engraved on worshing gems, Chinese scholars confirmed: Liangzhu people were "Wu people" or "Wu citizens" (羽人或羽民) with the bird and animal totem worship. It was a discovery. The ancient peoples were all totem worship. Russian totem was the bear, the French totem was the Rooster. Mongolian nomads still worship the white wolf ... In general, with mankind, the totems were only, either birds or mammals. Particularly, the Lac Viet had two totem birds and animals, were symbolized as Fairy and Dragon. Here we recognized the deep relationship in the past. They were two parallel lines engraved on the grinding stons in Bac Son culture that archaeologists call "Bac Son signs". Many scholars interpreted it as a symbol of the concept of "dualistic parallel " (two in one - dual unit) of the Viet people. This view was reflected in the legend of Hong Bang (鴻龐) legend. At that time, because in Viet language, the consonants and tones were not distinguished and the sounds couldn't be determined, so maybe there were formats such as: Krong -> hồng -> sông -> long -> rồng (dragon). So Hồng means Dragon. But Hồng 鴻 letters in Hong Bang were the Bird and the Giang letters, so we can make the letters to name just water birds, such as goose, also called Hồng Hạc (flamingos). Hồng was so birds. So, in Hong Bang, Red Bird, was the symbol of the Fairy.

Similarly, the word Mang (龐) may be the transcription of mạng, mãng, vàng. We popularly call the snake is mãng xà, but with the ancient people, mãng and xà were the snakes.

Remember the story that Liu Bang killed the big white snake to startup the career then finally he was killed by the Snake princess Wang Mang. Mang is a snake. A snake is also a dragon. In choosing the square letters to write the phonetics of the ancient Viet language, the first people used the Mang letter 厖 with the meaning of Mãng. If connected to other distortions of Bang 龐, the meaning of dragon and snake of the Mang was clearer. Hence, Hong Bang meant the Bird and Snake, ie. Tien Rong (Fairy and Dragon). Maybe Hong Bang letters were carved on ceramics or armors from the Kinh Duong Vuong at Liangzhu capital. The thing has been lost so the next generations couldn't found. From above connections, it can be said: the owner of the Liangzhu culture was Hong Bang clan.

With four criteria: the time, the boundary, the capital and people as analyzed above, we can see, there were clear similarities between the Liangzhu state in archaeological findings and the Xich Quy state in the Viet legendary. Between the silent evidence exhibits laid deeply in the ground for thousands of years and the fragile oral stories during 5000 years in folk, which there were such similarities, they were very ideal. These evidences helped us to assert strongly:

The Liangzhu State in the archaeological findings was the Xich Quy state in the Viet legendary.

As data and materials etc about Liangzhu, about 2,200 years BC, due to sea level rise, the Liangzhu land was low so it was submerged. Liangzhu residents evacuated around, many groups went far, to Vietnam and other Southeast Asian islands. Several tribes stayed in the old land with the difficult life, struggled to make a living to survive. Almost all the material culture of the Liangzhu state was buried. Not only the tools of stone, jade, ceramic, but more important ones were the characters (scripts) engraved on pottery, stone and jade also were lost.

A few hundred years later, due to dry weather returned,

the water withdrew, residents around to find the place deserted, broken land, ditches off, established new villages. Due to the alluvial soil, irrigation of crops was favorable so the crop harvest was rich and led to a growing number of people coming. These tribes remembered their ancestors so they gradually created Maqiao Culture. Maqiao Culture was inherited from the Liangzhu culture, had absorbed elements of Liangzhu culture. However, the times were different, so they couldn't re-creared the typical Liangzhu culture at Maqiao. So in the Maqiao period the pottery was less fine, the model was relatively simple, and only a few kinds of poor quality jade, poor and simple carvings, less than the level of social productive forces in the Liangzhu culture.

Along with better environment, people gathered more increasingly, on the old Liangzhu land forming the three new nations as Viet (越), Wu (吳) and Chu (楚) are all Lac Viet, Liangzhu's former inhabitants.

In this period, the Xia dysnaty also expanded southward. As Chr wrote, a branch of the Xia dysnaty to Guiji (會稽), cut hair, painted in harmony with the local population, became the leader of the Viet's States. Then there were wars to promote the competition between Viet (越), Wu (吳) and Chu (楚) and then annexation of the Qin Dynasty. People and lands of the Xich Quy (赤鬼) nation stepped into the ancient Chinese history.

2. Emperor Li (帝来)'s State

Around 2879 BC, Emperor Ming divided Shennong state into two countries: a dynasty reigned by Emperor Li (Đế Lai) in the Yellow River basin, with the center was the Delta of the Source River. Yellow River basin is the center of economic and cultural development of the Lac Viet people with Jiahu agricultural culture in Neolithic 9,000 years ago, Yangshao culture in 7,000 years ago etc until the Neolithic Erlitou culture,

Lungsan culture. Since discovering the Erlitou culture, Lungsan culture, scientists said that they were the products of the Xia dynasty. But now, looking at a comprehensive landscape, it was the continuous development of the Liangzhu culture in the Yellow River basin. Meanwhile, the Xia, Shang dynasties were the foreign factors to settle and took ownership of the Viet culture. After the invasion of the Yellow Emperor in 2698 BC, Emperor Li was sacrificed, Emperor Li's state was disintegrated, but many local leaders continued to struggle for long time. Later it formed the states of U Viet or Duong Viet (Yangyue), co-existed with the Shang dynastis and Zhou dynasties.

3. State of Xich Quy (赤鬼)

Being divided the land, knighted, Kinh Duong King founded the Xich Quy state (赤鬼) with the north bordering with the Yangtze, the west bordering with Ba Shu, south to central Vietnam, east to the East Sea. Liangzhu was the capital.

Kinh Duong Vuong passed the throne to his son, Lac Long Quan. Lac Long Quan passed the throne to his eldest son, Hung Vuong. Hung Vuong changed state name to Van Lang. In 2300 BC, due to rising sea level, Liangzhu capital was submerged, Hung Vuong moved the capital to Changtoushan in Northwest of Dongtinghu.

4. Ba Shu State

Maybe later little time compared with above period, in the western part of East Asia continent included Ba Shu, Thailand and parts of Myanmar, the Ba Shu state formed and led by the legendary king Cancong to have strength against the encroachment of the nomadic tribes from the west.

How were the Ba Shu states formed were atill mystery of history, but the outstanding achievements of the Ba Shu is the Xanxing tui culture. Archaeology suggested that: "The Xanxing tui archaeological site was a walled city located in the northeast city of Nanxing, Guanghan, Chengdu area, Sichuan Province today, and was built about 1600 BC. Many archaeologists identified Xanxing tui culture associated with ancient Shu kingdom and associated artefacts found at the sites belonging to the legendary king of the Shu state ... According to the Huayang nation journal wrote about the Jin dynasty (晋, 265-420), the Shu kingdom was established by Cancong. "[3]

Regarding the scope of the Ba Shu nation of ancient Sichuan people, Huayang nation journal wrote, "Its land spread to Yufu in the east, west to Ba Chu. The northern connected with Hanzhong and the southern lasted until Qianfu ". Kingdom of Ba Shu used to cooperate with the Zhou dynasty to overthrow the Shang dynasty. Though it was destroyed by the Qin dysnaty in 316 BCE but local leaders stil stayed to conduct the strong resistance, when the conditions allowed, they established of the states against the domination of the Chinese dynasties. Ba Shu nation's last descendants were the mighty Nanzhao dynasty lasted until the the Yuan Dynasty.

5. Yellow Emperor Dynasty

Conceivably, no later than 3000 BC, among the Mongolian nomadic tribes in the North and the agricultural Viet people in the South of Yellow Rivers often ocurred the disputes. The Mongols crossed the rivers, robnbed the food, cattle and arrested people to be their slaves. Agricultural population of the south bank of the River always resisted these raids. 2698 BC, Xuan Yuan clan leaders allied nomadic tribes attacked Zhoulu, occupied the southern lands. After the victory, a new stage opened: Xuan Yuan clan chieftain became stronger with a mighty army, a wide territory. He had to turn his warriors into rulers, arrested the local population to become his soldiers, pay taxes, and do service work ... Of course, he became a king and was called as

Yellow Emperor - King of the the Loess Plateau. And so, the state of the Mongols was born. But once entered the immense mountain and river area with a large Viet population, Mongolian with the small population and the undeveloped culture, quickly was assimilated by the Viet people. The mixed blood of Viet and Mongolian people born Huaxia people, with a half-Viet blood and increasingly imbued by the Viet culture. Many documents show, that after three generations, from Yellow Emperor to Di Ku (帝嚳), Huaxia people replaced their Mongolian father to lead the dynasty. Due to the combined quintessence of two nomadic civilization and agriculture, Huaxia people created a Golden Age in the history of the East, from Yao, Shun to Shang and Zhou. When Zhou dysnaty was eliminated, Huaxia lost its social leadership role, dissolved in large Viet community of Qin Dynasty, Han dysnaty etc. These dynastic though were unrelated to blood of the Yellow Emperor but for the Huaxia glory of the past so it still identify themselves as Huaxia and being grandchildren of the Yan Emperor and Yellow Empeor. Over hundreds of years, due to the hidden history, so the world only acknowledged the Shang dynasty was the first country in the East was formed. The fact was, there would be not the Shang dynasty if there were not the previous earlier state of the Viet people on this land.

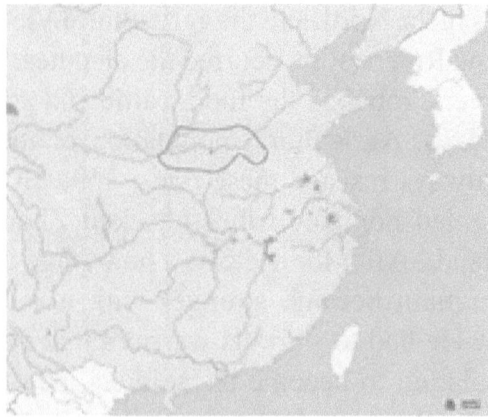

Xia state

II. The evidence from ancient books

The above was the history occured in the macro vision that only in today, thanked to new knowledge, we could see. However, we could also find traces of the ancient nations in the the ancient precious Chinese books.

- The Book of Documents (Shangshu尚書), Shun story 12 says: "Prohit the Xianmiao barbarians come to Xanwei land."

- Shun story 16: "Like that, though barnarina nations also must obey."

- Shun story 20: "Emperor said: Gaoyao! Barbarian Man di attacked Hua, many robbery invaders, many evils."

- Shun story 27: "To force Xinmiao barbarians had to move quite far away."

- Dayu 21: "In three weeks (30 days Youmiao barbarians still rebelled. Mr. Ich discussed with the Wu king, that only the virtue could touch the God though the God is far ahead. Who is complacent, he should be vulnerable; who is modest, he shall get the benefit; it is the Heaven's Rules? With the empathic heart can get the sympathy from the all the gods, not only the Youmiao barbarians.

- Yugong 36: "Outside the surrendered Zui region) 500 miles called "Yao" region. The Eastern Barbarian people resided in the nearly 300 miles. In 200 miles near there the slightly serious guilty sinners were exiled. "

- Yugong 37: "Outside the Yao region (surrendered Yêu) 500 miles, called "Wild" region. The Southern Barbarian people resided in the nearly 300 miles. In 200 miles near there, the serious guilty sinners were exiled. "

The first history book, recorded the important events of the Huaxia Dynasty, had to mention to suppress, assimilate the Man, Di people. Who the Man, Di people were? Two thousand years we did not know their origins. But now, from new knowledge, we understood that they were the Viet communities in long ago who mastered the mainland China. The resistance of the Viet people was the standing concern of the Chinese emperors. This said about the fact that, inside the Emperor's reign, there were the nations of the natives. These states had always opposed the invaders despite fierce oppression.

Zhou Yi says, "Gaozong of the En Dynasty (Yuting 1324-1266 BC) needed three years to win small Guifang country. The Guifang might be a small country of the Viet people in the South of Henan?

After Shangshu, Man, Di countries were never mentioned. However, we see them again in these pages from the Qin and later, with the name Bach Viet (Baiyue).

According Luoxianglin (罗香林) scholar, wrote in his book: 百越源流與文化 (The Origin and Culture of Baiyue) [4]:

"The Yuyue (於越), also was known as Vu Viet. When the Shang En dynasty was prevalent, Yuyue (於越) was restrained, was not very dormant. The Zhou dynasty appeared and it didnot strengthen the territory yet, on that occasion U Viet was rising in revolt. The Chr of Viet King Goujian writes: "Geographic magazine (輿地誌) said Viet throned almost 30 genarations, from the En dynasty to the Zhou Dynasty. In King wang period, there was a Viet Lord named Phu Hỗn, son of Doãn Thượng, expanded the land, proclaimed himself King." The Book of Bamboo Annals (竹書紀年, Zhushu jinian) wrote:" in 24th year of Zhou Chengtang King, U' Việt nation reformed". This showed that, during the early Zhou Dynasty, Viet nation had operated.

Tan nation sent messengers to offer things to the Emperor." This is the earliest documentation about Tan nation. In the Book of the Later Han Dynasty (Houhanshu, 後漢書) Nanman (南蠻) Xinanyi story, wrote: "In the Yungyuan 6th year (94), Rendunyi King of Khiếu ngoại county named Mộ Duyên Mộ Nghĩa sent the messengers to offer the rhinoceroses, large elephants. In the 9th year Khiếu ngoại man and Tan nation's Kinh namded Yongyou Tiao odered the servants to offer the treasures. "

One line of ethnic Viet, used to live in a strip of Burma today, created the Tan Nation. Tan nation's descendants distributed in Vietnam, Laos, Thailand and Burma nowadays. In the Later Han letter stated: "In the 9th year (97) of the Emperor Zhang Yongyuan, Tan nation sent the messengers to offer to the Emperor." This was the earliest documentation of Tan nation. In the Book of the Later Han Dynasty (Houhan shu, 後漢書) (Nan man) Xinanyi story: "In the Yongyuan 6th Year (94), Khieu Ngoai (Jiaowai) district, Rendunyi King sent the messengers to offer the rhinoceroses, buffalos and big elephants. In the 9th year Jiaowai man and Tan nation's King Yongyou Tiao ordered their servants to offer the precious and rare things. He above documents confirmed that, besides Shang and Zhou from Huaxia, there were the indigenous nations as U Viet (Yuyue, 於越), Ba, Shu etc. The problem now is to go back in time, find out how were these nations formed?

Ancient books wrote that Jiang Yuan, the Emperor Ku (Diku, 帝嚳)'s wife was the Thai ethnic people's daughter. This is evidence that, Thai people, a tributary of ethnic Viet have been here very soon. Access to more distant time, we know, Viet people from Indochina followed the west corridor to occupy Ba Shu land and continued to Shaanxi, Shanxi and midland Yellow, created the Yangshao culture. Thai clan may be descendants of those migrants. Delta of Source River (now the Central Highlands) in ancient time was the mountain and river, land (Jiangshan) of Ư Viet (Yuyue, 於越), people. Along with the line of the I Ching: "Fuxi surname faded, Shennong surname appeared", we had the legend that Fuxi created the I-ching (Classic of the Changes), Shennong taught peoplt to do the agriculture to plant the cereals. The legend that Ming Emperor, Shennong's grandchild in the 3rd generation, divided land, throned to Kinh Duong Vuong to set up the very deeply meaningful Xich Quy (Chigui, 赤鬼) nation.

Based on the legend and the rare inscription in ancient letters, we can imagine, in the third millennium BC, on the East Asian mainland existed at least three ancient nations: Emperor La's nation was in the Yellow River basin with the centered vast plain, fertile Trong Nguồn (In Source River delta). Kinh Duong Vuong's nation was in the basin of the Yangtze to Central Vietnam with Liangzhu was the center. Ba Shu nation was in the West, including Ba Shu land, Thailand, the Karen area of Burma.

References:

1. Vu Huu San. *North Viet Bay*, Republished 2004. Tripod.com.

2. Ha Van Thuy. Exploring the 6500 years old tomb of the Vietnamese in Henan China http://diendan.lyhocdongphuong.org.vn/bai-viet/33271-kham-pha-ngoi-mo-6500-nam-truoc-cua-nguoi-viet-o-ha-nam-trung-quoc/

3. Sanxingdui http://en.wikipedia.org/wiki/Sanxingdui

4. Lou Xiang Lin (罗香林) (Luoxianglin) scholar, 百越源流與文化 (The Origin and Culture of Baiyue), Chinese library. Taiwan bookshop, 1955. Handwritten translation of Vong Chi Nguyen Chi Vien.

CHAPTER IX

TWO CULTURES
ON THE CHINESE LAND

At Jiahu culture, they discovered in a ceramic vase keeping taste of honey and hawthorn were immersion in rice wine. From fragrance existing over 9000 years off, American scientists regenerated this olden wine. Wine was made from rice but the wine that was not rice any longer, it was the sublimated core and the soul of the rice. Thus, it was the essence, the core spirit ... alcohol was not easy to grasp, and still less easy to enjoy. So is the culture!

The bronze age replaces the stone era and the iron age replaces the bronze age ... humanity gradually was going up the ladder of evolution to today under the common roof Earth, the nations had gone to harmony in the electronic civilization. However, one thing was clear, though civilization was common but the nation being private. This nation was not mixed with other nations. What is the hallmark in order to each nation being its own? In other words, what made up a nation?

That was the culture, so that when lost it an ethnicity was no longer being it! Today, many people realized that culture was not only the identity but also the soul of the nation, was the arrow to guide nation in the arduous journey going to the future.

However, the culture was not naturally appeared. It was born only when the people community reached a certain progress on the road of evolution. The Westerners called cultivation is the culture and later, "culture" is also used to name the culture. That meant the culture was born only with farming. Though appeared later, the culture became the most important factor to lead the nation.

There was a thing that not many people thought of, that when there was no culture, so what led community? People didn't think much, because when we were born, the culture already was evident as the moon and stars, as close as the air to the point we never think from where culture appeared But it is impossible not to know if you want to go to the end of history.

From 70,000 years ago, after the long journey toward the sunrise, prehistoric people arrived in Viet Nam land. Due to natural conditions were governing, people settled and soon formed the society. And they also early raised the millet, rice paddy, chickens, dogs, pigs etc.

Settlement and doing the rice farming, Viet people had to care about the impact of the sun, moon, stars, rain, heat, cold, wind storms etc to their own lives and crops and livestock. From there, they had the conclusion that the man could only exist in harmonious relationship between the various elements of nature. This created that the oriental people to have the habit of the synthetic thinking that is respect for the relationship between the different factors of the environment.

On the other hand, agriculture soon formed and led to the important role of the mother, the woman in the clan. We could say, these two above traits were the genetic factors of the populations (fenotype) soon appeared and made the identity of the Oriental culture. When migrating to the America, Viet people had brought two such behaviors.

This was written by anthropologist Levi Strauss in the Sad

Tropical book: "The Caduevo aboriginal people in the northern Canadian habitually respected the women and the harmony between the different elements of the environment, similar to the South Chinese people. "

From synthetic thinking methods, Viet people realized the universe was made up of two elements i.e Yin and Yang: "One Yin one Yang was tao." Yin was static, negative. Yang was dynamic and positive. Although dynamic and static, positive and negative were opposite but both were inseparable from the harmonious unity in the same thing. Even on the most pristine new stone tool, we saw that Hoa Binh people were carve into it two parallel lines which archaeologists called as Hoa Binh sign.

That is the imprint encoding the original cosmic view of the Vietnamese: The universe exists in harmony between Yin and Yang, or is the double coincidence. From economic prosperity and wisdom such depth, until 4000 BC, people in East Asia had reached agricultural culture flourished in the world.

But more than 2,000 years past, that essence of Viet culture was located in Jing, Shu of the Chinese sages. This mades not only in East Asia but all humans believed, that wisdom arose from China and taught to other peoples.

Half a century ago, from the deeply researching on Oriental culture, through archeology, history and decoding legends, Philosopher Kim Dinh discovered that, because exploited China sooner, the Viet people had built the rice agricultural culture and the wisdom, which he called primitive Confucianism or Viet Confucianism on the China land. Occupying the land of the Viet people, Huaxia people learnt from the Viet people's culture and the saints as the Mr. Zhou, Confucius to summarize as Jing, Shu.

But then, due to the nomadic nature, to the turning point of the history, Chinese people took the path of civilization of their nomadic ancestors to deprave Viet Confucianism, became kingship Confucianism to suppress the common people and women, expanded the invasion to its neighbors. Thus, the East Asian culture existed in the confusion between the Primitive Confucianism and the decadent Confucianism.

The task of today is to distinguish, to separate the two Confucianism types to build the world's future culture. So here, before going deeply into the Chinese culture, we presented the basic features of Viet Confucianism.

II. Viet Confucianism, primitive culture of the East

In the famous fable of Aesop, there was a story that Aesop challenged his opponent to separate the river water from the seawater. Naturally his opponent lost. More than 2,000 years, the mankind was mistake when admitted: the great Chinese culture was the Han people's products. Only with his transcendent genius, Philosopher Kim Dinh, the first time shown that the Chinese culture began with the Viet ethnic's culture, the first owner of the Chinese land.

It was not just the too strange new issue but also it seemed paradoxical, so half a century had passed, it was still unfamiliar to the majority of humanity. Because the problem was too big, outside the scope of this book so here we only mentioned the primary focus.

According to Philosopher Kim Dinh, Viet Confucianism had the following characteristics:

1. The concept of the universe with three Yangs and two Yins. "One Yin and One Yang is Tao (道)! Yin and Yang, they are Tao -道 – the way! That Tao is the nature, and also the operation of the universe. It is true that Yin and Yang to make up the Tao. But the "Tao" that is circulating in the universe, how much is the Yin, with how much is the Yang? If it is static equilibrium with one Yin (-1) + one Yang (+1), the cosmic shall be eliminated, and it does not exist! In fact, the universe operates in an upward

direction, positive, which means the Yang dominates. But how much is that domination?

Oriental wise people realized that Yin and Yang's harmonious movement was within figure of 5: Yang + Yin = 5 = numbers of universe! But the question was, in that universe number, how many Yang and how many Yin? Only two answers: Either Yang 4, Yin 1 or Yang 3, Yin 2! It was two choices of people for development. Oriental wisdom realized 3 Yang + 2 Yin was the gold number of operating universes.

The life has been going on, growing, the Yang, but that is part of the Yang, the Sun is three, and the Land, the mother is two parts, will reach the highest harmony. Awareness of this great secret of the universe, but the East was not rigid when they said "three Yangs two Yins" that stated at wisdom "*tham thiên lưỡng địa*": true is 3/2 there but is not the rigid mathematical relationship which it is a correlated dialectic: at 3 but sometimes slightly greater or smaller than 3, to ensure the dynamic manner of development.

Such notions of oriental people were different with that of western concepts. From the hunters-gatherers, became the nomads and respected the movement, western conception was active life, fully exploiting natural and the competitive survival.

In the eyes of the Westerners, the universe and the life operated in proportion Yang four, Yin one. It was a hot growth, finally breaking the balance of nature and society, cause the catastrophic for nature and people.

2. Human's Concept: Human is the Owner, extrem Harmony and Spirituality.

From rice farming culture contemplated the human and the universe, the Oriental sage finds that the universe composed of 3 factors: The Heaven (天), Land (地) and Human (人), in which the Human (人) is central, owner.

As the owner of the universe, humans maintained the harmony relationships with universe as well as with others. And once people have become the owner and harmony thus it was human of spirituality, could be empathy, inspiration with the supernatural world.

3. Viet An Vi Tao

To survive in such a relationship with the universe and the fellows, humans needed to enforce the Tao An vi (tao an wei 安为导). Contrary with "Huu vi" (you wei 有为), meant all activities were the profit, so to be scrambled, appropriated. In contrast to "Vo vi" (wu wei 无为), it meant negative, without dreams, desires, and indifference, isolating with the world etc.

"An vi" (安为) is a way to live wholeheartedly positive, not by the impulse of self-interest, but by the necessity of mutual interest. While Westerners work and create for personal interests, the Oriental people also work and create with all the best for the mutual interest in the passion of joy and honor.

4. Average mechanism (平产)

Three nuclear elements existed by standing on the average mechanism (平产). It is a mechanism to ensure optimal fairness on income distribution. Not is the egalitarianism because no one has full rights to distribute the wealth, that is the average mechanism (平产) to reach the relative fairness in the community.

In memory of the East, it also recorded the dividing the assets in the ancient times, which is the "jing tian 井田": The community co-operated to break the waste land, people trying to make into square field, then divided into nine equal parts. Eight families cultivate eight pieces around and join hands to take care of the middle field, called "jing tian 井田". The part harvested from "jing tian 井田" was submitted to the King.

After this, the average mechanism was switched to "public field". Until 1945 in Vietnam, there was still 20% of the "public field", every three years, the village devided to the poor people for cultivation.

In the Oriental cultural diversity today, finding out four attributes of Viet Confucisim culture was the great contribution of Philosopher Kim Dinh. Thanked to the distinction, thanked to the finding out this source, future generations will determine the target for Eastern cultural renaissance, led humanity on the move.

II. The existence of the two cultures

The four factors are the nuclear of the Viet people's agricultural cultural wisdom. The question is on the land of China, how the culture had formed and developed?

We see that, the Neolithic culture on Chinese land had the same features, they had been living in settlements, and cultivation was the main, associated with livestock and hunting. Along with the grindstone standard kits with axes, hammers, shovels, hoes, chisels, knives, sickles, grinding table and farming tools were made of bone. The pottery included pots, jars, bowls, cups, vases etc although somewhat different in style but all were made of clay mixed with charcoals or husks. In large sites, they also found a significant amount of jade. Thus, we can say, the new rock culture in East Asia and China, was unified culture, in other words, the same culture.

But the cultures in the Bronze Age were different between Yellow River basin and the rest of China. At the Bronze cultural relics in Central Highlands, they found that the Bronze tools simulated the Stone Age tools. They were the three-legged pots, drinking cups and more popular as copper axes, copper hammers. The bronze axes and hammers replaced the stone axes and hammers.

Being the farming tools, the copper hammers and axes were also the effective weapons. But the axes and hammers were also represented the authority of leaders and royalty. Besides, here appeared the copper cauldrons, "ting 鼎" brasses were both the worship things, but also symbolized the authority of the leaders. Clearly, Bronze culture had inherited the tradition from the Neolithic culture enhanced the roles of the hammer.

Clear distinction of Zhongyuan culture with the remaining area, were here there were things made of bronze mixed with tin, while outside Zhongyuan the bronze tools of Van Lang, Ba Shu were mixed with not only tin, but also lead. Notably in this area appeared the traces of wooden wheels and typical tools of nomadic civilization. It could say that, in Bronze Age, in the Yellow highland, the factors of nomadic civilization appeared.

Meanwhile, in the remaining areas of China, was basically the same contract with the Central Highlands, which meant that the majority was the simulation of the Neolithic tools but swords instead of hammers as superiority weapons. Especially the bronze drums appeared as a kind of sacred instruments in worship, the music instrument and symbolizing of the leader's authority. In copper products, in addition to tin, the addition of lead was also characteristic of the South.

Thereby, we can see, to the Bronze Age, in the East formed two cultures. While the majority was still the traditional agriculture culture, in Yellow River valley appeared another civilization. Try to see what this civilization was?

Study Chinese history, we found:

Around 2698 BC, a great variation occurred, it was the invasion of the Xuan Yuan clans into southern of Yellow River. Living in the basin of the Yellow River, the southern agricultural people for thousands of years had suffered many pillages by the invasion of the northern nomads.

With the determination to open a living way to the south, many Mongolian clans allied into powerful forces. The big victory in the Zhoulu battle, the Mongolia led by Xuan Yuan clan occupied the Loess Plateau, established the Yellow Emperor dynasty. Chinese legend said that Yellow Emperor was in the tribal alliance led by Yan Emperor. When strengthened, Yellow Emperor defeated Yan Emperor in Fanquan (阪泉之战), won the league's hegemonic position. Then, Chiyou in the Yan Emperor tribe caused the treason. Yellow Emperor dispatched the troop and defeated Chiyou at Zhoulu. Legend has told that Yellow Emperor and Yan Emperor were brothers and the Chinese were their descendants.

In legend there was partially true: Zhoulu battle at the south of Huang River and Huaxia people were Yellow Emperor and Yan Emperor's descendants. But there were things to be processed according to a certain psychological trend. In fact, south of the Yellow River was the oldest residence of Viet people, often was invaded and pillaged by the nomadic Mongolians in the north. Zhoulu was a devastating battle. After the victory, the Mongols occupied the southern Yellow River and established the Yellow Emperor dynasty.

Yellow Emperor reigned from 2698 to 2599 BC and then passed to Shaohao (2598 - 2525 BC); Shaohao throned to Zhuanxu (2514 - 2436 BC), also known as the Qiandi in the North, surnamed Gaoyang. Zhuanxu throned to Emperor Ku (帝 譽, Diku) (2412 - 2343 BC), Emperor Ku (帝譽, Diku) throned to Emperor Yao (Diyao) (2337 - 2258 BC) and then Yao throned to Shun etc.

Looking the above genealogy, we saw something unusual: from a nomadic leader specialized in horseback riding, archery battle for conquest and plunder in the north bank of the Yellow River, downwards south more than 300 years, the descendants of next 4- 5 generations later became the saints of agricultural culture! A question arose: what created this miraculous change? I thought there were two reasons.

It is easy to see that, it was the mix-blood to create a new class: Huaxia people. If the Yellow Emperor, Shaohao and Zhuanxu were the Northern Mongoloid then Diku was a Viet ethnic's Southern Mongoloid. Not only the black skin of African ancestry but also a Viet name, name of the cormorant. Yao Emperor was more Viet. There might have occurred a situation like this: after the march of the Yellow Emperor, many Mongolian nomadic tribes swept through the river to occupy the land, lived with the brave Viet villages. All were expanding their land should not long after, a barrier was created, preventing the nomads from the north down. So, in the south, in the long time, there were no more Mongol residents. And with the meager number of intruders, the Mongols quickly mix-blood with the Viet, to born the Huaxia people, then they became the leading force of the kingdom.

The second reason: Huaxia was descendants of the Yan Emperor and Yellow Emperor, drank the Viet mother's milk, learned the voices, lifestyle, habits of the Viet. Because the human was born with the natural goodness, so Huaxia people were imbued with the goodness of Viet culture. Viet's ethnic qualities associated with the elite of the nomadic civilization gave birth to the saint as Yao, Shun to create Golden Age in Chinese history. After Yao, Shun, Golden Age ideas are transmitted through the Xia, Shang and Zhou, creating the splendid Chinese civilization.

In the documentation quoted above, scholar Zhou jixu commented:

"History was written in the traditional documents that the only to consider from when Yellow Empror's people entered the Yellow River valley and developed the civilization there. Those who had previously lived and created the glorious pre-historic civilization of the two rivers (the Yellow and Yangtze) were sunk after the fog of the history. They were excluded from the traditional annals, which covered almost all the history books of China, from Shangshu, Jijing to Chr etc. This was a history with the trend to reverse the location between host and guest. One reason for this situation was that the oppression and the exclusion by the strong Emperor's party. "

That was an insightful comment. But if we wanted to understand that statement, we needed to examine other incidents took place near thousand years later. It was the invasion of the Arian from Persia to invade the Indian land. With battle-mighty and civilized force, with Sancrit letters, Brahman religion and social caste system, Arian people practiced to destroy the Dravidian indigenous people and enslaved the natives, expelled them down to the south. In the occupied lands, they imposed to Brahman religion, with Vedas and the supreme authority of the clergy class and carried out adequately enforce prohibition of the external marriage, kept the pure Arian blood. This had changed the history and culture of India, turned the subcontinent into an agricultural production society but the superstructure was typical of nomadic civilization, created the separation of ethnic and religion that were cruel and persistent throughout the history.

Different with the Arian people, though the Mongolian people were combative, but the population was less and the culture was low. When entering in the land of Viet people, they saw the vast land, the rich economy, the large population, the high culture, the strong resistance fought against them. Therefore, the invaders had the appropriate behavior: they did not occupy too much land, did not force the people into slavery... They let the natives plow on their land and accepted to join in army, pay the taxes and serve the labor. Mongolian people ruled, traded and developed the industry. The Mongols did not prohibit the marriage with the natives. And the mix-blood progeny class was born, self-identify as Huaxia people.

Living in the communities where the majority was the Viet people, Huaxia people studied the Viet voice and Viet culture same time studied the ruling ways of their Mongolia fathers. At first, when there were not many people, they did not have a significant role in society. After the Yellow Emperor and Zhuanxu, Shaohao were Mongols, the kingship was moved to Diku, a Huaxia person. After Diku was Dizi. But because of incompetence, Dizi was deposed, the kingship passed to another son of Diku named Yao, in 2337 BC. Yao used the moral values, built the peaceful era on Central delta soil. Then Yao passed his throne to Emperor Shun. Continuing the moral foundation of King Yao, Shun had done many good things for the people and passed his throne to Xiayu.

King Xiayu continued to implement rule of virtue, had a great contribution and brought happiness to the Chinese people. Yu didn't throne to the sage. He passed throne to his son named Qi. The Xia Dynasty lasted from 2205 to 1767 BC. Yao, Shun, Yu lasted 1205 years. The Golden Age started from Yao, Shun and achieved the highest level of development in the Chu. In this time, the Viet's intellectuals with the Huaxia intellectuals improved the writing on animal bones and tortoise plastrons into writing on bamboo cards and silks for writing the Shangshu, the folk songs in the Jijing, Yijing and the Lejing, Lijing etc.

In the end of the Chu dynasty, humanism formed by virtue of Yao, Shun faded, the Mongol wolf nomadic blood flow hidden in veins of several leaders was no longer be restrained, brought them back to the greed, with aspirations to dispute and reave. Fierce battles erupted, pushed China into the Warring States, which led to the establishment of the Qin notorious brutality state. By burning the books, burying pupils, the Viet humanity culture was dead on the formal aspect. Continue the institutional Qin, Han Dynasty, the Confucian turned into the tools of the kingship for the absolute monarchy loyal advocates, highly patriarchal, suppressing women and ethnic minorities. After the Han Dynasty, due to historical circumstances, many millions of nomads came from the northern minority tribe to settle and dominate China. The northern nomadic people implemented the consecutive invasion and dominated, led China increasingly going into thoughts of nomadic civilization. And then under the rule of the Yuan, the Qing, China went deeper into the brutal greed vices.

It was *an upside-down history position between host and guest*. However, it was not the strong coterie of the Emperor but it was the talent of the leaders by learning successful agricultural Viet ethnic culture, along with Viet people to build the best golden age in history, bringing the glory for the Huaxia people. Due to the same of ethnicity and culture, the huge Viet population also brought the pride for the Huaxia.

The Yellow Emperor dynasty rulers understood the Huaxia' s biracial origin, they encouraged the Mongolian-Viet blood-intermixing. Not only that, they made the Vietnamese people be pleased by acknowledging the Huaxia people were descendants of Yandi and Hoangdi and worshipped the Viet's ancient ancestors from Suiren, to Fuxi, Shennong.

This success was so great that it was enchanting many Viet tribes which there were no any blood relationship with the Emperor, typically, the Qin, an ethnic Viet, during the time the Xia, Shang, Zhou was considered as Xiyi but when became the owner of Zhongyuan, they also self-called as the Huaxia. The Han also were Viet independent tribes living on the Hanshui basin. But when overthrowing the Qin, both Liubang (劉邦) and his Viet people also called themselves as Huaxia!

Thus, if being fair, the Chinese history and culture should be told as follows:

On the long-standing culture of Viet ethnic, in Bronze Age, the Huaxia people appeared. Being the Mongolia-Viet crossbred, born from the invasion of the Yeloow Emperor, Huaxia people studied the agricultural apprenticeship, voice, handwriting and abundant agricultural cultures of Viet people, i.e they became the Viet people both in term of genetic and culture. Due to receiving the elite elements of the two cultures, the Huaxia people conquered the large population Viet under its leadership, built the Chinese brilliant civilization. With such thinking, Chinese culture was not to usurp the culture of predecessor but it was the culture of a part of the Viet population that built.

Of course, there was a large part of Viet people was appropriated. They were Viet tribes that were not in the Chinese empire. Though keeping the ancestral lands, but they were often invaded by the Chinese dynastic aggression. They were also deprived of writing letters and the culture created by their ancestors. This fact was especially true with Vietnamese people, with nearly thousand years under the Chinese domination, was appropriated both handwriting and voice! Also, it had to mention the Viet people living in China under the ethnic, cultural oppression throughout history.

III. The limitations of Chinese civilization

Huaxia people absorbed the factors of Viet agricultural civilization including the voice, hieroglyphs and philosophical ideas in the texts of Viet Confucianism and thereby built the Chinese civilizations. However, being only the heirs so the Huaxia people and then their descendants could not understand the essence of Viet ethnic's agricultural culture.

Firstly, due to the Chinese language changed too fast towards nomadic trends, many words from ethnic Vietnamese were lost. They could not read and did not understand the words that were symbolized by the square literal characters of the ancient people. Since then, many of the ancient texts that later Chinese scholars could not read well, forced to replace it with the temporary means to the readers. This was seen in Shijing, Taotejing (道德經), Chuzi of Qu Yuan and from the many other texts as Yuerenge (越人歌, The Viet people's song) or Wei Jia Ling (维甲令, the order/command of Goujian) that cited in the previous chapter.

Also, due to being the heirs and the plunder that were not true creative owner so the Chinese people had so far struggled in the universal theory of the Five Elecments, a misconception about the Five Elements, thereby leading to the mistaken while decoding the Yijing and Horoscopes faculty.

So far, many contradictions in the theory of Five Elements, in Yijing was detected but Chinese scholars could not explain in a convincing way and still maintain the doubt. Another paradox was that so far, Chinese people did not know who the creators of the Yijing.

CHAPTER X

REWRITING THE CHINESE HISTORY

In Spring 2005, by publishing the essay: Finding again the ancestral origin, the cultural origin, we put the first steps to find the prehistory of the Viet people. This spring was coming, it turned round 10 years, more than a hundred articles and three books: Finding the origin of Viet culture (Literature Publishing House, 2006), Journey to find the source (Literature Publishing House, 2008) and Finding the origin through genetics (Literature Publishing House, 2011) were born. It could say, that the deepest secrets of Viet cultural history ever sunk in deep darkness were brought before the light days.

Something unexpected was while going deeper into Viet people's history, in my minds, the issue of Chinese cultural history gradually was being clarified out. However, it was not as a history as what the world knew, but the truth was opposite! Naturally, a question appeared: Why not rewrite the history of China? After laughing at my extravagant mind, I told myself: Yes, why not?

It was true, that China was a great culture. China had a long history. Chinese people were proud of 24 national historic volumes. And China also had a lot of big Confucians. But today if someone asked the Chinese people: who were your ancestors? Where did your voice come from? Who created your handwriting letters? And who created the I-ching (Book of Changes), the pride of China? I believed that all could only be the awkward silence! Ultimately, these questions did not get the answers not only with Chinese people but even the great scholars in the world! They couldn't be answered so far, because most of the wise men knew only Chinese history from the Qin Han periods and later. A limited period compared to the seemingly endless immensity of the ancient wild time. Yes, ancient wild time, but it was the most important point, the most decisive historical progress of all peoples because it was the first time.

So what should we write when rewriting the Chinese history?

On September 29, 1998, it marked a great milestone in the humanity history, when American scholars in the Project of Genetic Relationship of Populations in China, the first time, with the solid scientific evidence, published that Homo sapiens species were born from the only African homeland 160,000 years ago. Approximately 70,000 years ago, prehistoric man from Africa, along to the Indian Ocean coast arrived in Vietnam. Around 40,000 years ago, as the climate was improved, people migrated from Vietnam to China. The information shocked the scientists because it totally rejected the Multiregional theory of human origins that dominated in the twentieth century. By reliance on anthropological, the history of the Orient nation was oriented follow this theory, as compliance a scientific proposition. Not a few cases, scholars modified history data and bended archeological findings, the cultures to fit the theoretical directions.

In the East, the effects of the seismic were more tumultuous. Because the Oriental Studies of the French School of the Far East were dominated by notions of Multi-regional theory, had built on the notion the human civilization from Mesopotamia to Europe and from here, spread to Central Asia then to China, finally from China came to Southeast Asia. Historic books of most of the peoples of the East, including China wrote as that way.

Now, when theory that base on this postulate collapsed, of course, many history books lost their value, forced to be rewritten.

What the Chinese history should re-write? According to my narrow opinion, first of all there were following big problems:

1. About the Chinese origin

They were not the God's children, of course, the Chinese were not the descendants of the Yuanmou or Zhoukoudian people. Because, the Homo erectus, our predecessor species, extinct in Asia from 250,000 years ago. Chinese ancestors were not the Indo-European people from the west coming as "the most significant discoveries in modern history" of scholar Zhou Jixu. That was, of course, because 93% of Chinese people didnot carry the genetic codes of the Indo-Europian race, but they belonged to the Southern Mongoloid race.

Following the footsteps of pre-historic people, many genetic studies discovered that, 135,000 years ago, humans carried out the first immigration out of Africa towards the sundown. Unfortunately, after more than 40,000 years lived in the Middle East then 90,000 years ago, all buried in the ice of Levent area. 85,000 years ago, people made the second voyage, in the opposite direction, toward the Sunrise. Going means to live. It took 15,000 years, pre-historic people from Africa put their first steps on the East Sea shelf of Vietnam today. So after more than 200,000 years of the Homo erectus people's absence, Asia received the Homo sapiens. Well, Homo sapiens went to Vietnam but who they were? Geneticists did not take care about this. Through the survey more than 70 ancient skulls in Vietnam, anthropologist said, there were two big races: Australoid and Mongoloid. On the Vietnam land, the cradle of all Asian peoples, Australoid and Mongoloid races had mixed their blood born the four strains of the ancient Viet people: Indonesian, Melanesian, Vedoid and Negritoid.

In which, the Indonesian people were the majority, spoken the ancient Viet language, took the leadership role of the Viet community in the society and the culture. As the arrangement of the Creator, while the majority of the Mongoloid people mixed blood with Australoid, there were other Mongoloid groups lived separately and quietly in the northwest of Indochina. And 40,000 years ago, when a northern climate was improved, people from Vietnam land went to explore the China. The Mongoloid went to the North of China.

A mystery of nature that we could not understand, why people from more favorable place moved to the more difficult places with aimless footsteps? But today we must respectfully bow before the great exodus. Not only being the owners of the mainland, the Viet people had gone towards the west, crossed the Tibetan plateau, went to Central Asia to dominate the Europe. Here they mixed blood with white Europid race from the Middle East up and born the European ancestors.

Not just giving the Viet blood for Europeans, our ancestors left to our white skin and blue eye descendants many Viet words such as: sạn, cát -> sand; bí bầu, người -> people; nak, nước -> water etc. From China, towards the North, Viet people overcame the Bering strait to explore the Americas.

From Vietnam, our ancestors accrossed through Burma into India subcontinent, left the descedants latter called the Dravidian people, the creators of the Indus culture.

Owner of ax (viet) grinding pebbles, the most advanced tools of humanity at that time, our ancestors called themselves the Viet people. On Chinese land, Viet people created the innovative new stone culture with early agricultural culture and the most brilliant in the planet ...

Around 5000 BC, on Chinese land, an important event occurred, as in the Yangshao cultural area, the contact took place between the Australoid Viet people and the Northern Mongoloid. From there, the Southern Mongoloid race were born in the South of the Yellow River and increased fast the number.

Around 2698 BC occurred the invasion of nomads in South Yellow River and established the Yellow Emperor dynasty. So far, there was no final answer to determine who invasion was? Scholar Zhou Jixu thought that they were Indo-European people coming from the West. But Southern Mongoloid blood of the Han people, 93% of the Chinese population had rejected this thought.

If the Indo-European people entered into the Loess Plateau, they could not generate the Southern Mongoloid people. There were very, very many other people thought that it was the Han. But the archaeological found that it was not so. At the time of the invasion occurred, in the north and west of China, did not have the Southern Mongoloid people. That meant at that time the Han was unborn yet! The Hongshan culture's owners of Inner Mongolia were the northern Mongolia race. Therefore, occupying the Loess Plateau only could be the North Mongoloid people. And the Huaxia people were born from this invasion, by the Northern Mongoloid people mixed blood with the native South Mongoloid people. Thus, after 2698 BC, in the Yangshao culture of China, the Southern Mongoloid people born. Previous archaeology and later was the genetics that discovered: The Southern Mongoloid people appeared from Chinese land and expedited the process of Mongolization the populations of East Asia. Until 2000 years BC, the majority of East Asian populations was transformed into Southern Mongoloid race.

There was one thing that after much reflection, I have not

found a convincing answer: Why could Huaxia people achieve such a big role in the history of China? Being born later, the population was not much, but why Huaxia soon became the Leader of the crowded Viet people? From the Xia, through the Shang, to the Zhou, the Huaxia people occupied only a small of land between the vast Viet land

But why the Qin dynasty, a dynasty of Viet people, after defeating the six states, self claimed it to be Huaxia? With the Han dynasty, it was even more confusing. Both Liu Bang and Xiang Yu were Chu people, a powerful nation of Viet people, equivalent with the Zhou dynasty, to the end of the Zhou, it was independent state. So why defeating Qin dynasty and established its dynasty, Han also self called as Huaxia? Oddly, the only female Emperor Wu Zetian of China, while ruling the Huaxia nation, she used her Viet name. When at home, her name was Mi Nuong, commonly used name of the Viet aristocratic daughters. When being the King, she self-called as Viet Co Kim Luan Holy Emperor (越古金轮圣神皇帝) and from Tu Thi Viet Co Kim Luan Holy Emperor of the Tu family of ancient Viet ethnic (慈氏越古金轮圣神皇帝). It was worth noting that, in respect of her name, Wu Zetian used the "Viet Co" (ancient Viet) word with the main element was front and the auxiliary element was after, without using Co Viet as in Huaxia parlance! It was clear that while self-calling as Huaxia and ruling the Huaxia state, the Emperor did not forget her Viet origin!

How was this explained? In the folk words, the Huaxia people were the Mogolian people's agnation grandchildren and the Viet people's maternal grandchildren. Huaxia people proved their filial piety when they recognized the Viet people's legendary kings as Suiren (燧人), Fuxi, Shennong as their ancestors, while learning the Viet voice and Viet culture. It could be said, they were born in Viet land, in the heart of the Viet community, breastfeed from the Viet mothers, so the Huaxia people imbued with Viet ethnic culture and same time received from their Mogolian fathers the dynamic, creative, courageous, assertive spirit, so the Huaxia soon replaced their Mogolian fathers and led the Viet populace. By combining elements of the two cultures, among Huaxia leaders appeared Emperor Yao and Emperor Shun then created the Golden Age in Chinese history. Spirit of the Yao, Shun transmitted to Wu King and the Thang King. Succeeded the Shang dynasty, the Zhou dynasty acquired the Viet writing letters and created the brilliant dynasty in the history of the East.

That very nice thing attracted Confucius when he chose to follow the Zhou! Thus, might be to the Western Zhou, Huaxia was the best, the dream for everyone? It was the glory of the Golden Age of Yao Shun gave the Huaxia people the credibility in front of crowded Viet people. And by the same race, it was an important element making Viet people also self-called them as Huaxia!

So much later, the leadership role of Huaxia was maintained. End of Zhou period, because of the historical variability and the "wild strength" of the nomadic civilization of Huaxia leaders emerged, created the fierce fights, pushed the Chinese society into the Warring States period, led to the despotic monarchy. Chinese culture from the culture of Viet Confucious transformed into Han Confucious, Song Confucious.

This proved that the "gentleman" or "wild strength" was not by race but was determined by the culture. Same were the Viet people, but in the culture of the South would be "gentleman." When living in an atmosphere of civilized nomads will become "wild strength"!

2. Origin of the Chinese language

So far, the international philologist still followed the standpoint of Bernhard Karlgren Swedish scholar supposed that Chinese language belonged to the Sino-Tibetan language family.

However, throughout the twentieth century, they did not find the original language of the so-called Sino-Tibetan language (Proto-Sino-Tibetan)! This make the classification of the Chinese voice into Sino-Tibetan family was still an unproven hypothesis. The work would become clear when discovered that the ancestors of Chinese people were the people from Vietnam who had gone up in the long historical process.

As going up to the China, the Viet people carried their languages. Origin of the Viet people were Hoa Binh and Thanh Hoa, Nghe An, Ha Tinh, so the voice of these places was the oldest. When going to the Yangtze basin, firstly Viet people resided in Guangdong, Guangxi area. Then dominated the north bank of the Yangtze and then scattered throughout China.

Because living in areas where the terrain and land, climate was different, so the voice also segregated into many regional voices. Several tribes in western also contacted with nomads so they also learned the Mongol parlance with auxiliary element was front and the main element was after. The Mongols occupied Yellow River midlands and brought the Mongol parlance to impose on this area. Thus, the *Chinese language was the Viet words that were spoken by Mongol parlance.*

In the course of history, the Viet language was changed the umlauts in the speaking way of nomads making the language become manifold; people in different regions could not understand each other. Therefore, at Zhou dynasty, the imperial court advocated to take the voice of Guangdong region as the standard language, called elegant language (Yayu 雅語), applied to the entire kingdom. Later, Qin Han also took Cantonese as the standard language.

Next, due to turbulent history, the peoples in the West, North invaded, brought their voices to mix, made the Chinese language changed and became far more the Viet origin. Modern linguistics classified the Chinese language into the Sino-Tibetan family based on the reading of the Qing Dynasty's Mandarin speech with the auxiliary element was front of and the main element was after (adverbs, adjectives precede, the subject and predicate after).

But it could not find any original Sino-Tibetan language (proto-Sino-Tibetan) because there was never any language like that. Using the folk modern Cantonese language to track the Chinese language original could not be successful, because the original Chinese language was a dialect region of Nghe An, Ha Tinh on Vietnam land.

The traceability of the Chinese language was neccessary, but perhaps also was necessary that to use the existing ancient Viet language in the Dongyue (東越), Minyue, Taiwan, Hainan and Vietnam communities in an attempt to rediscover the meaning of many words altered to read correctly the Shujing or Shijing (诗经), Tao Te Ching (道德經) etc. From then, to restore the original meanings of these precious ancient Viet texts. On the other hand, it was also very necessary to compose the Lac Viet (Luoyue) great dictionary etc.

3. Origin of Chinese writing letters

Chinese characters origin was a matter of great interest of Chinese scholars and the world. However, so far there was no any convincing conclusion. The reason for such a situation was an important part that the scholars' prejudice thought that the Chinese culture was the culture of Huaxia, arising from the North. Therefore, the Chinese documents and the world just stopped from the fact that the Oracle bone script (甲骨文) characters appeared in the En dysnaty and they did not go further to find the root.

But no one found the ridiculous thing: in Central Highlands, the Xia dynasty did not have the writing letters. More than half of the Shang dynasty also did not have the writing characters.

But from when King Bangang left the Yan land to En land, then the writing characters appeared not only a great number but also the strangest thing that was the mature characters! It was true magic! So what made this magic? I was difficult to answer, or they did not want the real answer? A tree must have the original root before the top.

Archaeology discovered the Jiahu characters. Although they were the individual characters but due to their iconic similarities with the Oracle bone script or modern Chinese. Thus, despite not finding any important conclusions but it could not deny that there was a correlation: what simplicity in Jiahu could be the origin! From the Ming Dynasty, they had found the writing characters of the Shui clan. But because of preconceptions "the Chinese was the Center", they hastily said that they were the Chinese characters without any serious researches. In fact, because of its simplicity, because of the way its written was contradictory with the Kanji showing that it had a relationship with the speaking way of the Viet people and certainly predated the Enxu oracle bone script. But minded chauvinist could not believe that the Lac Viet people, ancestors of the Shui tribes living in obsolete, savage states in mountainous Guizhou area, had such civilization! Therefore, they only considered it as a child of Chinese characters. That would be alright on both the academic and politic aspects! But the reality was often stubborn, disobeyed the subjective will of the man, so in December 2011, in Gansang Guangxi appeared the letters on the stone shovels of the Lac Viet people. Archaeology had revealed the formation of Chinese characters. Maybe it was even more complex and interesting, but the simplest diagram would be: latest 9000 years ago, the Viet people created the first characters in Jia Hu culture. 3000 years later, about 6000 years ago, the Gansang characters appeared with noted records of divination. Also, during this period, the same hieroglyphs appeared in Liangzhu (良渚) culture.

A tribe of the Lac Viet kept these characters and created into the Shui characters, a kind of living fossil characters. Lac Viet texts in Gansang posted to the In Source (Zhungyuan now) area, Henan area today, a great cultural center of Dương Viet people and upgraded into the Oracle bone script. When occupying the En land, King Bangang learned and developed this kind of writing characters.

One thing should be clear: why the Chinese language is monosyllabic? In the speech "Effect of Yijing to Chinese culture" at the Peak cultural forum in Beijing on 03.09.2004, Nobel Professor Duong Chan Ninh said that "the Yijing used the monosyllabic words so the Chinese language was monosyllabic, too." In my idea, that was an illogical, the fact was contrary. The process of language phoneme not only appeared in the Chinese language, but also in Korea, Japan and Vietnam. The reason why the incident occurred and how, so far unsolved! We believed that it happened after the square letters appeared.

This process occured as follows: Due to square letters were single-letters, unable to make the syllables, so when using for the voice's phonetic transcription, each word only was used for one sound. Thus, polyphonic sound must rid one or two sounds for only a typical sound. And so, when the scripts developed, the voice became monosyllabic. It was monosyllabic word appeared before in the life and were used to write the Yijing making the words in Yijing were monosyllabic. This was also evidence that, the Koreans, the Japanese were also the Viet people. In the words of Professor Yang, it created a reverse process!

4. Unlike the Scholar Zhou Jixu's thinking. Chinese history was not the usurper of the location between Huaxia guest and Viet host. It was not that the Huaxia appropriated the culture of indigenous peoples. In fact, by their talents and virtues, Huaxia people united, gathered and led the overall Viet communities to make the Chinese history. After all, Chinese history was the history of Viet people living in the Chinese land.

5. In his works, scholar Zhou Jixu asked: "Why the archaeological discovery showed on Chinese land, the rice was planted from very early but the history recorded in written that Chinese agriculture was founded since Mr. Houji planted the millet, about 2300 BC?. A question was not only interesting but also made Chinese history rocked! Not satisfied with the answer of the author, I would like to present as follows: After killing the Shang dynasty and especially understood the texts, the Zhou dynasty advocated to assert the role of Zhou clan in history. The leading intellectual of the monarc knew that the greatest achievement for civilization was agricultural innovation.

Knowing that their ancestors from the King Yao period learned planted the millet from the Viet people, the Zhou dynasty was unable to admit merits of agricultural innovation for indigenous barbarian people. They won the great success for their grandfathers. The Zhou dynasty did not care about national history, but paid more attention to the family dynasty.

So, everything had to be started by the dynastic ancestor was Houji, after Yellow Emperor. Of course, at that time, Zhou people could not know when the rice was grown as archaeologists later. But history could not be written that the Zhou Dynasty enjoyed that great glory from indigenous barbarian people. It was due to intention of the Zhou kings to make Chinese history not only was shortened for thousands of years, but also was reversed.

In order to have this little book, the writer had learned much from the wisdom of humanity, through the legends, history, cultural studies, anthropology, archeology etc. But if there was anything further than the predecessors, it was due to the writer to read the texts that the Creators recorded in the Viet blood lineage. The texts were written in blood, wrote that: 70,000 years ago, people from Africa to Vietnam. Here, our ancestors met each other, and the Viet people were born. And from the Vietnam cradle, the Vietnamese had spread to dominate Asia and born the residents and Chinese culture.

With the position of the writer, the writer donates this book to his fellows on Chinese land, for the first time, after many millennia misled because of the misperception and the Chinese people can get back their Southern origin root!

Author
Hà Văn Thùy
thuyhavan@gmail.com

Publisher
Nhân Ảnh
han.le3359@gmail.com
(408) 722-5626